The Complete Book of Shotgunning Games

Tom Migdalski

MASTERS PRESS

A Division of Howard W. Sams & Company

Published by Masters Press
A Division of Howard W. Sams & Company
2647 Waterfront Pkwy E. Dr, Suite 100
Indianapolis, IN 46214

97 98 99 00 01 02   10 9 8 7 6 5 4 3 2 1

Library of Congress Cataloging-in-Publication Data

Migdalski, Tom.
        The complete book of shotgunning games / Tom Migdalski.
                p.   cm.
        ISBN 1-57028-142-4 (pbk.)
        1. Trapshooting. 2. Shooting. I. Title.
GV1181.M48   1997   97-28446
799.3'132--dc21   CIP

Acknowledgments

First and foremost, I thank my wife, Carol, and young daughter, Maggie, for their support and patience with the many hours that this work took from the family.

Second, I thank my friend, fishing and hunting partner and former member of my Yale Shotgun Team, Owen Wallace, Ph.D., for his outstanding work and commitment as the proofreader for this book. I'm also indebted to my fishing crony and weight training partner, Jerry Martin, certified strength and conditioning specialist, for his efforts in critiquing Part II — Body and Mind.

This book could not have been attempted in such a complete form without the inspiration and earlier teachings of my mentors. Gary Gesmonde, Ph.D., who introduced me to the exciting field of nutrition in an enlightening way that all subjects should be taught. And, Robin Glassman, my kind and talented journalism professor who helped me develop a keener eye and ear for good writing techniques and who helped me break into the outdoor magazine writing field.

I acknowledge Barry Wilson, coach of the University of Connecticut Trap and Skeet Team, not only for his efforts rebuilding that program, but for stepping up and doing such a fine job directing the Annual Intercollegiate Clay Target Championships.

I thank Jim Black and Ray Goydon at *Black's Wing & Clay*, Larry Cero at The Hunters Point, Millo Bertini at AmericanZZ and the people at Quack Sporting Clays, Inc., Beretta USA Corp. and Rosse & Associates, Inc. for their generous assistance with some of the graphics in this book.

I'm grateful to the people at the NSSA, ATA, NSCA, NRA, NSSF and USA Shooting, who provided much essential information on very short notice, and who genuinely care about the well-being of the shotgun sports.

I would be remiss without acknowledging the nationally recognized shotgun coaches and instructors with whom I have had the privilege of working with or learning from over the years: Duncan Barnes, the late Jim Dee, Terry Howard, the late John Linn, Phil Murray, George Quigley, Sr. and Lloyd Woodhouse.

I tip my hat to Rich Haigh, not only a longtime friend and outdoors companion; but also my skeet and trap colleague and confidant through our collegiate shooting years.

And last, I thank my father, Edward C. Migdalski, outdoors author, retired Director of Outdoor Education and Clubs Sports at Yale University and Coach of the Yale Skeet and Trap Team for 20 years. Without him, none of this would have been possible.

iv

Credits:
Cover design by Phil Velikan.
Technical assistance provided by Christina Smith.

Preface

As a trap and skeet shooter, I no longer have time to compete in matches and tournaments. My experience in serious competition occurred as a member of the Southern Connecticut State University Trap and Skeet Team in the late 1970's. I fondly recall our season finale each spring when we traveled to a different part of the country to compete in the Intercollegiate Clay Target Championships. For the past 20 years, except for an occasional round of skeet and trap, all my efforts involving the shotgun sports have been directed toward advising, instructing, coaching and writing.

During these years I have faced most types of problems associated with clay target shooting, from managing the trap and skeet fields at Yale's Outdoor Education Center to instructing groups and individuals to coaching the Yale Team at the Intercollegiate Clay Target Championships.

Because Yale's shooting programs are well known, many requests for assistance find their way to my Outdoor Education and Club Sports office. They come from a wide variety of sources. For example, fathers who are shotgunners seem, almost without exception, to want to teach their sons to shoot. From their inquiries regarding shooting facilities, it quickly becomes apparent that nearly all of them would go about the task the wrong way. Children and young teenagers need to be guided by specific teaching techniques. In these formative years the youngsters are easily influenced. A proud father, who may be a good hunter or clay target shooter, may in his enthusiasm, do irreparable damage by improper teaching. The result usually is a gun-shy boy or girl, a condition as final as that of a gun-shy dog.

Others who contact me are the "do-it-yourself" types, who wish to acquire all the information they can by asking questions before they join a trap and skeet club. Although I am pleased to help and to promote the shotgun sports, it is a time-consuming practice in a busy office.

Because the abilities of students who participate in recreational and competitive intercollegiate programs differ widely, the instructor or coach must be capable of recognizing and dealing intelligently with many variables. At Yale, where shooting instruction is offered to the entire university community through a non-credit physical education class, the instructor may be teaching gun safety to a freshman who is standing between a nationally recognized Ph.D. professor and a custodian.

Through various coaches' clinics, meetings and programs that my wife, Carol (also a shooting coach and instructor), and I have attended, it has become obvious that the inexperienced, volunteer coaches need information. Without a faculty advisor or coach, many collegiate shooting programs fold. The majority of these scholastic shooting programs have as their advisor a member of the school faculty who has limited time to spare for extracurricular activities and sometime no knowledge of clay target shooting. Unfortunately, such volunteer coaches take the students immediately onto the field to shoot rather than following a progressive plan of instruction which is so important in the development of new shooters. While their students shoot, they try hard to help, but do not have the foundation of knowledge to do so.

Aside from personally contacting a coach like myself, it is not easy for those and other interested parties to collect information concerning clay target shooting. For example, to become acquainted with the physical plant — that is, with field layouts, target throwing machines and the structures that house them — one has to dig through numerous folders, pamphlets and booklets. And, where do you look for answers to such simple questions as "How fast does a skeet target fly?" "What is it made of?" "Where can I go to further my learning?" "Will drinking coffee harm my shooting performance?" and "What are the right color shooting glasses for me?"

I have searched the literature for a book that covers all aspects of clay target shooting, a book that I could recommend to beginners, to coaches, to administrators, to my teams, to my classes, to veteran shooters — a book that contains information on all the shotgun games — in other words, a complete guide between two covers. I have found excellent books and videos, mostly by expert tournament shooters, and dozens of magazine articles dealing with one specific area in shotgunning, such as "how-to" improve one's trap, skeet or Sporting Clays shooting. To my knowledge, however, a single complete text involved with the shotgunning sports has not recently been published. Consequently, I agreed to write this book. I hope that even in a small way, the result is a contribution to the clay target sports. And, because shooting has added so much enjoyment to my life, I hope that someday it will do the same for my young daughter, Maggie.

A Word to Women and Left-Handed Shooters

The shotgun games are excellent sports for either the right- or left-handed shooters. And, shooting is just as much fun for the women as for the men. In fact, I often see female shooters beat males shooters in competition. However, in the following text, the shooter is often referred to as "him," and "he" is usually right-handed. This is only because the majority of shooters fit this category, and because it makes instruction writing more clear and less complicated. Of course, I wish neither of these groups any slight.

How to Use This Book

Almost everyone in the shotgunning community should be able to derive something useful from this book. The beginner will learn all he wanted to know about shooting clay targets and more. The coach and instructor will find valuable how-to information in the teaching chapters. And, the experienced competitor will be challenged with the information presented in the psychology, nutrition, fitness and vision chapters. But, the astute reader, and the one who really wants to get the most applicable information from the book, will read the related chapters. In other words, the tournament or league competitor who wishes to pick up those few extra targets shouldn't just stop at reading Part II — Body and Mind; he could peruse, for example, the chapter on how to coach. "But I don't want to know how to coach," you say. Perhaps true, but have you considered that the coaching chapter contains many fine practice techniques that you can apply to your own shooting? And the shooting coach shouldn't just stop at the "how to coach" and "how to instruct" chapters; he should analyze the sport psychology, vision, flinching, fatigue and diary chapters to see how best to apply that information to his students. The instructor may wish to draw highlights from Part I — The Games and Part IV — The Equipment to enhance his lecture material.

Of course, the best way to use this book is to read it cover-to-cover to get a complete understanding of the shotgunning games. Then, put it on a shelf and occasionally pull it out to use as a reference or "refresher" when you become rusty in certain areas. I hope that it helps. I think it will.

Tom Migdalski

For my father, Edward C. Migdalski, who instilled within me an early love and respect for shotguns and who gave me an interest in and appreciation for what it takes to be an outdoor writer.

Contents

PART I:
The Clay Target Games

1. The Standard Games

Men do it. Women do it. Corporate executives do it. Factory workers do it. Salesmen do it. Olympians do it. Students do it. And over 6 million other people a year do it.

Shotgunning. It's a sport for all types, ages, genders, and demographic profiles, which is why it's attracting 100,000 new participants every year, according to the National Association of Sporting Goods Manufacturers. A 1996 report by American Sports Analysis found that 6.93 million people participated in trap, skeet and sporting clays in 1995 and determined that the number of women in these activities doubled between 1990 and 1995.

So how do *you* get to do it? Read on!

WHAT IS TRAP?

Trap is a fast-paced game in which a flying target moves away from a shooter who fires at it with a shotgun. The target resembles an inverted saucer about an inch deep, slightly more than four inches in diameter and less than 1/4-inch thick. The target is brittle and will break when hit by lead pellets bursting from the shotshell (shotgun shell or cartridge). The target is thrown by a machine called a trap, hence the name.

Trap is a highly popular national and international sport. A shooter may be interested in it purely for recreation, or may compete in organized shoots ranging in pressure and intensity from home club events to the world's greatest single-sport contest — the Grand American Trap Tournament held annually in Vandalia, Ohio, in which over 5,000 shooters participate.

The standard trap games are: American Trap, Doubles Trap, Handicap Trap, International Trap, and Wobble Trap. The governing board for the first three is the American Trapshooting Association (ATA), located in Vandalia, Ohio, which boasts about 113,000 registered members, 79,000 of whom were active in 1996. In the United States, USA Shooting, based in Colorado Springs, Colorado, is the guiding organization for the latter two games. The Union Internationale de Tir (UIT) or "International Shooting Union" is the world governing body of international shooting sports whose headquarters are in Munich, Germany.

HISTORY OF TRAP

We assume that trapshooting as a sport was invented by the British because first mention of such activity, according to present-day knowledge, appeared in 1793 in the English publication *Sporting Magazine*. Although clay target shooting is a major sport throughout Europe, no records have been found that precede the 1793 article.

Trapshooting originated in England. Live pigeons were "trapped" under hats. When the gunner called "pull" the cord was pulled, thereby knocking over a hat and liberating the bird to make an elusive target.

In the early days of English shooting, live pigeons, rather than targets, were used; hence, the reason that clay targets are often referred to as "birds." The live birds were placed in shallow holes in the ground and covered or "trapped" with old hats attached to lines. At a signal given by the gunner the line was jerked and the pigeon took off in flight. Apparently, this type of pigeon-hole shooting was in vogue before 1793 because the article that appeared in 1793 in *Sporting Magazine* describes a more organized type of "box shoot."

In this sport, shallow boxes, about a foot high and eight to ten inches wide were placed in holes in the ground located 21 yards from the foot mark of the gunner. This box had a sliding lid with a line attached. The line was pulled upon command, thereby releasing the pigeon. The gunner was not allowed to place the gun to shoulder until the bird was in flight. If the bird fell beyond 100 yards of the box it was considered a lost bird. Wild and domestic pigeons, sparrows, quail and other birds were used as targets, but the larger pigeons were preferred. Pigeon shooting quickly caught the interest of English sportsmen, and soon the activity developed into one of England's most popular sports. Clubs were formed and various types of competitions were evolved.

Interest in trap in the United States started some time early in the nineteenth century. The first formal trapshoot, at least the first recorded, took place in Cincinnati, Ohio in 1831. Live targets were also used in early American trapshooting. The passenger pigeon, extremely abundant at the time, was a choice target, but English sparrows were also used. As in England, the sport quickly spread. In 1840, the Long Island, New York Gun Club was created and the New York Sportsmen's Club added trapshooting to its program.

Ten years later live pigeon shooting was at its peak in America, but non-hunters began grumbling; they abhorred the shooting of live birds for sport. One state after another introduced legislation to outlaw the competitions. Also, live pigeons in the wild were more difficult to obtain. And live birds didn't fly consistently, thereby presenting unexpected advantages and disadvantages to shooters in serious, financially rewarding competitions. Combined, these factors stimulated interest in developing a method of putting non-live targets into flight.

Charles Portlock of Boston was one of the key figures involved in influencing the movement away from live-bird shooting in America. In 1866, he improved on a "sling device" used in England. This English contraption, which threw glass balls from a trap, had major flaws. Neither the in-flight pattern of the balls nor the hardness of glass was consistent. Some targets were so hard that a direct shot at close range did not break them. All sorts of modifications to the glass ball were made by other designers. In some, feathers were glued to the outside of the target to imitate a live bird, and in others the feathers were inserted into the inside of the glass target. The feathers burst out when the ball was broken. Some inventors added powder to the balls, which, when hit, sent up a puff of smoke or a flash.

Another name, now familiar in the history of trapshooting literature, is Captain Adam Bogardus, who first made his fame as a market hunter and exhibition shooter. In 1876 he stimulated interest in glass-ball shooting by his exhibitions and also by developing a better trap that threw the target in a consistent flight path. In the next few years inventors tried numerous methods of throwing targets from traps, but the most significant turning point in trapshooting occurred in 1880 when George Ligowsky of Cincinnati developed a flat-disc clay target. In spite of some drawbacks, such as targets being too hard or too soft, the clay targets won instant approval from the trapshooting fraternity in England as well as in America. Ligowsky's successful demonstration of his new target in an exhibition shoot at the end of the New York State Championship live-bird trapshoot at Coney Island in 1880 contributed greatly to the demise of live-bird shooting.

A year after inventing the clay target, Ligowsky produced an improved trap for throwing his clay birds; he thereby established the first consistent trap and target operation. Many experimenters imitated Ligowsky's creations, and different forms of discs and traps were marketed. But an Englishman named McCaskey put the final touches to the Ligowsky target, creating what became, in essence, the target of today. Ligowsky's targets, made of finely ground clay mixed with water and then baked, were very hard and often did not break when hit. Instead of clay, McCaskey used river silt held together by pitch. Later limestone replaced the river silt, and so the target remains today, limestone and pitch. And although present-day targets have no clay in their composition, being composed of ground limestone with petroleum pitch as a binder, Ligowsky's name "clay target" has remained. Unfortunately, the petroleum-based pitch is not readily biodegradable and pieces of clay targets can remain on the ground for years. However, according to an article in *Sporting Clays* magazine, one manufacturer has promised to introduce biodegradable clay targets in the near future. The main ingredients will most likely be grain and food-grade starch. The clay targets would then not only be biodegradable, but could be eaten safely by livestock or wildlife.

When standard targets and reliable throwing machines finally arrived, interest in the sport of trap accelerated in the 1890's at an astounding rate. Equalized conditions encouraged the development and formalization of the game, with rules that would rate a shooter's ability, regardless of the shooting field location.

The first game in shooting clay targets involved five traps set in a straight line. One person was prepared to shoot or "on deck," positioned opposite the center trap, and was allowed five shots. The shooter did not know which target was being released, nor the angles at which the targets would fly.

Eventually, a series of changes were tried in an attempt to make the competition more difficult. For example, there might be five shooters in a squad, one person behind each trap. In the "walk-around system," the squad consisted of six shooters, the sixth person being located behind shooter number one. When the first five had fired, the shooter at Station 5 moved into the extra position at the first station. Under this system one shot was fired by each person at each station.

About 1885, an effort was made to reduce the number of traps. W.G. Sargent of Joplin, Missouri, conceived the "Sargent System," using three traps instead of five. The traps, four feet apart, heaved the targets at angles unknown to the shooter. Within a year or two, the game was being played with one trap, five stations, and a squad of five shooters. And that has been the dominant trap game ever since.

AMERICAN TRAP

The term "American Trap" is usually used to differentiate the sport from International or Olympic Trap; it is referred to as "ATA Trap" or simply "trap." The fact that the clay target throwing machine is also called a trap may confuse the new shooter, for the machine that propels skeet targets (skeet will be explained later) is known as a skeet trap and the type that throws trap targets is actually a trap trap.

In the American Trap game the trap is housed in a structure measuring about eight feet square and six feet high, with about half of the height being underground. When the gunner calls "pull," (a throwback term from the late 1700's when a live "trapped" bird was released from a box by a "puller" yanking a cord) the referee or puller activates the trap machine by pushing a button attached to an electrical cord; the target emerges from the house in any direction within an arc of 44 degrees. The trap action, that is, the swing of the metal arm, causes the target to rotate as it flies horizontally with a starting velocity of about 40 miles an hour; the target commonly reaches a distance of about 50 yards from the trap house.

The charge of shot that emerges from the gun barrel weighs 1 1/8 ounces and consists of about 400 hardened lead pellets, each about 0.09 inch in diameter. The shot, usually No. 7 1/2 or No. 8 shot, starts spreading the moment it leaves the muzzle (end of the gun barrel). At 40 yards, the shot spread encompasses a circle about 30 inches in diameter, with some stray pellets scattered beyond that area. Targets are generally hit between 30 and 40 yards from the gun, depending on the shooter's style and the distance he or she is standing from the trap house. In most trapshooting events the participants are stationed 16 yards behind the house. In handicap events, however, the shooter may shoot from a maximum of 27 yards. The shooting is done from five adjacent positions in a crescent-shaped formation. A target is scored, usually called "dead," if a piece or pieces fall from it or if it is completely shattered or "powdered." If no piece is broken the target is considered a miss or "lost."

A round of trap consists of 25 shots or one box of shells. Shooting is done in rotation with the person in Number 1 position firing first. Each shooter fires one shot at an individual target. When each participant has fired five shots from a particular station on the crescent, all move one station to the right until each member of the squad has

A typical American trapshooting scene: five people on the 16-yard firing line with a referee and a puller in the rear. The man of Station 5 is shooting while the man on Station 1 will be next to fire.

fired five shots from each of the five positions. The "lead-off" shooter always shoots first in each firing sequence regardless of which station he or she is on. Beginners usually score anywhere from five to ten hits depending upon their natural ability and the amount of instruction they have received. Good shooters will consistently score 21 or more. Experts are disappointed if they don't break 25 straight.

HANDICAP TRAP

The principles of the handicap in trap are the same as those that apply in golf and other sports: they are designed to equalize participants of different abilities. In trap, shooting distance provides the handicap. Good shooters are bumped farther and farther away from the trap house, up to the point where their advantage over the less accomplished shooters is minimized.

Handicap distances start at 19 yards and extend to 27 yards. In popular terminology, involving "hotshot" shooters, the 27-yard marker is known as "shooting from the fence."

Under the Amateur Trapshooting Association's system an individual's handicap is decided by committees within the association. "Known ability" is determined on the basis of handicap and 16-yard averages and/or scores in both registered and non-registered shoots. New shooters qualifying for a "Permanent Card" must shoot 1,500 targets of either 16 yards or handicap or a combination of both. All targets recorded must have been shot within the current year and/or the previous three years. Any shooter interested in the trapshooting handicap system should join the Amateur Trapshooting Association (see Appendix B for address). He or she will receive a copy of the association's "Official Trapshooting Rules," which explain the fine points in detail. Classification tables for Handicap Trap can be found in Appendix A.

Although the official handicap system is controlled by the ATA, some clubs prefer to use their own handicap rules for their local unregistered shoots. Obviously, the less proficient the shooter the smaller his handicap, and the better the shooter the greater the handicap. Inexperienced participants at local gun clubs must remember not to mix shooters with handicaps greater than three yards difference in the same squad because of the cross-fire risk. Contact the ATA for specific restrictions on handicap squadding.

DOUBLES TRAP

In the game of "Doubles Trap," which was first incorporated into tournament shooting in 1911, two targets are in the air at the same time. The gunner tries to hit them both, using two fast-swinging shots. It is not extraordinarily difficult to break both targets. In the skeet game, in fact, doubles are a regular part of the course. Still, doubles trapshooters are scarce. The reason, according to the authors of trapshooting books and articles, is that the game is thought to be much more difficult than singles trap. Perhaps comparatively few trapshooters indulge in doubles simply because a round is twice as expensive as singles and lasts only one-half the time.

Doubles Trap is shot in strings of 25 or 50 pairs. That means that two boxes of shells are consumed relative to every one fired in trap singles. Shooters who come to the trap field and clubhouse to spend the morning or afternoon will be finished shooting before they're really ready to go home — like the trout fisherman who plans to fish all morning, catches his limit of trout within an hour, and then is obliged by club rules to leave the stream. Besides, in trap, as in all shotgunning games, more is involved in the activity than just the shooting. Shooters, whether their goals are highly competitive or just recreational, enjoy talking about the round completed, giving excuses for their misses, offering advice to partners who missed and discussing the merits of various guns and shotshells. Sociability is involved.

The horizontal angle at which the target will emerge in regular 16-yard trap is not known to the shooter. In Doubles Trap, however, the gunner has the advantage of knowing the direction of the flying targets, the trap being set to propel the clays to the extreme left and extreme right. In other words, the trap angles are fixed so that the two targets travel straight-away from Stations 1 and 5. As in ATA Singles Trap, each contestant takes a turn at all five stations, but in Doubles he gets ten shots at each station instead of five. Registered shoots may consist of 100 targets shot over four traps, because a field rotation system is used. Three pairs are shot at each station on the first and third traps and two pairs are shot at each station on the second and fourth traps.

Doubles is a perfect game to include in a "field day" shoot, where fun-games and cookouts are programmed. And to those trapshooters who don't mind the extra cost, Doubles Trap is an exciting and challenging game. Doubles also makes excellent practice for the quail, grouse or pheasant hunting season.

INTERNATIONAL DOUBLE TRAP

Men's and Women's Doubles Trap was a first-time addition to the Olympic shooting program in 1996. More precisely called "Double Trap" in Olympic-terminology publications, the Olympic-style targets travel at up to 50 miles per hour — ten miles per hour faster than American Trap targets — from an underground trap house or "bunker." Three trap machines are used to throw these targets. The middle machine is set at straight-away while the two outside machines are set up to five degrees off center. And, the two targets are not thrown at the same elevation as they are in American Trap Doubles, making this sport all the more challenging.

Like International Trap, squads are composed of six shooters, one on each of the five stations and the sixth person rotating behind the firing line. Men fire three rounds of 50 for a total of 150 targets.

9

Women shoot three rounds of 40 for a total of 120 targets. In both double events, like other international shotgun games, the top six competitors advance to the final — 50 targets for men and 40 targets for women. Medals are awarded based on aggregate (match plus final) scores. Match scores of 135 for men and 100 for women are considered world-class. The women's 1996 Olympic gold medal in Double Trap was won by 17-year-old American, Kim Rhode. Kim shot an impressive 108 out of 120 in the initial match.

INTERNATIONAL TRAP

International Trap was known as Olympic Trap or International Clay Pigeon. According to Lloyd Woodhouse, coach of the U.S. Shotgun Team, all other countries call International Trap "Olympic Trap," but the U.S. Olympic Committee prefers that the word "Olympic" not be used in this country, substituting "International" instead. Woodhouse further stated that "International Clay Pigeon" is no longer in vogue because any words associated with live creatures (clay pigeon, clay bird, dead bird, lost bird, etc.) are being shunned by the target-shooting community.

International Trap differs significantly from American Trap. Six shooters rotate through the five stations as opposed to five shooters in American Trap. The great difference between the two systems is that in the International-style a 15-trap ground-level installation, called a trench or bunker, is used. The six shooters on the straight line (not crescent-shaped as in American Trap) stand 16 meters back from the straight line of traps. Targets fly a minimum of 70 meters or about 77 yards (compared to 50 yards in American Trap) and at up to a blazing 110 miles per hour, with extreme angles and heights prevailing. Instead of one shot at each target, two shots are permitted. The target is scored "dead" whether hit by the first or second shot. When the shooter calls for a target, a phono-pull (voice activated)

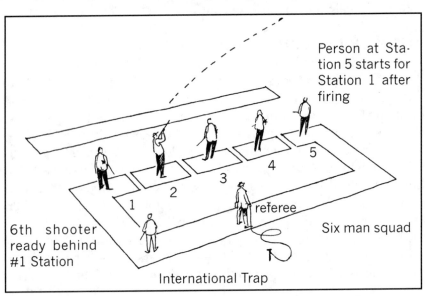

Person at Station 5 starts for Station 1 after firing

referee

6th shooter ready behind #1 Station

Six man squad

International Trap

release system is used (as opposed to a person pushing a button) to insure prompt and equitable target releases for all competitors.

The six-person squad changes stations after each shot, with one person always walking or "floating" from Station 5 to Station 1 while the other participants shoot. A round of 25 is shot. Twelve-gauge shotguns are used but to make the sport even more challenging, only 1-ounce shot loads are permitted, rather than the 1 1/8 ounce loads allowed in ATA Trap. Trap has been a men's Olympic sport since 1900 with the exception of two games (1988 and 1992) when it was open to both men and women.

As a consequence of the United States' poor showings in the World Championships of 1954 (at Caracas, Venezuela) and 1958 (in Moscow), the National Rifle Association (NRA), in conjunction with the U.S. Army Marksmanship Training Unit (USAMTU) at Fort Benning, Georgia, began a concentrated effort to develop International Skeet and Trap shooters.

With the continued help of the armed forces, particularly the USAMTU, the nucleus of the U.S. international shotgun program was developed. Eventually, the NRA inaugurated the annual U.S. International Shooting Championships. The growth in participation, in spite of the "invitation" system, was outstanding. In addition, to help attract more shotgun shooters to the international sports, the NRA began sponsoring and supporting teams to attend world championships in which the U.S. had never before participated. In March 1994, the NRA withdrew its leadership role in international shooting. Then in 1995, USA Shooting was officially sanctioned by the UIT as the new governing body of all international shooting sports in the United States.

Today there are fewer than a dozen Olympic-style 15-trap facilities in North America. The entire involvement in International Trap is too expensive, which is the main reason why interest in the Wobble Trap (described later) game is maintained. The first two official 15-trap fields in the U.S. were installed at military bases — at Fort Benning, Georgia, and at San Antonio, Texas. The first private International Trap installation in North America was constructed at Hamilton Gun Club in Vinemount, Ontario.

The U.S. recently had a great publicity boost in International Trap when Americans Josh Lakatos and Lance Bade won the silver and bronze medals respectively in the 1996 Summer Olympic Games in Atlanta, Georgia.

For more information on International Trap, contact USA Shooting (see Appendix B).

WOBBLE TRAP

The trap game originally called Modified Clay Pigeon is now known as the more politically correct names of Automatic Trap, Wobble Trap or Modified Clay Target. It was instituted in the world of clay target

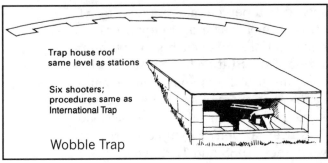

Trap house roof
same level as stations

Six shooters;
procedures same as
International Trap

Wobble Trap

shooting to encourage International or Olympic Trapshooting. In this game the above-ground trap houses used in American Trap are suitable (except in international competition), provided the roof of the trap house is not higher than 34 inches above the level of Station 3. International Trap (explained previously) requires an expensive 15-trap ground-level installation, and very few clubs with such facilities are found in the United States. Therefore, not many trap enthusiasts are participating in International Trap.

Although International Trap has been a part of the Olympic Games and World Championships almost from the beginning, it has had its ups and downs. It was dropped from the Olympics for a period because of the specter of "professionalism" due to the large number of live-pigeon shooters who participated. Following World War II it was reinstated to the World Championships and Olympic Games. For many years, however, International Trap wasn't added to the Pan American Games for two reasons: trap was not as popular among the Latin-Americans as skeet and the cost of an Olympic 15-trap trench was not acceptable to many host countries. Michael Tipa of the NRA was therefore prompted to develop the "modification" for the Winchester trap machine and worked hard on having the Modified Clay Target game adopted by the ISU (International Shooting Union). Tipa's efforts came to fruition in 1962, when the Amateur Trapshooting Association began registering Modified Clay Target ("Wobble Trap" is now the term in vogue).

Though an American trap house may be used for Wobble Trap, a house with its top at ground level is preferable, for it more closely meets the requirements of an International Trap facility. The trap house is equipped with a single multi-oscillating (vertical and horizontal) electrically operated trap. It may be manually or automatically loaded. The trap must throw targets at random and at continuously changing angles and elevations within limits designated by the official rules (vertical height varies from 1.5 to 3.5 meters, and the horizontal angle is widened from ATA Trap of 22 degrees to 45 degrees). And, the target is thrown at a greater speed and distance than ATA Trap targets (75 meters as opposed to 50 yards).

Firing is normally executed by squads of six shooters. Smaller groups may participate, but for safety reasons there should be no more than six in a squad. The procedures for shooting Wobble Trap are the same as for Olympic or International Trap. One shooter is positioned at each of the five shooting stations with the sixth participant placed towards the rear of the lane of Station 1 and ready to move onto Station 1. The squad rotates to the right after each shot. After the shooter on Station 1 has shot his target, he prepares to move onto Station 2, as soon as the shooter has fired on that station. The shooter from Station 2 moves to Station 3 in a like manner after Station 3 has fired at his regular target, and so on. When the shooter on Station 5 has shot his target, he will immediately proceed as standby to Station 1 to continue the cycle until all shooters have shot at 25 targets. Two shots may be fired at each target, with either one counting.

WHAT IS SKEET?

Skeet is similar to trapshooting in that the game involves shooting at flying clay targets with shotguns. The targets are exactly the same as those used in the trap games, that is, they resemble an inverted saucer about an inch deep, about four inches in diameter, and not quite 1/4-inch thick. The brittle target breaks when hit by pellets. The difference is in the machine that propels the skeet target. The skeet device throws targets in a constant or fixed pattern of flight, whereas the machine involved in trapshooting oscillates back and forth (except in Doubles Trap) and throws the targets at angles unknown to the shooter until they emerge from the trap house. The other major difference separating the two games is that in American Trap only one house, centered 16 yards from the line of shooters, is involved. In skeet, two houses are used, a high house and a low house. The high house is situated at the left end of a semi-circle that contains seven of the game's eight stations; the low house is at the right end of this "half-clock" arrangement.

Skeet is a more sociable game than trap. In trap, each contestant in the squad stands at an individual station, whereas in skeet one

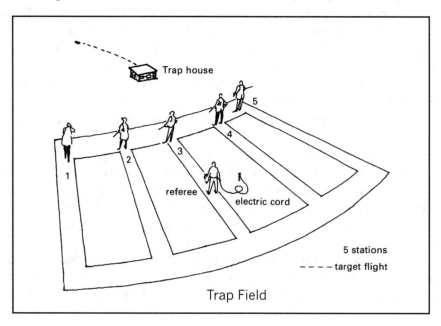

Trap house

5

4

3

2

1

referee

electric cord

5 stations

– – – – target flight

Trap Field

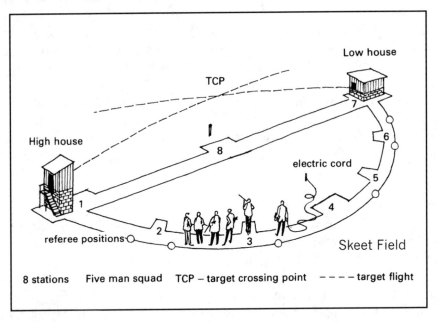

High house

Low house

TCP

8

electric cord

referee positions

Skeet Field

8 stations   Five man squad   TCP – target crossing point   – – – – target flight

person shoots from a station while the other members of the squad wait their turn behind him. In skeet it is easier for the squad members to observe each other's shots, and with eight stations to provide a greater variety of target flight, including doubles at four stations, there is much opportunity for the shooters to make excuses for missed targets and to criticize their friends' shooting. Generally, serious trap and skeet shooters stay with one game. Nevertheless, some of the world's best shooters do equally well at both games. The problem of becoming competent in both events is the time factor. To be a good shot requires practice. Field and personal time, as well as financial wherewithal, often make it necessary that a serious shooter choose to concentrate on one game.

The National Skeet Shooting Association (NSSA) is the parent body for official skeet events in the United States. It also has an International division for shooters participating under the rules used in International Skeet competition. The regulations for International or Olympic-style Skeet are governed by USA Shooting, with headquarters at the U.S. Olympic Training Center in Colorado Springs, Colorado. To contact the NSSA or USA Shooting, see Appendix B.

HISTORY OF SKEET

Compared to England's live-bird trapshooting activities in the late 1800's, skeet is a relatively new flying target game. And although Charles Portlock of Boston influenced the movement from live-bird to target trapshooting in America in 1866, the skeet game was not invented until 1920.

At that time, many hunters indulged in preseason trapshooting practice in the hopes of improving their bird shooting. Charles Davies of Andover, Massachusetts, a retired Boston businessman, was one such ardent shooter. He became dissatisfied with the practice sessions because the crossing and incoming shots of bird shooting were absent. Davies set out to devise a trap system that would more closely resemble real bird flight. He owned the Glen Rock Kennels, and it was on these grounds that, with the assistance of his son, Henry, and Henry's friend, Bill Foster, Davies began using hand traps to throw targets from different angles. Their enthusiasm grew with each innovation, and finally they decided to develop a shooting game that would provide practice for most of the hunting shots.

They tried and discarded many plans, and finally came up with one that was satisfactory. The field was laid out in a circle with a 25-yard radius with 12 positions identified on the circumference, similar to a clock face. The trap was located at the head (Position 12) of the circle so that it could propel the targets towards Station 6. Starting at Station 12, each shooter fired two shots from each of the stations. The last shell remaining in the original box of 25 was used at the center of the circle to shoot the incoming target released from Station 12.

In 1923, Davies and his associates reduced the radius of the circle to 20 yards. Then, the experimenters ran into trouble. A neighbor started a chicken business and built ten houses in the adjacent lot facing Stations 7 to 11. Consequently, one half of the circle had to be abandoned. The change prompted the placement of a second trap, this one at the "6 o'clock" station. The stations were renumbered, 6 became 1, 12 became 7, and so on. The scheme now contained seven stations in the semi-circle, with the eighth at midfield. This is the way the stations are situated today in the regulation skeet field. By adding the second trap the same target angles were presented in the semi-circle that were offered in the previous full circle plan. Next, Charles Davies and his crew realized that because both traps were operated from ground level, certain angles of birds on the wing were not presented because the targets were not flying out at the proper height. In other words, all the targets were rising. Therefore, a trap was secured to an elm tree trunk that was cut about 15 feet above ground. To further simulate hunting situations four sets of doubles were added.

Foster recognized the general appeal of this shooting game as a competitive sport and proceeded to formulate a set of rules to govern the activity. He then wrote an article giving an account of the new game. It appeared in February 1926, in issues of both the *National Sportsman* and *Hunting and Fishing* magazines, along with the announcement of a national contest that offered a prize of $100.00 to the person whose name for the new game was accepted. About 10,000 entries were recorded in the contest. The lucky winner was Mrs. Gertrude Hurlbutt of Dayton, Montana. Her offering was "skeet," an old Scandinavian word meaning "shoot." Hence, when you say "let's go shoot skeet," you are really saying "let's go shoot shoot." Because of the wide national publicity given to the new shooting game, skeet fields were soon cropping up all over the country.

The only book that I could find before World War II dealing with skeet was written by Bob Nichols, who in the 1920's was the skeet and shooting editor of *Field & Stream*. In 1926, he and a small group of shooters living in the New York suburban area started the Valhalla Skeet Club — the third skeet club organized in the United States. His book, titled *Skeet and How to Shoot It*, was published in 1939. The book still makes enjoyable reading. Especially delightful is an account of early skeet that bears on the history of this great game. It is worth introducing here:

Compared with the modern Skeet club, we were a motley crew back there in 1926. Our equipment was almost Spartan in its crude simplicity. Two flimsy traps threw the targets, one mounted on a rickety platform 10 feet above ground, the other slightly above ground level. The traps were entirely exposed, enclosed by no such structure as the modern trap house, and the trap loader was protected only by a sheet of corrugated iron nailed up in front of him. Incidentally, we took turns at functioning as "trap boys." Also, the trap loader was the puller. There was no central control even of the hand-operated type, let alone [an] electrically operated [one] with a timing device. Each club member who happened to be functioning as a "trap boy" at the moment, loaded and pulled at the shooter's command. One of the curious handdowns from that day to this is that many Skeet shooters still call "Pull" for the hi-trap target and "Mark" for the lo-trap target. It was necessary, of course, to have two different calls back in 1926. This was the only way the "trap boys" could understand which target was meant to be thrown.

The Skeet field of that day and on up until ten years later, in the summer of 1936, was slightly different from the layout we use today. The trap houses, facing each other, were 40 yards apart, just the same as today. Station 8 was located midway between the two traps, also the same. Thus, Stations 1, 7 and 8 have remained the same since the beginning of the game. Stations 2, 3, 4, 5 and 6 have been changed. Originally these stations were located equidistant from each other on the arc of a semi-circle swung on a 20-yard radius from Station 8. Today, these shooting stations have been moved inward, and the crossing-point of target flight has been moved outward. Today, the crossing-point of target flight has been moved out 6 yards beyond Station 8. And the shooting stations from 2 to 6 are now located equidistant from each other on an arc swung from the crossing-point of target flight on a 21-yard radius. Thus, instead of the targets being thrown directly over the trap houses, on a line between Station 1 and Station 7, they are now thrown at an outward angle.

How and why the game was changed to "Angle" Skeet may be interesting to the reader. The idea was first brought to the author's attention by Mr. Field White of the Poly Choke Company in the summer of 1935. It was acknowledged that shooters were constantly exposed to a shower of shattered target fragments under the field lay-out of the old game, when shooting at Stations 1, 7 and 8. A change in target line of flight to a pronounced outward angle would remove this hazard. It was also suggested that with targets thrown at an outward angle, instead of on a straight line between the two trap houses, it would then be possible to locate a series of Skeet fields in a straight "down-the-line" lay-out. This would not only save space, but would also speed up the movement of shooters from one field to another in our larger state, regional and national matches. Owing to the fact that Skeet targets are shot in practically opposite directions, this matter of providing for sufficient space and safety area in laying out Skeet fields has always been a problem . . .

We were immediately struck by the significance of the proposed change and strongly suggested in the Skeet Department of *Field & Stream* that such a change be made in the standard Skeet lay-out. The idea was received with no great warmth at the moment, primarily because the Skeet game at that time was entirely under the control of a rival sporting magazine publisher.

Subsequent articles, however, stressing the safety features of the new proposed lay-out eventually got results. In the summer of 1936, at the Great Eastern Championships at Lordship, Conn., so-called "Angle" Skeet was initiated. In the National matches, following in September of that year, "Angle" Skeet became the official game. At that time we referred to the old same as "Shuttle" Skeet. However, both terms of distinction have now faded out and the official game today, with targets thrown at an outward angle, is simply Skeet.

Because the skeet game simulated wild bird shooting with no closed seasons involved,

A view from the skeet field low house window shows the reason why (the houses face each other) modern "Angle" Skeet is safer and thus preferred to the old "Shuttle" Skeet game.

and because of the accompanying social aspects of clubs and club-houses, the sport grew rapidly in popularity across the nation. The shooters, looking for a guiding body, welcomed the formation of the National Skeet Shooting Association and its first National Championship, which was held at Cleveland, Ohio, August 16-31, 1935. The count of persons taking part in the 12-gauge event was 113, a surprisingly high number. The National Championship was rotated annually around the country — St. Louis, Detroit, Tulsa, San Francisco, Syracuse and Indianapolis. The last shoot under the original association was held in Syracuse in 1942. With the outbreak of World War II the championship came to an end and civilian skeet became practically non-existent. Most of the participants went off to war, ammunition and equipment became unavailable, and gun clubs closed shop.

Skeet did not die out completely during the war. In fact, in some respects it received a boost. The military recognized the value of skeet in training personnel to hit moving targets. Consequently, thousands of men were introduced to the shotgun and the game of skeet. The Air Force especially encouraged the activity. Not only was it pleasurable to be required to shoot skeet as part of the Air Force training, but it was doubly enjoyable because servicemen could shoot as much as they pleased in the off-duty hours with absolutely no cost to them!

With the end of the war the present National Skeet Shooting Association was organized and incorporated in December 1946. The National Rifle Association (NRA) played a leading role in the resurgence of the NSSA by financing a substantial, no-interest loan. The National Championship was reinstituted at Indianapolis and has been held annually ever since.

The original headquarters for the Association was situated in Washington, DC, then it was moved to Dallas, Texas. Dallas was designated as the permanent home for the Association, including the national tournament. The permanent home policy was abolished in 1952 and the tournament's name was changed to "World Championships" and held on various fields around the country. In 1973 the Association's headquarters was moved to the National Gun Club in San Antonio, Texas, which was formerly the Texas International Gun Club. A friend of my father's, Larry Sheerin, of San Antonio, was the leader of the small group of ardent skeet shooters who financed and masterminded the origin and construction of this magnificent gun club situated on 600 acres of rolling hills. This multi-million dollar complex is the largest and most complete shotgun shooting facility of its kind. The club's ranges include 40 skeet fields, 16 trap fields, three Sporting Clays courses and two NSCA 5-Stand Sporting fields. Besides hosting major skeet events such as the World Shoot, which draws an amazing 900 competitors shooting 534,000 targets, the National Gun Club has recently been the host facility of the Annual Intercollegiate Clay Target Championships.

Today, the game of skeet is recognized as a major sport nationally and internationally. It is highly regarded as a recreational pastime as well as a competitive pursuit. About 20,000 shooters are members of the NSSA, and many thousands more are either members of local gun clubs or participate without having any official affiliation. Although the 12-gauge event is usually the dominant part of skeet matches, the additional competitions in Doubles Skeet, 20-gauge, 28-gauge and .410-bore draw much attention, particularly in the larger tournaments.

AMERICAN SKEET

Skeet, also referred to as American Skeet when distinguishing the game from International Skeet, takes place on a field laid out approximately in a semi-circle, with eight stations for shooting. Seven stations are situated at equal distances from one another, along the circumference of the semi-circle with the eighth in the middle of the line between Stations 1 and 7. Station 1 is positioned at the left side of the field directly by the "high house" where the high targets emerge, and Station 7 is by the "low house" where the rising targets are thrown at the other end of the semi-circle. Although the flight path of the targets remains constant the gunner's perspective of the targets varies because he changes positions as the squad moves from one station to the next.

Five shooters make up a squad. A round of skeet for each shooter consists of 25 shots. Each participant shoots at a high house and a low house target at each station. Doubles, where targets fly from both houses simultaneously, are shot from Stations 1, 2, 6, and 7. The extra or 25th shot is called "optional." The option shot is used as a repeat of the first miss, and regardless if the option is hit or missed the original miss is still counted as a lost target. If the shooter hits all of the first 24 targets, the option is then taken as a second shot at low house Station 8. The correct procedure for a full round is as follows: the first shooter takes his position at Station 1 and first shoots the high house target and then the low house target. He remains on station and then shoots the doubles, shooting the high house target first. The second shooter takes the same shots and is followed by the rest of the squad in turn. When all members of the squad have shot at Station 1, the first shooter proceeds to Station 2 and shoots at singles high and low and remains on station to shoot doubles, again taking the high house target first. The same steps are followed by the other participants. Next the squad moves to Station 3 where only singles are shot, first the high and then the low. The same procedure is followed at Stations 4 and 5. Stations 6 and 7 are repeats of Stations 1 and 2 — first the singles, high house and low house and then doubles. In doubles at Stations 6 and 7 the low house target is always shot first. At Station 8 the first shooter in the squad shoots at the high house target and is followed by the others in turn. The same procedure is employed when shooting the low house target at the same station.

A scorer or referee releases the target when the shooter calls "pull." Usually, one person acts as scorer and referee. In formal matches and tournaments the host club supplies a scorer to mark the score sheet and a referee to push the release button on the electric extension cord that activates the "trap" or target throwing machine. The referee's word on the skeet field is law.

The majority of shooters use a 12-gauge gun to shoot skeet. In many tournaments, however, there are events for guns of four sizes: the .410-bore, 28-, 20- and 12-gauge. In recreational shooting the participant may shoot a round or two. Tournament events usually require 100 shots per shooter in each gauge. Beginners in skeet shooting usually break about nine or ten targets in one round. Intermediate shooters will hit from 12 to 16. Good gunners will usually score between 18 and 22. Experts will have sleepless nights if they don't disintegrate at least 24 out of the 25 targets. In major events, dozens of shooters may hit 100 straight. A few elite, world-class skeet shooters may compete for an entire year without missing a single target in the 12-gauge event!

Participants in NSSA registered contests are placed in categories or "classes." This classification system enables shooters of equal ability to compete against each other for awards. A new shooter must shoot at 200 targets to be initially classified. (See Appendix A for classification systems and tables for all clay target disciplines.)

INTERNATIONAL SKEET

International Skeet is a clay target game enjoyed by thousands of shooters throughout Europe and elsewhere abroad. It is one of the shooting events regularly scheduled in the Olympic Games, as well as being included in other World Championship events and even in the Intercollegiate Clay Target Championships. In the United States it does not come close to reaching the popularity of American Skeet, although interest in this Olympic-type clay target game is increasing.

What is the difference between International Skeet and American Skeet? The standard field layout is the same, but five basic requirements distinguish the International game from the American version. First, the shooter is required to start from a low-gun position; instead of mounting the gun to the shoulder he must hold the gun in a way that some part of the gun butt touches a line between the belly-button and the top of the hip bone. In other words, some part of the gun butt must be seen below the elbow when viewed from the side by the referee. Tape is usually placed across the top of the hip on the shooting vest or garment to make judgment easier for the officials. Second, the clay targets have to be thrown to 72 yards — 12 yards farther than in American Skeet. Consequently, they fly faster (about

55 miles per hour as opposed to 40 miles per hour) and their composition is harder in order to prevent them from breaking when thrown from the cranked-up machine. Third, the target may emerge from the house at any time up to three seconds after the shooter has called for it, which adds an element of surprise. Fourth, the "easier" shots were removed: low 1, low 2, high 6, singles on 7 and the option shot. These six extra targets were added as doubles on the more difficult middle stations 3, 4 and 5. And last, 1-ounce shot loads, instead of 1 1/8 loads, must be used.

In International Skeet, unlike American Skeet, the shooter is required to maintain a low-gun position until the target emerges. The gun butt must touch the body somewhere along a line from the belly-button to the top of the hip, which makes the stock visible below the elbow.

Since skeet originated in America, why has the form of the game changed in Europe? Actually, International Skeet has not changed as much from the prototype game as it may appear. Originally, skeet was shot with the gun held in the low position when the shooter was ready on station. An indefinite time release after the shooter called for the target existed. To illustrate this point I include the following excerpt taken from the first skeet "gun position" rule approved by the National Skeet Shooting Association, effective January 1, 1931:

> The shooter shall not raise his gun to his shoulder to shoot until the target is seen in the air. When ready to shoot he shall take his position at the shooting station with his gun in an informal field position. He shall then order the target. The puller shall release the target at any time after the order is heard, during an indefinite period of about five seconds. The referee shall count any target as lost where the shooter places his gun butt on his shoulder to shoot before the target appears.

The "informal field position" gun rule was confusing and caused bickering among shooters and between shooters and referees whenever a participant raised the gun "closer to shoulder." Referees were also put in the awkward position of having to make "judgment calls" or personal interpretations about the proper field position of a gun. The NSSA was forced to first modify and then eliminate both the low-gun position and the delayed target release. On the other hand, the Europeans, who adopted the skeet game from us in the mid-1930's, retained the "informal field game position" and cut the maximum

21

target delay to three seconds.

Until recently, the format, that is the station-to-station sequence in shooting, remained the same in both games. In tournaments, the order in which the gunners shoot is determined by lot, and each squad shoots only one round (25 targets each) at a time, spreading the shooting over an entire day. However, as attendance grew at International Skeet tournaments, it became apparent that squads were taking too much time to complete their rounds. Too many shooters were "fiddling around" on station before calling for the target. Consequently, the International Shooting Union revised the rules, which became effective January 1, 1977. The shooter was now required to load the gun and call for the target within 15 seconds. The number of shooters per squad was increased to six, the shooting sequence was changed, the "optional" shot was eliminated and two shotshells had to be loaded for single shots (on stations where two singles occur).

The rules have continued to change over the years to make the game more efficient and more difficult.

Sequence Of International Skeet

Station   Procedure

1 — 1 single from high house + 1 pair doubles
2 — 1 single from high house + 1 pair doubles
3 — 2 singles (1 from high & 1 from low) + 1 pair doubles
4 — 2 singles (1 from high & 1 from low) + 1 pair doubles
5 — 2 singles (1 from high & 1 from low) + 1 pair doubles
6 — 1 single from low house + 1 pair doubles
7 — NO singles, only 1 pair doubles
8 — 1 single from high house & 1 single from low house

NOTE: Shooters will move from Station 7 and line up in order behind the field referee on a line between Stations 8 and 4. The first shooter takes his position on Station 8 in the normal manner, loading ONE shotshell only, shooting at the target from the high house then, turning in a clockwise direction (rotating to the right) take his position for the low house, load ONE shotshell and shoot at a target from the low house. Each succeeding shooter follows the same procedure.

The leading proponent of developing International Skeet in the United States was the International Shotgun Department of the National Rifle Association. In 1994, the NRA withdrew from that responsibility and in 1995 a new governing body was formed called USA Shooting, based at the Olympic Training Center (OTC) in Colorado Springs, Colorado. (See Appendix B for address information.)

As mentioned previously, International Skeet is not nearly as popular in the United States as American Skeet. There are signs, however, that this "low-gun" type of skeet has been attracting more shooters, especially the younger ones. For example, in the 1997 Intercollegiate

Clay Target Championships held in San Antonio, Texas, students from 24 colleges and universities participated. Within those teams were 150 individuals registered in American Skeet and 118 in International Skeet.

Is International Skeet less popular because it is a more difficult game? Probably. Experienced American-style shooters like to shoot perfect scores — that seldom happens in International Skeet. However, if a person concentrates on the International game he or she will become proficient at it. While doing so, the American Skeet scores may drop. Perhaps the shooting relationship between American Skeet and International Skeet is similar to that between trap and skeet. If a shooter desires to become truly proficient at shooting any one of these events his efforts should be expended on the one game of his choice. Another reason why American Skeet is vastly more popular than International-style is simply because it has been in existence in the United States for many more years. Furthermore, facilities for shooting International-style are comparatively scarce. True, on an American Skeet field, the shooter can practice the low-gun position, and the referee can vary his pull of the target for up to three seconds, but the pinch comes with the target throwing machines. The machines used at nearly all skeet fields are not geared to throw International targets. First, the club manager does not favor cranking-up the American Skeet machine because it is a nuisance to him. And second, his reluctance to "beef up" the mechanism and reset the field to throw faster targets is well founded because special springs are required and must be set heavily enough to throw the target the extra distance required for the International game. The change produces an undue strain on the equipment, and the housing on the older trap machines may break. Also, special International targets must be purchased and stored. Another obvious problem is squadding. An American-style skeet shooter at any field may enter into a scheduled squad that has an opening, but an International Skeet devotee cannot mix into such a group. Special time and field arrangements have to be made for him and the other followers of his game if the shooting grounds do not possess an International-type skeet facility. Efforts to encourage more shooters to participate in the challenging International game will therefore be frustrated until more clubs include permanent International Skeet fields.

International Skeet shooters, like American Skeet shooters participate in a classification system, which permits shooters of similar ability to compete against each other for awards. Classification tables for the International games can be found in Appendix A.

SPORTING CLAYS

The game of Sporting Clays, also referred to as "Sporting," dates back to England in the early twentieth century when trapshooting used live pigeons. When clay targets were introduced, the sport began to evolve as it is known today. But instead of using the standardized distances, target angles and target sizes of skeet and trap, Sporting Clays courses are designed to simulate hunting conditions and live-game shots, including ducks, grouse, pheasants and rabbits. Six different sizes of clay targets give the shooter the simulated experience of actual hunting conditions. Additionally, hunters can shoot as frequently as they like in a time with dwindling wild game resources, polish their skills and extend the "hunting season."

The national governing body of Sporting Clays is the National Sporting Clays Association (NSCA), which is the largest Sporting Clays association in the world. Nearly 600 NSCA clubs exist with representation in all 50 states in the U.S. and in 10 foreign countries. The association was founded in March of 1989 and it is headquartered at the National Gun Club in San Antonio, Texas. The NSCA currently has about 12,000 members and hosts the National Sporting Clays Championship, which attracts over 1,000 participants annually.

Though intended to simulate hunting situations, all stations or "stands" in Sporting Clays must be shot from a standing position; walking, sitting or laying in or on stations is not permitted. Sporting Clays targets can be thrown as singles or pairs. Unlike doubles in other shotgun events, the pairs in Sporting are not always thrown simultaneously. Three types of pairs exist, which may be launched from one or more trap machines: Report Pair — two sequential targets where the second target is launched at the sound of the gun firing at the first target; Following Pair — two sequential targets where the second target is launched at the official's discretion after the first target; Simultaneous Pair — two targets launched simultaneously. Target number and selection for any competition are at the discretion of the shoot officials, but must be the same for all competitors. A plastic or wooden menu card is posted at each shooting stand citing the type and order of targets that the shooter can expect.

A minimum of 50 targets is required to be thrown in registered NSCA events, with additional targets being thrown in 50-bird increments. Sporting Clays is also unique because the number of shooting stations and the number of targets at each station, on each field, are determined by the shoot officials. Hence, every Sporting Clays course is different from the next, although certain shots recur from course to course. After all, there are only so many ways a pheasant can fly or a rabbit can run. These recurring-type targets are given names: The Springing Teal is normally a pair of targets thrown steeply; the Woodcock is a flushing, outgoing target; the Driven Grouse is incoming clays that might start low and rise up over the shooting station; and the Passing Mallards and High Pheasants are often targets launched from tall tower-mounted traps. These towers may be up to 120 feet high, or they could simply be lower towers mounted on hills. The Rabbit is thrown to roll along the ground on edge giving its "flight" a very challenging erratic, bouncing nature. Recently, some shooters, unhappy with their low scores, have voiced an opinion that Sporting Clays has become too difficult.

Some Sporting courses also offer a "Poison Bird," which is usually established by color. On a particular shooting station, for example, the shooter may be told that the green targets are "poison" and, thereafter, any shooter hitting a green target will be penalized. This provision keeps the shooters unusually alert, similar to having to identify an illegal hen mallard or black duck while duck hunting. However, in NSCA registered shoots, Poison Birds are not allowed.

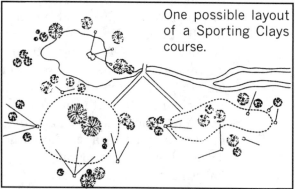

One possible layout of a Sporting Clays course.

A group of two to six competitors makes up a squad, which walks along a meandering trail to various shooting positions or stations incorporated into the natural surroundings. An average Sporting Clays course is laid out over ten, 20 or 30 acres, ideally in a rough, hilly terrain. The path that the shooters follow is usually circular or horseshoe shaped, which enables the shooters to start and finish in about the same location. Along the path targets are thrown from ten to 14 shooting stations. The shooter steps onto a station that has a confining wooden, metal or plastic structure surrounding it, which prevents a dangerous overswing of a loaded gun. Unlike the other clay target sports, the order of competitors within the squad usually rotates from station to station. As in International Skeet, after a shooter calls for a target it may be thrown with up to a three-second delay.

The original ruling on the gun-ready position required the gun stock to be held off the shoulder at armpit level, but not down at the hip as required in International Skeet. As of January 1, 1997, the rule was rescinded and a "free mount" position became legal in all NSCA sanctioned events. This means that the shooter may start with a low gun or a previously mounted gun. The Federation Internationale de Tir aux Armes Sportives de Chasse (F.I.T.A.S.C.), with headquarters in Paris, France, is the international governing body for Sporting Clays. All F.I.T.A.S.C. sponsored events still require the low gun ready position.

Other special rules make Sporting Clays refreshingly different from other regimented shotgun sports: certain single targets are only allowed to be shot at once, yet other single targets may be fired at twice, with the target scored "hit" if broken with either shot. When shooting report or following pairs, the shooter may shoot a missed first target with a second shot instead of firing at the second target of the pair, the result being scored "hit" on the first target and "lost" on the second target. Should the shooter break both targets with one shot, both targets are scored as "hits."

NSCA 5-STAND SPORTING

One of the most popular new clay target games is called NSCA 5-Stand Sporting, or just "NSCA 5-Stand." According to Martin Jones, Manager of the National Sporting Clays Association, it is important to differentiate "NSCA 5-Stand Sporting" from the original "5-Stand" because the NSCA adapted their own version in about 1991. NSCA 5-Stand events consist of groups or rounds of targets shot in 25 or 50 clay target increments from five shooting stations or "stands." Each participant rotates to the next station upon completion of shooting at the previous one. The shooting stations are set between four and six yards apart in a straight line, similar to stations in American Trap, whereas regular Sporting Clays consists of a minimum of ten shooting positions scattered across a large area. The new game of NSCA 5-Stand offers several different skill levels and utilizes six to eight automatic clay target throwing traps to simulate live birds. Targets can be thrown from such diverse directions as from high and behind, fast crossing angle shots, a "rabbit" thrown on its edge along the ground or springing shots traveling vertically and away. Targets are released in a predetermined set sequence marked on a menu card in front of each shooting cage. These cages on each station are constructed of metal, wood or plastic and are intended to prevent an aberrant swing with a loaded gun. Targets are registered separately from regular Sporting Clays under a special set of rules, however, NSCA 5-Stand uses the same classification system as NSCA Sporting Clays (see classification systems and tables in Appendix A).

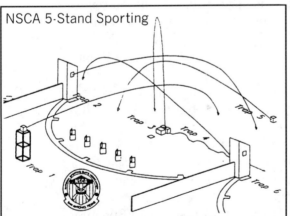

NSCA 5-Stand Sporting

NSCA 5-Stand fills a need of many gun clubs because it provides clay target shooters and hunters with additional original and challenging shots similar to Sporting Clays, yet requires much less cost and space. 5-Stand can be set up in the limited area of any skeet or trap field. Only one person is necessary to run the automatic traps used in NSCA 5-Stand, whereas a minimum of two, and usually more, are needed to handle the manual traps positioned throughout a sprawling Sporting Clays course. And, an NSCA 5-Stand course can be transported from club to club via a tractor-trailer truck.

2. The Competitions

THE EVENTS

Competitions involving the formal shotgunning games are many and varied. They range from half-day, low key, 50-target shoots in a winter league at the local club, to the ultimate in national, international and world championships where individual gunners fire at hundreds of targets over several days just to qualify for the finals. Some types of competitions are postal matches (honor-system competitions where scores are submitted through the mail), summer and winter leagues, state and regional championships, registered and non-registered shoots, tournaments sanctioned by specific associations, open-to-all tournaments, intercollegiate matches and intercollegiate national championships. Many of these have classification and qualification systems governed by national and international associations. Others are simply junior championships, senior championships, wheelchair tournaments for the physically challenged, holiday shoots, celebrity shoots, memorial shoots and programs that honor an individual. And then there are club, industrial, individual and team leagues. And the list goes on.

The most prestigious international shotgun competition occurs every four years in the Olympic Games. Other noteworthy international tournaments are the World Shotgun Championships (WSC), Pan American Games and Championship of the Americas (CAT).

In trapshooting, the Grand American is by far the most prestigious of the national tournaments. The Golden West Grand American Trapshoot, another famous competition, is a further example of a large and popular trapshoot. .

In skeet, some of the NSSA national events of prominence are the World Shoot, Mini World, the Great Eastern, Mid-West Open, Pan American Open, Great Southern, Annual North/South and US Open Championships. In 1996, each of these major skeet shoots drew at least 164 competitors, more than 50 of which were AAA and AA shooters. These tournaments threw a minimum of 73,400 targets apiece. Numerous other major competitions are held throughout the country, most of which involve a great many skilled shooters attracted by substantial cash prizes. To cover all the different big, national and international trap, skeet and Sporting Clays events would require a volume in itself. However, to give the reader some insight into the enormous scope of shotgunning games and their importance in the world of sport, a brief review of a few of them is in order.

OLYMPIC AND WORLD INTERNATIONAL GAMES

International shooting matches became popular in the nineteenth century. Officials of the first modern Olympiad, the 1896 games held in Athens, Greece, encouraged this type of competition by including a few shooting contests in the program. The first formal International Rifle Shooting Championships were held in Lyons, France, the following year. The interest aroused by this competition led to the formation in 1907 of l'Union des Federations et Associations Nationals de Tir, the forerunner of the International Shooting Union or Union Internationale de Tir, which today provides rules and controls the formal international shooting sports. The UIT is headquartered in Munich, Germany.

Target shooting as a competitive riflery sport in the United States did not take place until the formation of the National Rifle Association of America in 1871 by a group of National Guard officers. It was the leaders of riflery who eventually stimulated the shotgunners to be involved in the Olympics. The International Trap event was initiated as an Olympic sport in 1952. And International Skeet followed in 1968. At the 1996 Summer Olympics, in Atlanta, Georgia, 160 shooters representing 65 countries took part in the international shotgun competitions. The participation distribution, broken-down by discipline, was as follows: Men's Skeet — 54 shooters, Men's Trap — 50 shooters, Men's Double Trap — 35 shooters and Women's Double Trap — 21 shooters.

As the National Governing Board for International Skeet and Trap, USA Shooting is responsible for selecting and training the National Team (NT), the National Development Team (NDT) and the U.S. Shooting Team (USST) annually. The USST represents the United States in world-level shooting competitions.

This squad is concluding a round of International or "Olympic-style" Skeet. Note that the shooter on Station 8 high house is maintaining a low-gun position while waiting for the target.

Every year there are one or more of these world-level events for which the USST must be selected. According to Lloyd Woodhouse, U.S. Shotgun Team Coach, these world events run on a four-year rotation that begins anew the year after the Olympics, which were most recently in 1996. The events for the first year include the Championship of the Americas and the World Shotgun Championships (1997). The next year of the cycle consists of the prestigious World Shooting Championships — the largest shooting competition of its kind (1998). The Pan American Games and the World Shotgun Championships comprise the events of the third year (1999), and the cycle ends in the fourth year with the Olympics (2000). Each year the UIT sanctions a series of five World Cups in Men's Trap and Skeet and four World Cups in Men's and Women's Double Trap, which are hosted by shooting federations around the world. Usually, a World Cup is hosted in the United States by USA Shooting. Shooters from different countries must participate in these Cups to achieve individual qualification and win country quota slots to take part in the Olympic Games. Each year the top shooters from the World Cups are invited to participate in the World Cup Final. This competition ranks next to the Olympics and World Championships in importance and prestige; it is similar to an annual World Series of shooting sports.

MAKING THE OLYMPIC TEAM

According to Randy Moeller, Director of Competitions for USA Shooting, headquartered at the U.S. Olympic Training Center in Colorado Springs, Colorado, (see Appendix B for information) his organization continually receives calls and correspondence from individuals requesting information about qualifying for the Olympic Shooting Team. Mr. Moeller writes this concise description of the process:

First, you must be a member of USA Shooting. As a member of USA Shooting one of the benefits you will receive is *Quickshots*, a publication which lists upcoming competitions

29

throughout the country.

You must shoot in a preliminary trials competition (PT) sponsored by USA Shooting and shoot a minimum score which has been established in each discipline, then receive an invitation to participate in the USA Shooting National Championship (USASNC), which is the first step for National Team / National Development Team selection. In all of the disciplines there are a series of shooting team selection matches held before and after the USASNC, which are a part of the final selection process for at-large NT and NDT positions. You must compete in the final selection competitions when the Olympic Team is selected based on scores fired. There are no subjective methods used to select the Olympic Shooting Team.

ATA GRAND AMERICAN

The Grand American Handicap is the single largest participation sporting event in the world. Annually, about 5,000 trapshooters from all parts of the United States and Canada participate in this greatest of all shooting tournaments, with men, women, and children competing on equal terms for the championship. Held in Vandalia, Ohio, the Grand American Trapshooting Championship is actually the National Championship of the Amateur Trapshooting Association, the organization that supervises and promotes registered tournament trapshooting in the United States and Canada.

Ten days of non-stop shooting are required to complete the 16 major championships. In order to expedite this crowded and intense competition, all of the 72 tournament and practice traps, strung along a mile and a half of trap fields, are used.

Much more is involved with the Grand American than the actual gunning. The shooting facility is the home of the ATA and the ATA Hall of Fame Museum. It is also the place where many of the most important commercial companies involved with the huge clay target shooting market maintain year-round headquarters from which they promote their products. During the tournament the products and their makers are very much in evidence: shotshell loading machines, the finest of trap guns, the best stock makers and gun engravers, manufacturers of top-grade shooting and apparel accessories. Although the actual shooting programs are extremely serious, the surrounding atmosphere is like that of a large annual fair.

The Grand American Handicap started in 1900 at a shooting club at the Interstate Park, Queens, Long Island, New York. The original four-day tournament ran from June 12 to 15. The feature of the shoot was a 100-target event at handicap distances ranging from 14 to 25 yards. Any reader interested in more details about the Grand can find it in *The Grand — A History of Trap Shooting*, by Jimmy Robinson

HOW DO YOU MAKE THE U.S. SHOOTING TEAM?

• U.S. Shooting Team •
Competes in Olympics, Pan Am. Games, World Championships,
World Shotgun Championships, Championship of the Americas

• U.S. Shooting Team Selection Matches
• Training/Competitions including World Cup
• Junior Team for World Shotgun Championships, Championship
of the Americas

• National Team
• National Development Team
• USA Shooting National Junior Olympic Team

• National Team Selection Matches
• USA Shooting National Championships
• ACUI Intercollegiate Clay Target Championships
• USA Shooting National Junior Olympic Championships

• Preliminary Tryouts Matches
• State/Regional Championships
• USA Shooting Olympic Training Center Summer Camps
• USA Shooting State Junior Olympic Shooting Championships

• Junior Clubs
• Grassroots Programs
• Club Shooting Programs and Competitions

31

and Jim Nicholas. For specific information concerning procedures for entering the Grand, inquiries should be sent to the Amateur Trapshooting Association. *Trap and Field*, the ATA's official monthly magazine, carries a wealth of information relating not only to the Grand American, but also to other trapshooting tournaments. All persons interested in trapshooting should join the ATA and subscribe to this attractive and informative magazine. Annual memberships and membership applications are available at gun clubs and from the ATA office (see Appendix B).

NSSA WORLD CHAMPIONSHIPS

This greatest of all American Skeet events, sponsored by the National Skeet Shooting Association, takes place annually in the United States because it is here that nearly all of the American Skeet (gun mounted to shoulder) is practiced. Representatives from a few foreign countries do participate, however. The World Shoot is held every year at the sprawling 600-acre National Gun Club in San Antonio, Texas. The National Gun Club is the home of the NSSA Museum, and it is where many important vendors involved with the clay target shooting market maintain headquarters from which they promote their products.

It takes about a week to complete all the events in the World Shoot, which include the .410-bore, 28-, 20- and 12-gauge and Doubles competitions. Concurrent events or divisions include: Open Champion, Runner-up Champion, Lady, Junior, Sub-Junior, Collegiate, Military, Industry, Two-Man Team, Five-Man Team and all class categories: AAA, AA, A, B, C, D and E. The .410-bore, 28- and 20-gauge are 100-target events. Shooters are required to fire at 250 clays in the 12-gauge event. Many shooters enter all events hoping to place in the High Overall (HOA) Championship.

One of the rows of skeet fields at the 600-acre National Gun Club in San Antonio, Texas, home site of the annual NSSA World Championships and recently, the ACUI Intercollegiate Clay Target Championships.

In 1996, 882 shooters competed in the World Shoot, 288 of these competitors were classified as AAA or AA shooters (see Appendix A for classification tables), and an astounding 533,754 targets were thrown. During the week preceding The World Shoot is a "warm-up" tournament called the Mini World, which is also hosted at the National Gun Club. In 1996, the Mini World drew 589 skeet shooters, 204 of whom were rated AAA or AA, and 223,900 targets were launched.

The NSSA publishes an excellent monthly magazine called *Skeet Shooting Review*, which regularly carries information about the World Shoot and other major events.

NSCA NATIONAL SPORTING CLAYS CHAMPIONSHIP

In September of each year the National Sporting Clays Association sponsors the National Sporting Clays Championship at the National Gun Club in San Antonio, Texas. Originating in 1989, this five-day shoot has grown steadily, and it currently attracts over 1,150 competitors from around the United States and abroad. The NSCA Championships include a wide variety of activities to suit most gunners' interests, including NSCA Sporting Clays, NSCA 5-Stand Sporting, F.I.T.A.S.C. Sporting Clays, small-gauge events and side-by-side and pump shotgun events.

One of the NSCA 5-Stand Sporting fields at the National Gun Club in San Antonio, Texas, host site of the NSCA National Sporting Clays Championship.

The second most important Sporting Clays event in the United States is the three-day U.S. Open. The NSCA sponsors the U.S. Open each year at different locations around the country. The purpose of the rotation system is to give those shooters who might not be able to attend the National Championships a chance to participate in a major Sporting Clays event. The rotation pattern used for the U.S. Open is East, West, Central, East, West, Central and so on.

Becoming a member of the NSCA (see Appendix B) provides the shooter with information about the U.S. Open and the National Championship as well as other Sporting Clays tournaments. Most of this information is distributed through the NSCA's fine publication, *Sporting Clays* magazine, which is included with your membership.

ACUI INTERCOLLEGIATE CLAY TARGET CHAMPIONSHIPS

Many intercollegiate trap and skeet shooting competitions occur around the nation, including countless matches, leagues and regional shoots, all taking place during the school year. The major collegiate event is the Intercollegiate Clay Target Championships, sponsored by the Association of College Unions International (ACUI). I was first exposed to the Collegiate Championships as a freshman member of the Southern Connecticut State University Shotgun Team in the spring of 1977 when our squad traveled to Omaha, Nebraska. I recall that we placed fifth out of about 30 teams in American Skeet — that was big-time stuff for us. And 20 years later, I still get excited attending the largest collegiate clay target competition as the coach of the Yale University Shotgun Team.

The Collegiate Championships started on the University of Iowa campus in 1969 when 56 students from 16 schools competed in American Trap, American Skeet and International Skeet.

In 1997, the just-completed 29th Annual event was held at the National Gun Club in San Antonio, Texas. The Intercollegiate Championships now draw about 180 student shooters representing about 30 institutions from 20 states. Scores for these collegiate athletes are highly competitive; winning team scores of 490 x 500 in American Skeet and 970 x 1000 in American Trap, on average, are posted.

Perennial powerhouses at the Collegiate Championships include Purdue (Indiana), George Mason (Virginia), Trinity (Texas) and Texas A&M. Examples of other competitive teams traveling from diverse locations include the US Naval Academy (Maryland), Pine Technical College (Minnesota), US Military Academy (New York), University of North Dakota, Arizona State University, University of Wyoming, University of Kentucky, Colorado State University and Yale University (Connecticut).

The Collegiate Championships are challenging and unique because rather than competing in various events within one clay target discipline, the participants compete in five disciplines over a four-day period, all in the 12-gauge. These events are International Trap (100 targets), International Skeet (100 targets), American Trap (200 targets), American Skeet (100 targets) and NSCA 5-Stand Sporting (50 targets). Winchester has been a strong supporter of the Collegiate Championships by providing the shooters with all of their competition ammo. Winchester is on track in assisting these students — some of whom could not afford to participate without Winchester's support. For more information on the ACUI Championships, see Appendix B.

3. The Novelty Clay Target Games

The informal or novel shotgunning games do not receive as much attention as formal trap, skeet and Sporting Clays activities do. The informal or "fun" games of clay target shooting bear the same relation to trap and skeet as the game of touch football does to regular football games. We are all aware of the great number of football games that take place regularly throughout the country. But who, aside from the participants themselves, ever takes note of the innumerable touch football contests and the associated spontaneous activities of passing and catching the football?

Trap, skeet and Sporting Clays games require organization and formality, just as football does. The shooter's scores are noted on specially designed score sheets each time a round of 25 targets is shot. The individuals' scores are also kept in clubhouse books and sent for tabulation to regional and national associations to which the participants belong. Also, various organized shoots, matches, tournaments and championships are available to any shooter who desires formal competition. On the other hand, in a situation similar to "do it yourself" football, there are thousands of shooters who prefer to do their clay target shooting informally on their own with their own equipment. Hand traps, practice traps and clay targets, which are readily obtainable at most outdoor sports shops as well as large discount sports and department stores, encourage shooters to try the novelty shooting games. Regardless of age or gender, everyone can enjoy the sport year round.

As I look back at many years of instructing shooting sports, I realize that some of my most rewarding experiences have been teaching families. In retrospect I recognize that these outings proved to be an immensely valuable family activity. I was able to instill in these groups — especially the children during their most formative years — the discipline, etiquette and courtesy lacking in many modern-day family relationships. The parents and children were able to share a unique and challenging recreational activity on equal ground; it was often the 14-year-old who outshot mom and dad.

Before we delve deeper into the games of informal shooting with hand traps and practice traps, it is safe to assume that some readers may not be acquainted with such mechanisms and how they are used. Therefore, a brief description is warranted at this point, even though the subject is discussed in detail in another chapter.

HAND AND MANUAL PORTABLE TRAPS

Hand trap designs vary, depending on the manufacturer. Some are more elaborate than others, and consequently the price varies. Basically, the hand trap consists of a wooden, metal, or plastic handle or grip with an extension of about eight or ten inches, to which is attached the two-pronged device that holds a clay target. A spring holds the target firmly until the target is released. Some new models are all plastic and hold the target in place simply by the pressure of the two prongs. The release comes when the thrower's arm, in its swing, reaches proper momentum. The simpler hand traps have only the two heavy prongs to hold the target; others are arranged to harbor two or three targets within parallel tracks for throwing "doubles" and "triples." The better grade hand traps have a flexible spring that connects the handle to the target holder; the whipping action of the spring adds speed and distance to the target when cast.

The portable manual trap machines are also available in different designs, but their mechanics are similar. Each has a metal base to which are attached an oblong-shaped, smooth-sur-

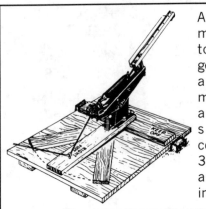

A trap can be made versatile to throw targets at various angles by mounting it on a "do it yourself" base construced of 3/4" plywood and supporting boards

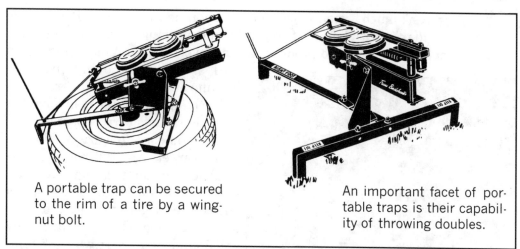

A portable trap can be secured to the rim of a tire by a wing-nut bolt.

An important facet of portable traps is their capability of throwing doubles.

faced arm and a heavy spring. To throw a target, the arm is cocked in place, then released by means of a cord attached to the trigger. Some portable traps are equipped with "hold down" anchors which, when stuck in the ground, hold the trap rigidly in place. Others are held down by foot or are mounted over a tire rim, with the base of the trap secured to the hub with a bolt. In regular shooting areas a permanent wooden base is usually constructed. And I have seen a portable trap mounted on top of a discarded oil drum. Weighted with field stones, the drum made a perfect base.

Portable manual traps are light in weight, most are adjustable without tools, and all can be easily transported by car. They propel single as well as double clay targets, and the targets' angles of flight and distances are adjustable. Moveable traps are available wherever guns and ammunition are sold. If the shop manager has none in stock, he or she will probably order one or supply the customer with the name and address of one of the companies that manufactures traps. Most shotgunning magazines and *Black's Wing & Clay* carry ads for these devices (see Appendix C).

The hand trap, and then the more substantial portable or practice trap, was invented by bird hunters who, before the start of the season wished to sharpen their marksmanship by shooting at flying targets. Clay targets thrown merely by hand were not satisfactory because their flight distances were too short. All sorts of contraptions were subsequently tried, such as broom handles and elastic bands cut from rubber tire tubes, but they

Proper position of a hand trap in preparation to throw a clay target. Unlike its predecessors, which had wooden handles and metal springs, this new hand trap is made from lightweight, one-piece plastic.

weren't much better. When some entrepreneurs devised a home-made hand trap with handle, two prongs and a spring, manufacturers took note and started to produce an improved device. As a result, informal shotgun shooting practice became attractive to gunners.

The target thrower must stand beside and slightly behind the shooter for the safety of both participants.

A certain technique is involved in heaving targets correctly, and in order for someone to learn to shoot at flying targets, the thrower must be proficient at that technique. It is important for the newcomer to know where the target is going to fly, but if the targets are badly thrown they will flounder out every which way, including vertically, instead of horizontally, causing the clay bird to dive suddenly to earth. Because instructions for throwing targets do not always accompany the hand trap in the store-bought package, a few hints on the proper throwing procedure are in order.

Some hand traps have a leather thong or strap attached at the upper end of the handle. Use of the strap is recommended. The thrower puts his hand through the loop before grasping the handle. Should the thrower lose his grip on the handle, the thong, when secured around the wrist, will prevent the trap from flying out and possibly hitting the shooter; the thrower, of course, should stand to the side and behind the shooter for safety reasons. Also, if the strap is of the proper length and feels secure around the wrist, it will increase wrist support, enabling the thrower to propel the target farther with less effort.

Four basic directions in which to throw a target exist: left and right, high and low. Let's start from the beginning, using a right handed thrower — left handers can simply reverse the instruction. The throwing sequence can be separated into three components:

1. Stance

The legs should be positioned comfortably in the direction of the intended target flight with the left leg forward and the feet spread apart, about shoulder width, in the same position used in throwing a ball.

2. Weight Distribution

Initially, all of the body weight will rest on the back leg, remaining in that position for as long as the throwing arm is cocked behind the body in preparation for the swing. The body weight is shifted from the rear (right) leg to the forward (left) leg in one smooth motion at the same time the throwing arm is being swung forward. Halfway through the swing, body weight should be equal on both legs. As the arm swings ahead of the body, releasing the target, all the weight should be on the front leg for a good follow-through.

3. Arm Position

The arm is held in a "side-arm" throwing position behind the right shoulder. The elbow, about equal level with the wrist, and extended about three-quarters of the way, should create an angle of about 135 degrees. With the wrist cocked back as far as possible, the arm is swung forward, accompanied by a strong wrist action. The arm swing is very much like the throw one uses to skip a flat stone across the water, or in fly fishing, when putting the rod into action under low-hanging tree limbs.

The entire swing is kept waist high for a target flight not too far above the ground. When targets are being thrown at an average height to the extreme left or right and to all the angles in between, only the stance shifts; the arm and wrist movements remain the same. The higher the target is intended to fly, the higher the forward swing will end. But, good snappy wrist action is important regardless of the height of the flying target. With practice the thrower can become proficient at throwing accurate high and low targets as well as fast and slow ones.

Not long after the emergence of the factory-made hand traps, gunners discovered that practicing with them was more than just preparing for the hunting season; it was fun. Because of the popularity of the hand trap, manufacturers produced a more sophisticated portable trap machine known as the practice trap. Fathers who used these traps found it much easier to introduce their sons to shooting. Today, however, family shotgunning games are no longer only a "father and son" affair. Daughters and mothers have become strongly involved. And nowadays, it is not unusual to see an entire family enjoying a combined shoot and lunch at a local gun club.

During the past decade, sportsmen have given more attention than usual to the clay target games. And with the continuing decline of available hunting areas not only has individual interest in the informal, fun shotgunning games increased, but shooting clubs in general have incorporated "fun games" into their programs. Now, many clubs use their trap and skeet fields for informal games, combining parts of regular trap and skeet shooting with such games as Sporting Clays, Grouse Walk, Duck Tower, Dove Shoot, Turkey Shoot and Doubles thrown from one or more portable traps. For example, many university trap and skeet clubs run an Annual Shotgunning Games Field Day for students, faculty, staff and alumni, with an exciting mixture of shooting sports as well as a cook-out and an awards presentation. These field days have also become an effective means of fundraising for collegiate shooting programs.

The games described below are ones that have been used successfully by many organizations; some have been invented at the Yale Trap and Skeet Club or modified to meet college student interests. Any chairperson, manager, or coach of shotgun shooting activities can easily modify these events or add his or her own ideas. The one extremely important restriction to the formulation of these games is that the chairperson be someone with years of experience in gun safety. The informal shooting games are designed for fun and recreation, but the leader should maintain a strict "no nonsense" attitude. And he or she should insist that participants wear eye and ear protection. Placing a quick call to your insurance company is wise if you are inviting non-club members to participate. These "outsiders" may not normally be covered by your policy.

PORTABLE AUTOMATIC TRAPS

A large market exists in portable automatic trap machines. These traps are an overkill for the do-it-yourself, weekend shooter who simply wants to drive to a desolate field and break some flying clays.

Automatic traps can be battery or electrically powered (sometimes by portable generator). They are ideal for Sporting Clays, NSCA 5-Stand and various other novelty clay target games offered at both small private and large commercial gun clubs. These machines are significantly larger and heavier than the portable manual traps, but they throw the targets with more velocity. Targets in the automatic machines can be hand-loaded or automatically fed from a large carriage, which sits atop the machine and holds up to 100 targets or more. The other advantages, besides increased target velocity, are target flight options, remote control and an automatic cocker, which resets the arm against the spring after each target is launched. The automatic traps range from simple and portable to large, heavy-duty commercial-grade models costing thousands of dollars (see *Black's Wing & Clay* in Appendix C for manufacturers of portable trap machines).

TYPES OF NOVELTY GAMES

The novelty shotgunning games may be grouped into five categories:
1. Those that involve hand and portable traps.
2. Games adaptable to a trap field.
3. Games adaptable to a skeet field.
4. Games that require special facilities or equipment.
5. The "Field Day" games that may combine activities of the previous four.

HAND TRAP GAMES

The evolution of the clay target and the availability of the inexpensive hand trap have opened unlimited possibilities for individuals and families to participate in private shooting at low cost. Hand trap games are economical, versatile and adaptable to any terrain, provided only that a safety area of 300 yards can be maintained. If you intend to shoot on private property be sure to obtain permission from the owner, and clean up any trash and hulls (empty shotshells) before you leave.

The hand trap method of throwing the clay target into flight is still the least expensive way to participate in shotgunning games. All you need are some targets and an open area where shooting is legal. Two people are needed, one to shoot and the other to toss the targets, and not including the price of the gun they can shoot 50 clays for only about $22.00. Priced at a discount sporting goods store, two boxes of 12-gauge target loads cost $12.00. A half-case of clay targets is priced at about $4.00, and a plastic hand trap, a minor, one-time investment, goes for just $6.00. The cost breakdown comes to a reasonable 32 cents per shot for the targets and ammo.

The arrangement for a shooting sequence or the set-up of a game will vary depending upon the individual shooters. Easy targets, thrown straight ahead, should be presented to the novice. If the participants are experienced, the height and angle of the flying targets are limited only by safety factors. Obviously, the thrower should stand to one side and far enough behind the shooter to be safe and not a distraction.

Regardless of the degree of expertise of the gunners, the efficient execution of the games will be hindered if the thrower is unable to control the direction of the target's flight. Anyone taking a turn at target throwing should first practice with the hand trap without a shooter on station. The inexperienced thrower should not be trying to master the proper arm swing and target release when a shooter is patiently waiting for the target to appear. Before any hand trap shooting is attempted the thrower should have had enough practice launching targets so that each throw is under control; that is, the target flies in the direction the thrower intends. If the shooter is apprehensive about the ability of the thrower the consistency of his shooting will suffer.

Although many gunners are introduced to shotgunning through the use of hand traps, the use of a stationary trap is preferable for teaching shooting, especially when teaching children. The new shooter will be nervous enough without having the added concern of not knowing which direction the target will fly. The beginner first becomes acquainted with proper stance, shouldering, gun hold position, shell sound and gun recoil before he or she starts thinking about swing and lead. It is important that the targets all be straight-aways until such time as the student is breaking them consistently. More detailed information on how to teach shooting is found later in this book.

Games Consisting Of 25 Shots

In most games, the shooter is given a total of 25 tries because that is the standard number of shells contained in a box. For example, if the gunners are primarily interested in a "rabbit" shoot, all 25 shots can be used at targets thrown as low as possible to the ground, or six shells can be used at each of four different heights of flying targets in order to simulate field shooting at rabbits, quail, pheasants and waterfowl. As in skeet shooting, the 25th shell can be used for an option shot — as a repeat of the first target missed.

Skish — The No-Gun Clay Target Game

Before discussing the various hand target-shooting games, I'll describe a clay target game that requires no gun — a game that my father, Ed Migdalski, retired Yale University Shotgun Coach, developed during one of the Annual Field Days sponsored by the Yale Trap and Skeet Club at Yale's Outdoor Education Center. Among the scheduled events was a fly casting competition, in which the participants cast flies (artificially created fishing lures) at a set of five targets, called "Skish" (the hook points were removed for safety). The targets were hoops 30 inches in diameter, each a different color and each floating in the trout pond at a different distance from the caster. If a fly fell into the hoop or touched it, the cast was called "perfect," with scores being determined by the number of direct hits and the distance of the misses from the hoop. While watching this game, it suddenly occurred to my father that a similar contest might be developed as an additional event in the shooting program. "Clay-Target Skish" is a hand-trap, clay-target throwing competition. Heading for the trap and skeet area, he laid out the same colored hoops used in the fly casting game (colored Hula Hoops or old, painted bicycle tires can be used as well), but placed them farther away. The referee called out the color of the hoop that the thrower was to aim for.

As in the fly casting contest, each competitor had ten tries and started with a total 100 points. A throw was called perfect if the target fell no more than ten feet from the center of the hoop. If the target dropped between ten and 20 feet from center, five points were deducted. If the clay hit the ground between 20 feet and 30 feet from center, ten points were taken from the score. To measure the distances, a peg was inserted at the center of each hoop, and the referee placed a marker at the spot where each of the thrower's casts hit the ground. After the ten throws were completed, it required but a few moments to establish the score by measuring the distances between landing points and center pegs. The game proved to be great fun, and helped introduce shooters to the hand-trap method of throwing clay targets.

Upland Game Shoot

The Rabbit Run, Quail Shots, Flying Pheasants and Dove Shoot are hand-trap shotgunning games that can either be treated as individual events or scored in combination in the inclusive game called "Upland Game Shoot." These games are especially helpful for shooters who enjoy Sporting Clays but have no course available nearby. The objective is to throw the targets so they ride at heights that will simulate the flight patterns of real game. In all four events the shooter, standing in one spot, has a try at targets tossed by the thrower in three directions: to left, straight ahead and to the right.

The Rabbit Run or "worm burner" targets are cast as close as possible to the ground. In Quail Shots the targets are thrown to fly at a height of about eight feet to simulate quail in the wild, which do not fly very high when they break cover. From my pheasant shooting experiences, I judge that a hand-trap clay target, coasting along at an average height of 15 feet, is about right to imitate the live bird in the Fly-

Hand-trap games resemble most every type of shot that a hunter can expect in the field. With practice, a hand-trap thrower can vary his tosses to afford shots very similar to the close-to-the-ground rabbit shot, the somewhat higher quail shot, the still higher but straight-flying pheasant shot, and the high-flying duck or goose shot.

ing Pheasants event. The target for the Dove Shoot should be thrown to fly 20 feet or more above ground.

If the combined hits of all four events are to be counted as a final score, each shooter takes four turns at each shooting station, thereby consuming 24 shells. The first gunner shoots two rounds (shooting left, straight ahead and right twice in succession) at the Rabbit Run targets. Then the other gunners take their turn at the same targets before the first contestant returns to station and shoots his next two rounds at the quail event targets. The same procedure is followed until all contestants have shot six times at each of the four-event targets. Each shooter takes his 25th or option shot as a repeat of the first target missed.

WATERFOWL SHOOTS

Pass Shooting

One of the most common shots in duck shooting, often referred to as a "pass shot" or "pass shooting," is when ducks do not intend to stool, that is, to come into the decoys; instead they swing by "to take a look." Also, duck hunters off the New England coast, for example, operate from points along the shore or from small islands not too far distant from shore. Scoters, eider and oldsquaw are quarry in this type of rock shooting, but often these ducks don't decoy, especially later in the season when they become "rock shy." Nevertheless, as they swing by in range at tremendous speed, these big, hardy birds offer challenging targets to the gunner. Unquestionably, the main reason for missed shots is because the hunter does not lead the duck enough. This was once amusingly illustrated when a hunting partner of mine, Rich Haigh, fired at the lead bird in a line of five scoters and the third duck folded cleanly! Whether the gunner is a duck shooter practicing "lead" for the upcoming season or whether he is interested only in hitting clay targets, the game of Pass Shooting is a good one.

Three persons are best for the Pass Shoot. The gunner takes a stand in line with two throwers, one on each side. The distances between gunner and thrower should be changed after each round and the crossing angle of the flying targets should also be increased making them more difficult to hit. If the shooters wish, a box of shells may be consumed at this exercise. For example, each gunner shoots at a right and left target alternately. The second and third time the right and left targets are shot, from the same station, their height is increased. After each shooter has shot at six targets, three from each side, the throwers move farther away, but equidistant, from the shooting station. If the throwing action takes place from four different distances on each side of the shooter, 24 shells will have been used, with the 25th used as a repeat of the first target missed. Or, the shooter with the best score out of 24 gets to shoot his partners' extra (25th) shells as his award.

Ducks Decoying

With ideal conditions prevailing and the wind at the gunner's back, the ducks' final descent into the decoys will come from directly in front, that is, into the wind. The Ducks Decoying game is an attempt to have the clay targets simulate ducks swiftly dropping into the decoys. And it makes an interesting shoot because the targets are coming at the gunner and dropping down a short distance ahead.

The best way to execute this game is for the thrower to be situated atop a cliff, clay bank or a high sand dune and, of course, far enough behind or below the edge so as not to be in danger of being hit by shot pellets. The gunner's position will be designated by the area in which the targets actually hit the ground. The thrower must attempt to heave the targets into the dropping zone with some degree of consistency. The gunner may move forward or backward in order to reach the desired distance for shooting.

High-Flying Ducks

In hunting, it often happens that ducks or geese will come flying high and fast past the gunner. Most often such flights occur at dusk when the birds travel, without pause, from feeding areas to the marshes, ponds or lakes where they spend the night. In such cases, the ducks or geese have no intention of decoying, but when approaching the area of descent, they will often fly within gun range. At such times, the shooter, crouching behind brush or in a ditch, experiences some magnificent overhead pass shooting, as opposed to pass shooting over decoys, when the birds come in much lower and pass in front of the gunner.

The High-flying Ducks game is much the same as the Ducks Decoying, the targets being tossed toward the shooter from the top of a clay bank, sand dune or steep hillside. However, in the Ducks Decoying event the targets fall in front of the shooter, whereas in the high-flying game the clays are hurled hard enough to pass at a good height over the head of the person on the shooting station.

The gunner can provide himself with another type of high pass-shooting shot by simply moving 30 or 40 feet to one side and standing at a right angle to the path of the flying targets. A fast swing and a substantial lead are then necessary to break the targets.

If a scoring game is desired, three parts can be included in the High-flying Ducks game. Each gunner in turn shoots six targets at each of four stations. The 25th shell or option shot is used as a repeat of the first target missed. Shooting Stations 1 and 2 are located in a line perpendicular to the cliff so that the targets pass overhead. The first station should be positioned a convenient distance away from the base of the cliff, the second station about 30 or 40 feet farther back. Station 3 could be located 30 or 40 feet to the left of Station 2, while Station 4 might be a similar distance to the right of Station 2.

Duck-Blind Shots

As an explanation for non-hunters, a duck blind is a structure intended to conceal the gunners when ducks, attracted by decoys floating on the water, fly overhead. The blind is usually constructed of local materials that will blend with the surrounding landscape.

Hunting from a duck blind is intended for water-side shooting but it can be practiced from a replication of a real hunting blind in an open field. The hunter need not wait until the hunting season to enjoy this type of shooting.

A blind can be quickly improvised with plywood, snow or branches. An actual hunting blind is positioned so that the prevailing winds are at the shooter's back, because ducks decoy into the wind. Clay target blinds should also be placed, when possible, so that the wind comes from behind.

If the objective is to simulate duck hunting the best procedure is to have at least three persons participating — the gunner sitting in the blind and two throwers, standing with one on each side. Since ducks seldom fly into decoys directly overhead from the rear, it would be unrealistic to throw clays from behind, as straight-away targets. The throwers should position themselves about 30 or 40 yards from the shooting spot and throw the targets so that they present "passing across" shots. For the sake of practice, the gunner may want to shoot singles thrown from both sides. But with doubles, both throwers should be positioned on one side of the blind. In my many years of duck hunting I have never seen ducks cross in front of the blind simultaneously from opposite directions, as in skeet doubles. Therefore, in doubles, the throwers, standing about five yards apart, toss out the clays at the same time, or one thrower can hold his throw momentarily so that the second target will fly behind the first, but in the same direction. Because of environmental contamination, this game should not be shot over water.

OTHER HAND TRAP GAMES

Walk-up Shots

Not all hunters are fortunate enough to hunt with dogs, that is, to have their game found, and pointed to, before walking up to flush out the birds from cover. So, they do it the harder way, walking the fields hoping to scare up a pheasant, grouse, or quail.

The game of Walk-up Shots is not only a challenging sport for experienced clay target shooters, it is also a practical way of preparing the hunter for the upcoming season. It sharpens the eyes and reflexes and, if done regularly, gives the sportsman exercise in the field — an important factor in reducing fatigue and accidents resulting from fatigue while hunting.

The shooter and the hand trap person — who carries a shoulder bag of clays so that they don't break in transit — decide on a path or a course to negotiate. The thrower, walking with a loaded hand trap at a convenient distance behind the shooter, unexpectedly yells, "Bird!", while releasing the clay in a direction that presents a feasible target. From a safety point, the thrower must have had enough practice tossing clays so as not to hit the gunner. An ideal situation in the Walk-up is to have two throwers following and flanking the gunner. All sorts of challenging angles then can be presented to the walking shooter, including doubles. The throwers can signal each other occasionally. For example, displaying a raised arm with two fingers extended would signify doubles.

A meandering New England trail is an ideal place to play the game of Walk-up Shots, which simulates the wily ruffed grouse. The thrower must be experienced enough with the hand trap to toss the targets into a clear area and not hit the gunner.

Floaters

All of the preceding games involve fast targets mostly simulating the quarry in speedy flight. As a change-of-pace shot and also as a way of presenting newcomers with easier targets, the "floater" can be of value. A well-practiced thrower is needed to float out slow "teasers" for the experienced shooter as well as tossing up slow moving targets for the beginner.

FUND-RAISING EVENTS

The Turkey Shoot and other special events have been shooting games ever since Americans started using guns recreationally. The Turkey Shoot is usually held in the fall around the Thanksgiving holiday, and it is usually sponsored by a local gun club to raise money for their own organization, a church or other worthy cause. The program may consist of several shooting games, including or combining regulation trap, skeet or NSCA 5-Stand with the novelty clay target games. Turkeys or hams are awarded as prizes. A fee is charged either to enter individual events, or to participate in the entire program.

The multiple event program is often offered by gun clubs whose membership is composed exclusively of experienced shooters. Other organizations, however, may use a single shotgun event with other activities such as archery and .22 rifle target-shooting.

An excellent one-event game for fundraising at a church outing, for example, is called Lucky Target. A steel plate with a three-inch hole cut out of its center is positioned at a distance of 20 or 25 yards from the shooter. A white piece of paper is taped over the hole on the back side of the plate. The number of pellets that go through the paper are counted and a record of each shooter's score is kept. The highest number of pellet holes wins the turkey. In case of a tie, the participants have a shoot off. The gun used in this event is a .410-bore shotgun. The cost of entering the shoot is set by the outing committee, at usually something like a dollar or two per try. In this type of public event where many participants have never before fired a shotgun, extreme caution must be exercised by the supervisors running the contest. They must be experienced shooters, thoroughly familiar with the shotgun. The gun must be loaded and handed to the shooter with safety on. The overseer must also stand by the shooter and release the safety after the participant shoulders the gun. A table should be placed immediately ahead of the shooter's station. The gun, when not in actual use, should rest with the action open on the table. As an added precaution to prevent the neophyte from swinging inadvertently away from the direction of the steel plate, a framework or "stand" can be constructed of wood 2 x 4's or plastic PVC pipe, similar to those used in Sporting Clays. All shooting then takes place within the stand, in an area about three feet wide. The sponsors must also provide eye and ear protection for each participant.

There are other ways of playing the Lucky Target games. A card-

A Turkey Shoot

board or stiff paper target, about three feet square, is tacked to a frame. Marked on the paper is a circle about a foot-and-a-half in diameter. The circle is marked like a thinly sliced pie. Each contestant pays a fee to write his or her name in one of the slices. When all the slices are signed, the coordinator of the event, using a 12-gauge shotgun, shoots at the diagram from a distance of about 30 yards. The slice that receives the most pellets wins the turkey.

In another version of the same event, each contestant draws a circle, on any part of the cardboard, using the base of a paper cup, for example, as a form. The participant signs his name in the circle. The circle getting the greatest number of pellets wins the prize.

One of the most popular of the Lucky Target methods involves skeet shooting. It is called the Lewis Clay System because, I suppose, it was invented by a Mr. Lewis. Like the preceding games, the cost of the turkeys or other prizes is taken into consideration, and the number of winners is determined by the amount of profit the club expects to make. For a needy cause, such as raising funds for a local child with cancer, the shoot coordinator should contact area food stores and get the turkeys donated. The scoring system works this way: the gunners' scores are posted in order of the number of targets hit in one round of skeet. A turkey is presented to the shooter with the highest score. Ties can be decided by a flip of a coin. But the remaining turkeys reserved for the event go to lucky shooters, not to the best shooters. It might be decided, for instance, that if 35 shooters take part, shooters scoring in the tenth, 20th, or 30th places will receive a prize.

Two other novel shooting games that are often employed in turkey shoots, sometimes as part of the whole program, sometimes as individual events with specific prizes, are Handicap Trap and Mo-Skeet. The trap game involves five shots, the first shot from the regular 16-yard middle station and the other four from 18, 20, 22, and 24 yards. Ties can be broken by "shoot offs" or coin flips.

Mo-Skeet involves a mini-machine and mini-clay targets. The gun used is a smooth bore .22 rifle and the ammunition is a .22 rim-fire cartridge loaded with No. 11 shot. The gunner stands directly behind the trap. Usually, the required number of targets for the competition is five. However, the rules can be varied depending on the particular situation. For example, the elevation or the angle of the flying targets can be changed after every two or three shots by each shooter. Or the gunner's position may be changed to the right or left of the trap.

4. Portable Trap Games

Both the hand trap and the portable trap machine throw standard clay targets, but that's where the similarity ends. The portable machine has many advantages over the hand trap, but it is not as easily transported as the hand trap, which can be placed anywhere in your automobile. When attached to a base, the portable trap takes up most of the room in the trunk of a conventional car, and it is best conveyed in a pick-up truck or recreational vehicle. Once set in place in the field, however, it is far superior to the hand trap for use in the informal shotgunning games. It is lightweight and easily moved from one spot to another; it can throw regulation trap, skeet and Sporting Clays distances; it throws singles and doubles, and some models throw triples. The manual trap is simple to operate, is set up quickly and can be held rigidly in place without permanent anchorage. Most models are adjustable without tools, and in some types the angle of flight is designated simply by the position in which the clay target is placed on the throwing arm.

Inside:

UPLAND GAME SHOOTER

DUCK SHOOTS

OTHER PORTABLE MACHINE GAMES

49

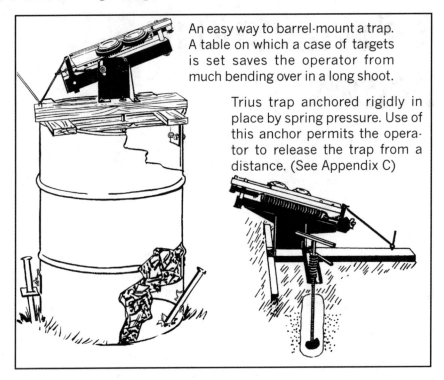

An easy way to barrel-mount a trap. A table on which a case of targets is set saves the operator from much bending over in a long shoot.

Trius trap anchored rigidly in place by spring pressure. Use of this anchor permits the operator to release the trap from a distance. (See Appendix C)

The one aspect in which the portable machine is greatly superior to the hand trap is the consistency of flight of the clay targets. Once the tension of the spring is set for distance and the mechanism adjusted for height, the targets are thrown with a steady flat flight and high speed rotation. Discounting wind influence, the direction, height and speed of the target are always about the same, an obvious advantage over the hand trap when informal clay target games are being played. When instructing new shooters, and especially youths, the portable trap again is greatly advantageous because it can be positioned for straight-ahead shots. And the anxiety of the new shooter not knowing exactly where the clay is going to fly — as is the case when a hand trap is used — is eliminated.

Readers interested in trying the Portable Machine Games should first study the corresponding section in the previous chapter.

UPLAND GAME SHOOTER

The shooter, in comparing the practice trap with the hand trap, will quickly realize that some of the informal shotgunning games conducted with the hand trap cannot be conveniently carried out with the practice or portable trap. For the Upland Game Shoot, for instance, which consists of four events — Rabbit Run, Quail Shots, Flying Pheasant, and Flying Doves — three traps would be necessary because left, center, and right flying targets are required. However, if three traps were used (one for each direction) the Upland Shoot would be one of the best of the clay target games. The throwing machine is easily adjusted to change the height of the flying targets after the shooters complete each event.

Duck Shoots

The Passing Ducks shoot is another hand trap game that is not easily adaptable to the portable trap (see Hand Trap Games). Two machines are necessary, and they have to be moved during the exercise because the procedure requires that the distance between gunner and the throwing machines be increased after each round is completed. In this event, however, the trap can be easily adjusted to throw a higher target after each gunner shoots a round at a right and a left target.

Ducks Decoying

The use of a practice trap is ideal for the Ducks Decoying game. If the machine is set up on a high cliff, clay bank, or a sand dune, as mentioned previously, it can be adjusted to drop the targets at the correct spot in front of the gunner. Also, since the trap's pull-cord can be any length, the trap can be placed closer to the edge of the embankment, and the puller can move farther back, making the game safe and less distracting to the shooter.

High-flying Ducks

Similar to the Ducks Decoying game, this is a perfect game for the stationary practice trap. This event is described further in the preceding chapter.

High-Flying Ducks

51

Duck Blind Shots

The Duck Blind Shots game may best be carried out by use of hand traps because it may be inconvenient to carry practice traps to a replicated duck blind, especially if the area is a good distance away from a road. However, if two traps can be placed in an isolated area, the Duck Blind Shots game is a valuable addition to any outdoor recreation plan.

OTHER PORTABLE MACHINE GAMES

Doubles And Triples

In order to make any "do it yourself" practice trap game more interesting or more difficult for experienced shooters, Doubles and Triples may be included as a special event or added to the various other games. But target velocity must be taken into account — the more targets placed on the throwing arm, the less the velocity they can be thrown with. Hence, distance and speed of the targets may suffer.

Walk-Up Shots

The practice trap game of Walk-up Shots differs from its hand trap counterpart. The walking gunner, instead of being followed by the thrower or throwers, starts from a distance of about 20 yards from the practice trap and then walks toward the trap with his gun in the alert position. The puller may pull a long cord to release the arm of the trap as soon as the shooter is standing on the mark, in the ready position, or at any time during the walk up to the trap. This game is also called Grouse Walk and it may be played with single or double targets.

Protect your operator at all times from both the direct discharge of the gun and possible ricochet of the pellets. The illustration shows a trap pit for permanent set-up. Always remove at least the spring and arm when trap is not in use so that children and trespassers will not be injured.

Various other practices and games can be initiated, depending on the ingenuity of the participants. For example, Rabbit Run singles and doubles can be shot while the gunner stands on a solid platform, about four feet above the ground. The height supplies a new dimension of shooting down at the targets, just like trying to hit rabbits. The trap can also be secured to a barrel top several feet above ground, thereby adding another type of shot.

Cruise Ships

On several occasions when asking a group of new pupils in a shotgunning class if anyone had experience shooting clay targets, some students replied that they had. Upon further query, they said they had shot "trap" on a cruise ship.

What cruise ships call "trapshooting" is simply a portable trap machine bolted to a railing at the stern of the boat. Little formal instruction is provided, and the instructors are often the ship's safety or security officers. Fees are steep, as you might expect, making cruise ship "trapshooting" the most expensive of the shotgunning games. One popular cruise line, for example, offered "trapshooting" at $3.00 for four shots. Unfortunately, most cruise lines have recently dropped clay target shooting as a recreational activity due to environmental concerns. Perhaps with the advent of biodegradable clay targets and non-toxic shot the cruise lines will reinstate this fun and worthwhile activity.

5. Trap Field Novelty Games

The regulation trap field offers a facility for some unusual and exciting shooting. The Rabbit Run, Grouse Walk, and Protection (also called Back-up Trap) are the three games most commonly used as fun games arranged at the trap field. At the Yale University Shooting Fields we tried a new game that I named Jump Shooting, and it became so popular that we now use it regularly as one of our informal games.

RABBIT RUN

In the Rabbit Run game, the trap machine is lowered so that the targets fly as close to the ground as possible. The shooter stands centered on top of the trap house, assuming, of course, that the roof is substantially built and will safely hold the gunner. This creates a unique angle of shooting down onto the target. The first participant takes three shots; the other gunners follow in turn. This procedure is followed seven more times and each person therefore uses 24 shells. The 25th or extra shell may be used following the first miss

Inside:

RABBIT RUN

GROUSE WALK

PROTECTION

JUMP SHOOTING

To shoot the Rabbit Run, lower the target flight as much as possible and stand atop the trap house roof to accentuate the angle.

or the agreement may be for everyone to shoot four shots the last time on deck.

If the rabbit game is carried out with doubles targets, the gunners can shoot two rounds, that is, four shots at each turn. If this system is followed six times, 24 shells will be consumed with the 25th shot offered as an additional single target the last time each gunner shoots. If more challenge is needed, the trap machine can be set to throw wider angle targets.

GROUSE WALK

The Grouse Walk or Quail Walk is another contest that quickly separates the adaptable shooter from the regimented shooter. This game can be played with one or two shots allowed at each target; or the game could involve doubles. Regardless of the system employed, the shooter loads his gun at Station 3 and walks in a straight line towards the center of the trap house. The puller may release the target immediately upon hearing "ready" from the gunner on Station 3, or he can release the target at any point along the shooter's path between Station 3 and the trap house. At times, the puller will allow the shooter to walk all the way to the trap house before releasing the target. Or he may have the gunner wait for several seconds before the target emerges. A wait of not more than three to five seconds is fair to the gunner standing up against the trap house. The participant can walk at any speed, but at no time can he stop or use a hesitant gait.

The astute puller will note whether the shooter shoots left or right handed and will release the target when the gunner has his opposite foot forward, thus forcing him to take an extra step to get to the essential shooting position. For example, biomechanically speaking, a right-handed shooter can't shoot with his right foot forward.

When playing the Grouse or Quail Walk game, the shooter holds the shotgun in the low gun-ready position to help simulate hunting conditions.

PROTECTION

The Protection or Back-up Trap game calls for five teams of two persons each to take positions, one team to each station, 20 yards or more from the trap house. The shooters stand next to each other only a couple of feet apart. The game is the same as regulation American Trap, except that two shooters on the same team have a chance to hit the target. Both shoulder their guns in a ready position. When the target is called for, the person on the left shoots first. If he hits the target his teammate does not fire. If he misses the clay, his partner then shoots at it. If the second shooter fires at a target his teammate has hit, or before his partner fires, the target is automatically scored as a miss.

"Protection" is a two-man team game for trap. This is an ideal game for husband-wife and parent-child combinations, but should only be played by experienced gun-handlers. If your club has a superimposed trap-skeet field, with the No. 8 skeet station coinciding with the No. 3 16-yard trap station, it's possible to enjoy "Protection" shooting at skeet targets from trap positions, starting back at the 20-yard marker or more distant. Throw singles targets only from unannounced houses. While the target source is unknown to the shooters, the fun and laughter are predictable.

The sequence of shooting is the same as in regulation trap, except that two gunners, instead of one, are standing at each of the five stations. Shooting is done in rotation with the team on Station 1 firing first and the others following in turn. After each team has fired at five targets from a particular station, all move one position to the right until all teams have fired from the five stations.

JUMP SHOOTING

I call this game Jump Shooting because the flight of the clay targets, rising at fairly close range from the trap house and veering off suddenly from the shooter in an unexpected direction, is reminiscent of waterfowl bursting from cover when startled by an oncoming duck boat — say in a shallow marsh or around a river bend. The same type of "jump shots" are presented when the hunter, trudging towards a marsh pothole, "jumps" an unsuspecting duck into the air.

The game plan requires eight stations aligned with the front edge of the trap house, four to the left of the house and four to the right. The two stations closest to the house should be marked about 12 feet from it. The second station on each side is marked six feet from the first, and the other stations are also six feet apart. The first shooter positioned at the first marker on the left side of the trap house (Station 1) calls for the target and shoots at it. After the rest of the squad has done likewise, the procedure is repeated twice more at the station. The same order is followed at the other three positions (Stations 2, 3, and 4) on the left side of the trap house. Then, the squad moves to the right of the house and repeats the same action. By shooting three shots at each of the eight stations, 24 shells are expended. The 25th or extra shell can be used as an extra shot at the station where the first missed target occurs. Or it can be fired as a fourth shot at the last position, Station 8.

Care should be taken to avoid participating in Jump Shooting while shooting is occurring on an adjoining skeet field. Trap houses may be in the line of fire from Stations 1 and 7 on the flanking skeet fields.

To add a further dimension to games like Rabbit Run, Grouse Walk and Jump Shooting, have the participants keep a low gun-ready position, similar to that used in International Skeet or hunting, until the target emerges.

Except for Protection, all of the above games are best played with skeet or Sporting Clays guns.

6. Skeet Field Novelty Games

The skeet field is an excellent facility for experimenting with different types of games where clay targets resemble field shots in wingshooting. Double targets at all stations is one of the favorite contests. Another scheme, and variations of it, may be called Pigeon Shoot or Dove Shoot, in which the contestant is presented with a target unexpectedly while walking with gun at the ready position, as in hunting.

DOUBLES ALL STATIONS

In this game the action is just as the name implies. Two targets are released simultaneously, one from the high house and the other from the low house. Each shooter takes his turn at all stations, thereby firing at 16 targets. The game can end at that point, or the nine shells remaining in the box may be used for "walk-up doubles" from Stations 3, 4 and 5. In this second or "walk-up" part of the event, the gunner starts walking towards Station 8 with gun lowered in a typical hunting position. The puller releases the targets unexpectedly at any distance between the beginning

57

station and Station 8. The gunner, while walking, must not stop or hesitate in stride before the clay target is released. The firing sequence is two sets of doubles at Station 4 and at one set of doubles at Stations 3 and 5. The extra or ninth shell can be shot as a repeat of the first miss, or given to the winner.

The Doubles game can also be played as it is in American Skeet. That is, shooting doubles at Stations 1 through 7 and then working back around the stations and ending up on Station 2. The leftover shell is then used on 2 high house. If shooting two rounds (50 targets), the extra shell from each round can be saved and used as a double at Station 1 on the second round. In this game, the shooter always shoots the going-away target first, that being the one from the closest house. On Station 4, which is equidistant from the two houses, the shooter shoots the high house target first on the initial trip around (from 1 to 7), and on the return (from 7 to 1) he shoots the low house first.

DOVE SHOOT

The following description of a walk-up shoot gives an idea of the type of fast shooting game that can be developed on the skeet field with target opportunities that resemble field shots in hunting. I have named this scheme Dove Shoot, because it presents the shooter with excellent reproductions of the various, fast swinging shots required to bring down a white-wing dove or mourning dove.

The Dove Shoot is entirely a walking game using regular skeet stations. Each station, except No. 7, is used as a starting point from which the gunners, in turn, walk towards Station 8. The puller may release the target anytime during the gunner's advance toward Station 8. For safety reasons, Station 7 should be eliminated as a starting area because the shooter would be at risk of being hit by a low house target. Instead, a position between Stations 6 and 7 can be used; it is called Station 7B as a reminder against using Station 7. The scheme is as follows:

1. Each gunner shoots at a high house single from all stations (1 through 7B).
2. In reverse order of stations (7B through 1) the squad members fire at a low house single from each station.
3. Next, each person shoots at a single at Stations 2 through 6. In this series, however, the target may emerge from the high house or the low house at the discretion of the puller.
4. Doubles are shot at Stations 3, 4, and 5.

HANDICAP SKEET

The novelty Handicap Skeet game consists simply of having an unusually good shooter stand two or three yards behind the regular stations when shooting with gunners of lesser ability. Caution must be exercised here. The other members of the squad must also move back the same distance while the handicap shooter is "on station."

DUCK-BOAT DOUBLES

Duck-boat Doubles is a game I invented to help prepare for the upcoming waterfowl season. My partners and I hunt sea ducks directly out of our duck boat or we sit on a tidal rock in Long Island Sound. In either case, the shooting platform (rock or boat) is too slippery or unstable to safely stand and shoot. Hence, we do all our shooting sitting down.

Duck-boat Doubles involves shooting following pairs while seated! In this case, a "following pair" is two sequential targets thrown from the same house, where the second target is launched at the puller's discretion after the first target. Care must be taken, however, to resist throwing the second target until the machine has had a moment to reset itself, otherwise, no target or a broken target will emerge. The reason for throwing sequential targets

Duck-boat Doubles challenges the gunner by requiring that he shoots while sitting; the low gun-ready position adds to the difficulty! A plastic milk crate or five-gallon bucket makes an ideal seat.

from the same house is that pairs of ducks usually fly in from the same direction. I have never seen two ducks fly past simultaneously from opposite directions as the targets do in skeet doubles.

To further add realism and challenge to Duck-boat Doubles, I request a surprise or "delayed" target release of up to three seconds and I hold the gun across my lap until the target emerges.

Sequence Of Shooting Duck-boat Doubles

Station	Procedure
1	1 pair from high house + 1 pair from low house
2	1 pair from high house + 1 pair from low house
3	1 pair from low house
4	1 pair from high house + 1 pair from low house
5	1 pair from high house
6	1 pair from high house + 1 pair from low house
7	1 pair from high house + 1 pair from low house
8	No shots

The extra or 25th shell can be used to repeat the first miss, or given to the winner.

HALF-STATIONS SKEET

Half-stations is a game I developed to help train the Yale University Shotgun Team, which I coach during the school year. This shot-gunning game is serious, at least for our team, but it is a refreshingly fun change of pace. The purpose of Half-stations Skeet is to help my team members adapt to odd target flights created on windy days or to prepare for an NSCA 5-Stand Sporting match, for which we have no practice facilities.

The game rules are simple: for the most part, we shoot a regular round of skeet, but the shooting stations are all moved to the right. In other words, our "Station 1" is halfway between the normal Stations 1 and 2. "Station 2" would then be halfway between the actual Stations 2 and 3, and so on. For safety reasons, we don't shoot to the right of Station 7. Instead, we shoot singles at "Station 7" halfway between Stations 4 and 8. For "Station 8" we take two big steps off Station 8 toward the high house. The shooter on "Station 8" then shoots one shot, moves two more big steps toward the high house, reloads his gun, and shoots again. After the entire squad has shot their high houses the procedure is repeated on the low house. The extra two shells used on "Station 8" are the result of no doubles being fired on the "Station 7" position. The 25th shell can be used as a normal option shot.

7. Special Facility Games

Several of the most unique novelty clay target games require special facilities (or equipment) and management by a gun club, shooting preserve or independent group of shooters. Many gun clubs have constructed such specialized installations on a permanent basis. Unfortunately, some of these fine games have become scarce due to the recent rise in Sporting Clays popularity. If for no other reason, some of these shotgunning games are presented here for their historical value.

CRAZY QUAIL

Crazy Quail, developed in Texas, is one of the most exciting clay target games. Targets, emerging from a pit, are thrown in a 360 degree circle from a single trap, with safe distances of 300 yards in the direction of the firing. The practice trap is welded onto a vertical shaft. At the bottom of the pit, attached to the shaft, is a seat for the puller or target releaser; the seat swings around the shaft in a circle. The gunners usually stand at a 16-yard marker, but longer distances (up to 27 yards) may be used. The puller may release the target

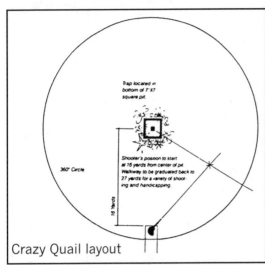

Trap located in
bottom of 7'X7'
square pit.

360° Circle

Shooter's position to start
at 16 yards from center of pit.
Walkway to be graduated back to
27 yards for a variety of shooting and handicapping.

16 Yards

Crazy Quail layout

to fly in any direction, including directly at the shooter. And the target may be withheld for up to ten seconds after the shooter yells "Pull." The gunner, for reasons of safety, is not allowed to shoot at the target once it has passed him. Some installations include a wooden frame to prevent the shooter from swinging too far.

The seven-foot-square pit is usually about six feet deep. Pit sides may be corrugated aluminum or galvanized steel. A mound of dirt may be placed in front of the pit as an added safety feature for the target releaser. The mound can be made to look natural by planting local shrubs around it. Some clubs set up full-sized, realistically painted, silhouettes of dogs at point at each end of the mound.

Drainage in the pit can be a problem. In an area of poor drainage, the trap can be situated at ground level and a higher protective mound built up around it. In a permanent, first class arrangement, a drainage pipe can be installed in the bottom of the pit.

Crazy Quail is a fun game, and shooters may make up their own rules for competition. The facility is also adaptable for teaching beginners to shoot. The trap can be held at a constant angle and the spring tension can be eased for a slower target. Also, the novice can move in closer to the pit.

Duck Tower. The shooters can also be positioned in front of the tower to shoot at targets flying directly overhead.

DUCK TOWER

Duck Tower is another of the clay target games that is especially enticing to hunters. The tower can be of any convenient height depending upon the site. The house on top of the trap can be just large enough to hold an automatic trap, or it can be big and strong enough to protect the person who is working a hand-loaded machine. When using a trap that throws in a single direction, the shooters can change stations in order to be presented with targets at different angles.

An attractive permanent layout can be created by erecting three to five stations, appropriately separated and arranged in a semi-circle so that they face a tower, in which is housed an automatic throwing machine similar to one used in trapshooting. The stations can be built to resemble actual duck hunting blinds. Gunners may change blinds after every five shots. And they can make up their own shooting rules.

RIVERSIDE SKEET

This clay target competition was developed in 1948 by shooters at the Riverside Yacht Club, Riverside, Connecticut. The scheme includes five stations arranged to resemble a standard trapshooting facility. The stations are wooden platforms four feet square and about six inches above ground. A hand loading machine (manual trap), anchored in a concrete block, is safely located at each end of the line. The traps are angled so that when doubles are thrown the targets cross at about 25 yards.

The shooter at Station 1 gets a left-hand single, then a right-hand single. His third shot is a single at the option of the trappers. (A signal system is used by the two trappers.) After the third shot, the gunner at Station 2 takes his turn, and so on until all five gunners have fired three rounds. Station 1 then fires doubles. After all shooters have fired a double they rotate in the same manner as in standard trapshooting. Shooters can create many variations of the game, and trap angles can be varied to make shooting more difficult.

63

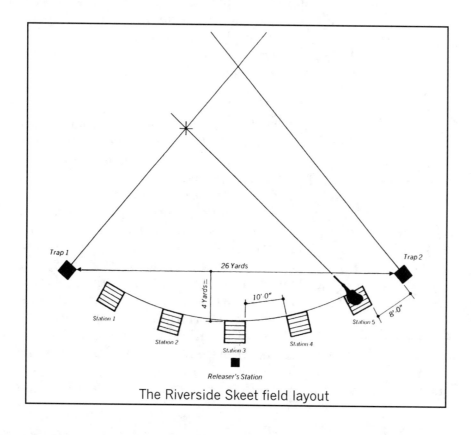

The Riverside Skeet field layout

This is a multiple-trap walk. As few as four or as many as a dozen or more traps may be used. The traps can be adjusted for various angles. The targets are released as the shooter walks along the path. If one shooter participates he can shoot at any and all targets. If two shooters travel the course, one takes the right targets and the other, the left.

MINI-TRAP

The Mini-Trap, a course for .410-bore shotguns, was introduced years ago by the NRA. Although Mini-Trap uses standard clay targets, the shooting field is half the size of a regulation trap field. The field is set up in a clearing about 210 yards long and 75 yards wide. The stations are located 25 feet from the front edge of the trap house. The distance between stations is five feet on centers.

The trap should be adjusted to throw the target approximately 35 yards, and it should be mounted so that it inclines at an angle of 30 to 35 degrees, with the front higher than the back.

Any .410-bore shotgun may be used, with shot not heavier than No. 7 1/2. A round consists of ten targets. The gunner fires at two targets from each of five stations. Of course, all the safety precautions used in regular trapshooting should be observed.

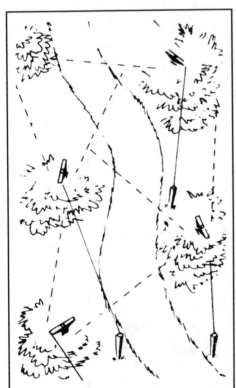

Mini-Trap has several advantages over regulation trap. The .410-bore shotgun is light and the recoil is minimal compared to that of regulation trap guns. The targets are thrown at slower speeds, hence, they are more easily hit, thereby encouraging the novice. And .410-bore shells usually cost less than 12-gauge ammo.

GROUSE WALK

Another clay target game that closely simulates field shooting is the multiple-trap Grouse Walk. No limit is set on the number of traps employed. As few as four or as many as a dozen traps may be used. The traps are laid out along a winding path, where they are hidden behind shrubs, rocks, embankments, etc. Their long release cords are also camouflaged. The puller follows a few yards behind the gunner and pulls the cords that release the traps. If only one shooter walks, he will shoot at targets emerging from both sides of the path. If two gunners negotiate the course side by side, one takes the right targets and the other, the left. After each round, the angle of the flying clays can be easily changed by turning the portable traps slightly. For safety, common sense dictates that the throwing machines are positioned so that the clay targets fly out in directions that do not jeopardize the gunner. And it takes a bit of experimenting when setting the release spring of the trap. The tension should be decreased to more clearly resemble the flight speed of grouse, especially if the course site is a wooded area or in heavy, high brush.

QUAIL WALK

The Quail Walk closely resembles the Grouse Walk. But instead of the throwing machines being set along a winding path they are hidden on both sides of a railing fence or a hedgerow. Two gunners, shoulder-to-shoulder, walk along the fence, one on each side. The shooter on the right fires at the targets emerging on his side, and his companion on the left shoots only at clays emerging on his side. The long release cord to each trap can be set through eye-hooks under the rail of the fence. The puller releases the concealed machine by pulling a ring attached to the end of the cord. For both Quail and Grouse Walks, the loaded firearm is held in a low-gun "hunting" position with the safety on until a target emerges.

INTERNATIONAL SPORTING CLAYS

International-style Sporting Clays is a really tough new shotgun game. Unlike the American Sporting Clays targets, which usually finds the participant faced by repeated pairs of the same double shots, International Sporting Clays presents a different target on each shot. If, for example, there are five single shots on a stand, all five may differ in size, speed, color, distance and angle. The traps are often set to take advantage of natural terrain and make the target flight deceptive.

Tripping device. Shown is a wobble stick, which lets the shooter release the trap from a distance without use of hands. This is used primarily when the shooter wants to shoot alone. The shooter trips the trap by leaning against the stick.

In one variation of the Quail Walk, a number of traps are hidden along both sides of a fence. Two gunners walk along, shoulder-to-shoulder, one on each side of the fence. The gunner on the right shoots targets appearing on his side ony. The gunner on the left takes shots on his side only.

Doubles are thrown on each stand or station in International Sporting. And when they are thrown they usually come from two different traps and are not a simultaneous (true) pair. This unique sport uses many target throwers to achieve this level of diversity — as many as five or six per station is common. International Sporting more closely simulates live target opportunities due to the variable nature of its doubles.

This sport, like hunting, also allows full use of the gun — two shots are legal on every singles target, and 1 1/4-ounce shot loads are still permitted though that may change in the future. Long targets of 45 to 65 yards are commonplace in International Sporting. The main governing body for this event is the Federation Internationale de Tir aux Armes Sportives de Chasse (F.I.T.A.S.C.), which is based in Paris, France.

A simplified variation of this game is similar to NSCA 5-Stand Sporting (see Chapter 1 — The Standard Games); however, a menu card is not present. When the shooter calls for the target, he or she has no idea from where the targets are originating. Three stands are used and a total of 150 targets are shot per shooter. A computerized program insures that although the shots are random, all shooters will receive all the target flight options during the match; in other words, nobody will get all the "easy" shots. The governing body for this game is Sporting Clays of America (SCA). (See Appendix B for information on SCA).

ZZ BIRD

ZZ Bird, or "Helice" as it is called in Europe, is another one of the latest shotgunning games and, according to *Shotgun Sports* magazine, it is becoming very popular at shooting

The ZZ Bird launcher oscillates horizontally like a table fan; five of them comprise a field. When the shooter calls for a target, any one of the five machines will release the propeller-driven target, which may fly in any direction or hug and "run" along the ground for a short distance before rocketing skyward.

Reprinted by permission of the AmericanZZ Company.

ranges nationwide. ZZ actually predates clay target shooting. Before the advent of the clay target, young boys used to wind up a propeller-type target and upon command, pull it with a string to spin it and make it fly. This type of target shooting never caught on and after the creation of the saucer-shaped clay target the propeller-driven target faded from the scene.

Millo Bertini, General Manager of AmericanZZ, said that the need for a live-pigeon replacement started in the late 1950's when, during a live pigeon shoot, a wounded or dead pigeon dropped beside the Queen of Monaco. The Queen was so taken back by this awful spectacle that she outlawed live pigeon shooting in all of Monaco. Hence, a substitute had to be found.

The Louise Mandrell Celebrity Shoot, the Charlton Heston Celebrity Shoot and the Holland & Holland Shoot have all featured ZZ Bird. State shoots with ZZ have occurred in Michigan, Ohio and Pennsylvania. Some of the fields around the country offering ZZ Bird include the Dallas Gun Club in Dallas, Texas; the Nevada Gun Club in Wellington, Nevada; the

Veach Road Gun Club in Gambier, Ohio; the Arrowhead Hunt Club in Whiteville, Tennessee; the Hopkins Game Farm in Kenndyville, Maryland; and the Orvis/Sandonona Shooting Preserve in Millbrook, New York.

ZZ Bird replaces the game of live-pigeon shooting by employing a reusable mechanical target. According to Mr. Bertini, live pigeon shoots are still available in the U.S. in states such as Texas, Pennsylvania and California, however, they are becoming more widely prohibited. In a ZZ Bird match, the gunner can get one, two or several "birds" at once. One feature of a ZZ target is that it flies, like a real bird, with unpredictability — it can change direction in mid flight. ZZ Birds are vastly different and more challenging than clay targets. Being an expert shot in Sporting Clays helps a shotgunner to hit these erratic fliers. But it doesn't help much!

The ZZ target is made of a steel propeller with a plastic dome mounted on it called a "witness." The witness has to be shot down within an area of 50 yards diameter from a 25-yard handicap. The gunner can shoot from a handicap of 20 to 30 yards away and may take two shots at each target. If the shooter hits the "witness" and it drops outside the 50 yard boundary it is a lost target, similar to the rules in live-pigeon contests. The ZZ game rules allow the gun to be pre-mounted on the shoulder, as do the most recent (January 1, 1997) NSCA Sporting Clays regulations.

The exciting game of ZZ Bird can be installed by the AmericanZZ company (see Appendix C for information).

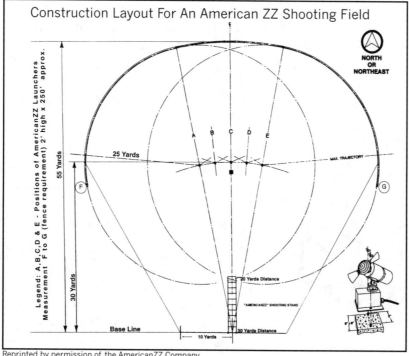

Construction Layout For An American ZZ Shooting Field

Reprinted by permission of the AmericanZZ Company.

MODERN SKEET AND MODERN TRAP

Modern Skeet mirrors regular skeet with one major alteration: the standard target machine is used with the addition of an oscillator beneath it. The oscillator lifts and lowers the target thrower, with the high house and low house working independently of each other. This creates a game of surprise, which much more closely simulates hunting conditions and prepares skeet shooters for targets on windy days. The shooting sequence is similar to American Skeet, thereby eliminating confusion. Singles on all stations are replaced with report pairs, meaning that the second target is released when the puller hears the shot at the first target. Doubles are shot as in American Skeet on Stations 1, 2, 6 & 7 — these are true or "simultaneous" doubles. And, unlike American or International Skeet, Station 8 is shot as a simultaneous pair. The rules of Modern Skeet are the same as NSSA Skeet. Modern Skeet may be shot with a low-gun position or an on-the-shoulder position.

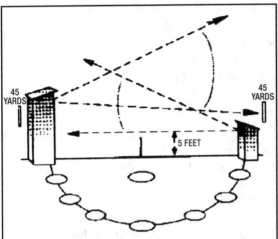

The game of Modern Skeet simulates American Skeet, except that a vertical oscillator has been added to both the high and low house machines, which provide varying target heights.

Reprinted by permission of the creator of Modern Skeet, Quack Sporting Clays, Inc.

Modern Trap uses an oscillator beneath the trap machine to throw trap targets that curl as they travel away from the shooter, rather than flying straight. Both Modern Skeet and Modern Trap games have the advantage of being an inexpensive way to add some Sporting Clays-type targets to regulation skeet and trap fields. For information on adding oscillators to your skeet or trap machines, see Quack Sporting Clays in Appendix C.

PDQ TWISTER

The shotgunning game of PDQ Twister entails the throwing of a series of clay targets at different patterns in up to a 180- degree arc at various elevations. Singles, report pairs, following pairs or simultaneous pairs may be thrown. At level one (there are five levels), for example, first a random single is thrown, which is followed by a report pair. Two shots are allowed at the single targets, with either one counting. Next, a following pair and a single are thrown,

Dual traps are at the heart of the game PDQ Twister.

Photo courtesy of Larry Cero at The Hunters Pointe

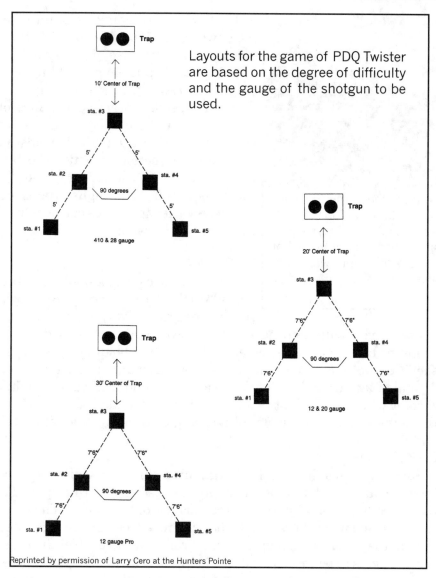

Layouts for the game of PDQ Twister are based on the degree of difficulty and the gauge of the shotgun to be used.

Reprinted by permission of Larry Cero at the Hunters Pointe

and then two simultaneous pairs are launched. All shooters complete Station or "pad" 1 individually, then move as a group to the other pads. Shooting stations are posted a various distances from the trap to accommodate 12-, 16-, 20- and 28-gauge as well as the .410-bore shotguns. For more information about PDQ Twister contact "The Hunters Pointe" listed in Appendix C.

STARSHOT

Starshot is a clay target sport that was created primarily for ease of viewing by spectators and television audiences. A Starshot layout consists of a vertical, semi-circular tubed steel framework. The shooters and the viewers see the steel framing as being divided into pie slices. Each "slice" is subdivided by smaller semi-circular arcs, which make the structure appear similar to giant dart board,

The backdrop for the game Starshot appears like a giant dartboard, half of which is above ground. Clay targets originate at the base or "bullseye" of the grid and are thrown upward; the sooner the targets are shot the higher the score.

half of which is above ground. The framework sections are marked from one to 12. At the base of the structure or "bullseye" is a large pit holding four trap machines, which throw targets at different speeds up across the face of the grid structure. The total points scored for each target hit depends on the sector or section in which the target is broken — the lower or "quicker" a target is broken, the higher the score will be. A variety of games can be played by teams in Starshot.

TWO-MAN FLUSH

This sport uses a Modified Clay Target or "Wobble" trap. Targets are thrown in any direction away from the trap house — vertically and horizontally. Two shells are loaded in the shotguns of each of two shooters, and a railing holding ten shotgun shells is placed in front of each shooter, which makes reloading faster. A total of 24 targets are launched at 1.5 second intervals. The first shooter will take the first two shots and the second shooter will take the next two shot, and so on until each has fired at 12 targets.

SUPERSPORT

Supersport is a "high-tech" shotgunning game, which is said to be the ultimate simulation of a live bird hunt. This shooting sport utilizes 10 to 30 automatic traps spread across 10 to 30 acres. The traps can be buried in bunkers, hidden behind hills, trees, shrubs or placed high in towers. The participant uses a computer to control the number of targets to be thrown and the degree of difficulty. As the shooter walks through the course, sensors, which are located along the course, receive signals from transmitters worn by the individuals. The signals are relayed to the course-control computer, which adjusts the machine angles and number of targets thrown. A noise that simulates the particular bird (target) is sounded prior to it being launched.

CHINESE TRAP

Also called "Scrap," this game is played by using a skeet and trap field that is overlaid (to save space), as appears at some gun clubs. Shooters use the skeet Stations 1 through 7 and shoot at regular trap targets. Most often, a low-gun mount is used and two shots may taken at each target with either shot counting.

FOLLOW THE LEADER

Reminiscent of childhood games, as the name implies, Follow The

Leader is a game without many rules. The sport can be played on any shooting field, but a combination skeet and trap field probably works best. Shooters in a squad are picked randomly to determine order. Shooter 1 calls for the target(s) to be attempted — any combination from any position. If he or she is successful, the remainder of the squad must try to duplicate the shot(s). Participants who don't match the leader's score are eliminated. Of course, the last shooter remaining wins.

SLAPSHOT

Also called "Simulated Live Pigeon," this is a new shotgunning game that is increasing in popularity. Originally from England, Slapshot simulates the fun of live-bird shooting. A reusable white marker is snapped beneath a standard clay target, which is thrown from a regular trap. To score a hit, the shooter must break the target and drop the marker inside the perimeter of a fenced-in area. For more information, see Slapshot in Appendix C.

THE RED BARON

Used primarily for fund-raising events, this lively game requires the shooter to knock down a miniature remote-controlled airplane. See Sporting Planes in Appendix C for more information.

PART II:
Body and Mind

8. Sport Psychology

At least four principle human factors have a direct bearing on a competitor's shooting ability, whether that person is a beginner, a world champion, or somewhere in between. These four factors are psychology (thought processes), nutrition (food, beverages and supplements), vision (eyesight) and fitness (exercise habits and conditioning). Each has a significant influence on a shooter's scores. The great majority of shooters are unaware of these controlling factors, but any shooter who has a weakness associated with any of the human elements can improve his or her shooting considerably by confronting and remedying the problem. These four elements, plus fatigue and flinching, will be reviewed in detail in this part.

At this point, it is reasonable to introduce the term "shooter-athlete." Shooters, especially national and world-class shotgunners, are highly skilled athletes. In fact, no less so than other sports requiring little power or all-out physical effort. Clay target shooting and similar sports are composed of complex skills, which combine speed, vision, concentration, maximum

Inside:

PSYCHOLOGY IN CLAY TARGET SHOOTING

SUPERSTITION

STRESS AND THE AIMING SPORTS

NEGATIVE THINKING — BLAMING YOURSELF

NEGATIVE THINKING — BLAMING OTHER THINGS

A WINNING ATTITUDE

CONCENTRATION

REACTION TIME

VISUALIZATION AND IMAGERY

NERVOUSNESS AND PHYSIOLOGICAL RESPONSE

accuracy and some endurance. Examples of comparable competitive sports might include archery, riflery (biathlon and running target), table-tennis, golf, badminton, tennis, racquetball and handball. Hence, any of the aforementioned elements that could help athletes in these sports may also assist the shotgun athletes. I will begin with the most important human element in clay target shooting — the mental game.

PSYCHOLOGY IN CLAY TARGET SHOOTING

Every knowledgeable coach, regardless of sport, recognizes the importance of the psychological factor in individual and team performance. Individual team members are influenced to some degree by the psychological responses of their team as well as by the opposing teams or individuals. And, the team as a whole is influenced by the psychological impact of each individual. As shooters and shooting coaches should be aware, psychology plays a large role in the shotgunning games, whether indulged in competitively or only recreationally. "Psychology" alone, however, is too broad a term. Therefore, we will review some of its components as they apply to shooting.

SUPERSTITION

One way many clay target shooters allow their own behavior to have a detrimental effect on their shooting skill is by indulging in practices that are nothing more than superstitions. Take, for example, the shooter who, in reloading his hulls, avoids reloading those that have missed a target. Such superstition will have an adverse effect on his shooting because he is thinking negatively. Subconsciously, he will be thinking about throwing away hulls rather than hitting targets.

A superstitious trapshooter takes the time to place the brass so that the words are readable. When he is about to call for the target, he may wonder, "Did I or didn't I align that shell?"

Again superstitiously, some trapshooters take great care to place the shell in the chamber in such a way that the base-stamp can be read. Psychologically, this type of behavior is detrimental to total concentration, because as he calls for the target, somewhere in the recesses of his mind, the shooter will be wondering: "Did I or didn't I insert the shell correctly?"

How about the shooter who blows the smoke out of his gun barrel after every shot? The feeling among "smoke blowers" is that if they don't blow into the barrel they increase their chances of missing the next shot, the theory being that some of the energy of the shot charge is lost if it has to first push the smoke out of the barrel. Again, to be preoccupied with such irrelevancies while on station can be more of a detriment psychologically than a benefit.

Another common sight at shooting fields is the gunner who refuses to be lead-off person on the squad. Does he believe that his performance will be improved if he observes the targets beforehand, or does he fear that a miss will be more noticeable if he is the first person to shoot at each station? Either way, his attitude is self defeating. Instead, he should view the lead-off position as a challenge.

"Smoke blowing" often goes beyond practicality. It may be detrimental to the shooter's mental management process when it becomes a preoccupying ritual.

Many years ago an acquaintance of mine won a major skeet tournament in the .410-bore with a 100-straight. Coincidentally, he had the urge to urinate for the four rounds of the competition. Now, despite the fact that he hasn't won any other major shooting event since, he will only compete with a full bladder!

Consider the person on station who accidentally drops a shell on the ground and kicks it aside rather than picking it up and placing it in the gun chamber. His action may have nothing to do with superstition, it could be good, common sense. Bending over sends blood rushing to the head; straightening up quickly may affect equilibrium. Also, some persons' eyes do not focus quickly when shifting from looking for the dropped shell close by and then searching for the distant flying target. Such behavior has a sound physiological basis. Conversely, some national-class shooters always pick up a dropped shell. These shooters feel that they will be too preoccupied trying to remember to pick up the loaded shell, rather than concentrating on the target they are shooting. In this case, individuals must weigh the trade-offs and make their own decision.

Superstitions or rituals also have a positive effect in competitive sports. For example, if a shooter feels that a certain brand of ammunition is lucky or that it will help him hit more targets, it probably will. The reason is not that brand-X ammo is any better than another type, it is that the shooter believes it is better. This phenomenon can be described as a "self-fulfilling prophecy." If he believes it or expects it to be so, then it usually becomes so. In this instance, the ammunition brand doesn't become a distracting factor. The shooter always buys and carries brand-X and when calling for the target is not thinking: "Did I remember to load brand-X?" But, once again, the shooter must weigh the trade-offs of the idiosyncrasy: if he makes it into the shoot-off and the gun club has run out of brand-X, is he

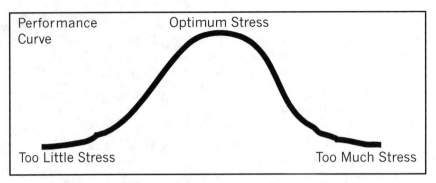

Performance Curve — Optimum Stress — Too Little Stress — Too Much Stress

going to let that affect his mental state and hinder his score?

STRESS AND THE AIMING SPORTS

Studies have shown that unique psychological stresses are inherent in "aiming" sports such as pistol, riflery, archery and shotgunning, which involve tremendous hand-eye coordination. The lack of physical activity in these sports does little to relieve stress, and usually just the opposite is true. The participant is put under more stress as he approaches a perfect or near perfect score and as his competitors' scores becomes known.

Yet, sports requiring all-out physical effort usually dissipate psychological stress, for example, once the starter's gun goes off in a 400-meter dash, the runner's "nerves" disappear. Participants whose anxieties require them to act out aggression in direct ways, (boxing, football and wrestling, for example) often do not do well in "aiming" related activities. And, participants who can't control themselves physically and emotionally while under stress will also fail to achieve high levels of performance in the shooting sports. Stressful and negative thoughts only serve to aggravate tense situations and increase the likelihood of poor scores.

The challenge, therefore, is for the shooter to learn to focus on the task at hand and use stress to his advantage by means of concentration and development of a positive attitude. This helps to create optimum competitive conditions. From another perspective, anxiety can be graphed as a bell-shaped curve. At one low end of the curve is not enough anxiety, which produces a casual attitude and weakened performance. At the other low end of the curve is too much stress, which also produces poor athletic results. However, at the peak of the curve is an optimum amount of anxiety (neither too much nor too little), which enables the athlete to perform at his best.

NEGATIVE THINKING — BLAMING YOURSELF

During the last 25 years I have taught and coached hundreds of shooters. In every physical education shooting class, recreational shooting course or shotgun team at least one individual — and usually more — is a negative thinker. He offers a bewildering set of comments that down-play himself and his own shooting ability. Often these individuals are successful, top-notch business managers, or confident, straight-A students. But on the shooting fields these same people lack self-esteem, have no self-confidence and possess a negative outlook concerning their shooting abilities. I take note when I hear them state: "I'll never be a good shot," "I know I'm going to miss at least five targets this round," or "I always choke under pressure."

Negative-minded thinkers become increasingly upset as they miss targets. Instead of relaxing, they swear to themselves, call themselves names and scowl. This attitude makes a pleasurable activity into a chore. Instead of enhancing their leisure, they create an environment that adds tension, stress and anxiety to the sport.

When shooters of this type realize that they are performing poorly, they bear down harder and become intensely serious. This, of course, only worsens the matter. Their muscles tighten and their minds strain in more self-defeating thoughts, "If I miss this next target it'll really ruin my score." Being tense and thinking negatively means that they anticipate a miss. It becomes a negative type of self-fulfilling prophecy — they get what they expect, and they expect to miss.

On the other hand, try observing AAA, AA and Master-class shooters. Sure, they concentrate intently on the task at hand. But that's all it is — mental focus and concentration. They are not "getting down on themselves" for a poorly broken or missed target. And how do they act between rounds or events? They appear oblivious to the pressure. They joke, kid one another, throw a Frisbee or play cards in the clubhouse. Meanwhile, Mr. B-class shooter is pacing, straining, stressing and shaking his head, getting down on himself for his "poor" score. The great shooters have not only learned the proper way to concentrate, they've also learned how to be their own best friend and how to have a good time.

NEGATIVE THINKING — BLAMING OTHER THINGS

Some "negative thinkers" blame other people or things for their poor performance — fellow shooters, referees, their guns, the ammo, the field, the targets or the conditions.

How about the skeet shooter who says, "If I didn't always get the slow pulls I'd have a better score," or the trapshooter who says, "If I weren't the one to get the hard-angle targets I could win this event." These self-defeating attitudes focus the blame on people or objects and prevent the shooter from taking responsibility for his own performance. When the weather is bad, it's easy to say, "I am not going to shoot well because of the rain (or sun, or wind, or snow)." But somebody is going to win the shoot with a good score, and it won't be the "blame-it-on-something-else" shooter. Instead, the negative-thinker should realize that many good scores have been shot under identical conditions. The attitude should be, "If the target is in the air and I can see it, I can hit it." With a change of attitude the negative thinker will believe that he can shoot the winning scores — no matter what the conditions. Remember, somebody has to win.

The U.S. Army Marksmanship Unit — International Trap & Skeet Guide has this to say about negative and positive thinking:

1. **Response to a Problem.** Psychologists have determined that there are four basic methods of responding to a problem. Two methods are positive and are classified as direct or indirect. Two methods are negative and are classified as retreat or evasion.
   a. Positive response.
      (1.) The direct, positive approach. This is the self-confident, self-sufficient, direct, positive attack. You realistically face the facts, analyze them, identify and evaluate the obstacles to a successful solution. You know what you want to accomplish and you take direct steps to attain it.
      (2.) The indirect, substitute or compromise approach. This is the small, diffident, tentative, indirect action. Sidestepping leads to seeking short-cuts. When the probable solution is tried, there is much fervent hoping that the fates are on your side. You are only hinting and probing instead of establishing definitely what you need to do.
   b. Negative response.
      (1) The negative retreat. The failure to give the honest try to see what you are capable of accomplishing. Surrendering without a sincere effort. The flight habit can become chronic. This is the man [or woman] that cannot accept the responsibility for a mistake or failure. A bad shot produces excuses.
      (2) Evading the issue. Evasion is the lack of incentive. "Why?" is the approach. "Why do I have to do better than anyone else?" If the desire to excel is not there, you will never aimlessly, or otherwise, achieve the degree of accomplishment that crowns the champion.
2. **Analyze the Problem.**
   a. Psychologists have discovered that one of the chief reasons for difficulty in the solution of problems is inability to soundly analyze. Pose a clear-cut plan of action in full array. Face the specific difficulty and make a determined effort to break it down. If it can be identified, there is a solution for it. There are shooters on your team or some other team that are operating without this specific problem putting a brake on their performance. Talk it out. A communal pondering session will break it wide open.
   b. There is a four-point system of analyzing and solving specific problems. It reduces the whole, big problem to many specific small ones. Head four columns on a sheet of paper with the following titles: one, 'STEPS IN THE PLANNING'; two,

'SPECIFIC DIFFICULTIES'; three, 'SUCCESSFUL SOLUTIONS'; four, 'DOUBTFUL OR NO WORKABLE SOLUTION'. Following this approach reduces a major problem, such as the delivery of an accurate shot, into many smaller specific steps, which can then be addressed individually.

Perhaps you are not interested in breaking down the problem into so many specific components. However, the points listed above are good ones and are worth considering and applying to your own mental management system. In other words, you can respond to a problem positively or negatively; it is up to you to determine which way to handle it.

A WINNING ATTITUDE

A positive or "winning" attitude, like the fundamentals of shotgunning, is something that can be learned. Attitude makes the difference between enjoying the shotgunning sports and posting good scores or stressing over every competition and shooting poorly as a result.

Here are a few tips from a friend of mine, the nationally renowned shotgunning coach and author from George Mason University, the late John R. Linn. He wrote:

> Start by realizing all pressure is self imposed. In many cases, it may be a way of not facing the realities of competition. The shooter who is the hardest on himself is often looking for scapegoats. Beneath the self-criticism, he is blaming his poor performance on squad members, pullers, wind, gun, shells or what have you. Accept the fact you missed the target and realize you are putting pressure on yourself.
>
> If being your own best friend is the first step to being a better shooter, the second is to own up to your mistakes. It is only when you accept the fact it was your own poor technique or execution that lost the target can you begin to work on improving your shooting style and movements.
>
> Since all pressure comes from inside, you can control it. Encourage yourself at every opportunity. The next time you get a good score going and suddenly miss a target, do not turn your nice day into a nightmare. Do not grab yourself from inside and call yourself stupid or careless. Never tell yourself you are a poor shot or you choked. Instead, give yourself some encouragement and support. Concentrate on all those smoked targets you had, and dwell on your mistakes only long enough to record them in your mental and written shooting diaries. Keep a diary so you will know what you have to practice. It will also show the progress you are making and help overcome weaknesses in your shooting technique; that in turn builds confidence.

Do not weaken yourself with negative thinking. If you believe you are going to miss, you will. The top shooters know this and work to stay "up" all the time they are on the [firing] line. If you feel negative thoughts creeping into your thinking, stop and get control of yourself. Reassure yourself you can break any target thrown out of the house. Return your thinking to the shooting fundamentals. Tell yourself to keep your head on the stock, and see the target before you move the gun.

Another way to have a winning attitude is to act like a winner: walk, talk and handle the gun with self-confidence (not to be confused with being conceited or "cocky"), and don't look intimidated by the competition. Smile when you miss a target! Acting confident will not only help you feel like a winner, but it will also distract or "psych out" your competitors because you appear unbeatable.

CONCENTRATION

Concentration is the single most important aspect in successful, competitive shotgun shooting. Webster's Dictionary defines concentrate as: "gather to one point; come together; devote all attention." Coach John Linn wrote: "Forget about Webster's Dictionary, my definition is something like putting together everything you know about a certain skill for a certain period of time." In the Winchester film *Skeet Well*, world champion skeet shooter and shooting instructor, Fred Missildine, defines concentration this way:

Concentration is the ability to get keyed up but yet relax. The ability to concentrate on breaking one target at a time. The ability to forget the second bird on doubles until after you've broken the first one.

Concentration, I guess, is the ability to take the last shots one at a time when you're shooting targets 98-, 99- and 100-straight in a tournament and not think about shaking hands until you've broken the last one.

The shotgunning games are often referred to as "seeing and reacting" sports. Matt Dryke, 1984 Olympic Gold Medalist in International Skeet, while describing an intense, "sudden-death" shoot off, said, "I was really moving well, and I knew I had a medal going into the final... I just tried to relax and keep it simple — see the target, break the target." What Matt was probably alluding to was being in "the zone" — concentrating on each target individually, thinking positively and just "seeing" and reacting. Whatever your definition of concentration, it is a valuable performance tool that must be mastered and practiced.

One of the most common tips used by coaches is "watch the ball," or in our case, "watch the target." To most shooters, especially novice and recreational participants, this advice may sound painfully obvious, "Of course I'm going to watch the target, what else is there to look at?" In reality most shooters look at the target but don't really see it; an analogy similar to saying you "hear something but don't listen." To do either properly, both "seeing" and "listening" require concentration. And, ironically, one of the best ways to concentrate is to really see the target. Some of the world's greatest athletes say that when they are "seeing" well — really visually concentrating — that the moving object of their attention (ball or target) appears to get larger or slow down. World-class batters claim that they can see the seams on pitched baseballs as it rockets toward them. Professional tennis players routinely watch the patterns of the seam on a moving tennis ball. Elite skeet shooters state that they can see the target spinning or rotating as it travels through the air. The target appears too big they say, so they focus on and shoot at a specific spot on the target. For example, Brad Simmons, friend and member of the 1976 U.S. Olympic Skeet Team, once said to me, "How can anyone miss these targets, they look like big 'ol watermelons floating out there!" Let me try to explain how this type of visual concentration is done.

Most shooters look at the target, or the general area surrounding the target, but this is not enough to achieve true visual concentration. The shooters look at the flying target, but simultaneously they are thinking about the lead, or when to hit it, or the follow-through or about what their score will be if they miss. The shooter who has mastered concentration does not let these or any other thoughts creep into his mind when truly seeing the target.

One way to "see" the target and deepen concentration is to look at one part of the target. A good focal point is the edge where the top of the rim or "flange" meets the dome (See Chapter 24 — Targets). This point occurs at the dead center of the target on straight-aways and at the nose of the target on angle or crossing shots.

Most novice shooters have difficulty mastering this technique. If the shooter is new, trying to find the focal point is a significant distraction; they are more concerned with noise, recoil, the weight of the gun and just tracking the target — and understandably so. Once all the basics are mastered, however, then it might be time to take concentration to the next level.

The look of concentration is often easy to spot. Here the former coach of the Yale Shotgun Team, Ed Migdalski, age 80, is unwavering as he prepares for a target.

This method of concentrating works because the mind becomes engrossed with watching the target. In doing so, the mind forgets to think too hard and instincts take over. The focal point is always in the present, preventing the mind from straying into thoughts of what has just happened or what might happen later. Visual concentration preoccupies the mind with a single, important purpose.

Visual concentration does not mean staring hard at the target. It does not mean you are thinking about trying to concentrate. It is not thinking intently about anything. It is what world-class athletes refer to as "being in the zone." The mind blocks all thoughts by focusing on the object of its attention. The experience should be enjoyable, thereby allowing yourself to get into a "relaxed concentration" mode. If your eyes are straining or squinting then you are trying too hard. While watching the focal point of the target, you should also observe whether it is rising or falling, if it is traveling left or right. "See" (imagine) the pellets leave your barrel and impact the target at the spot you are focusing on.

REACTION TIME

The term "reaction time" is often used interchangeably with the term "reflexes" by athletes and coaches. However, the two are not synonymous. Good reflexes are when an athlete is able to move quickly and accurately in a highly skilled act. Few people realize that during "reaction time" the athlete does not move! "Reaction time" is the time between the stimulus and when the athlete first reacts to the stimulus. In other words, for the shotgunner, it's the time from when the clay target is first seen to the time when the shooter first moves his gun. Reaction time is critical to the clay target competitor, especially the International-style skeet and trap shooters. Steps should be taken to reduce this time lapse as much as possible.

Reaction time is especially important for the International-style shooter.

As with any other natural ability, some shooters are born with faster reaction time than others. But, like learning to concentrate, some techniques are available to help shorten reaction time.

Studies have shown that what the athlete has his or her mind "set" upon while waiting to move will lengthen or shorten the reaction time. If, for example, the shooter achieves a "motor set," (referring to motor-movement skills) by thinking "move" while waiting for the target, the movement is started more quickly than if the shooter does not think about anything (a difficult task) or if he achieves a "sensory set" (referring to the body's senses) by thinking "listen for the noise" or "look for the target." The differences caused by the two styles of mental pre-start conditions could make the difference on whether a fast target gets a jump on the shooter or not.

Research has also found that flexing the muscles in the body parts to be moved (see Chapter 9 — Fitness and Conditioning) an optimum amount — neither too little nor too much — will significantly shorten reaction time. A moderate amount of muscular tension will cause a quicker reaction time than a lot of tension or not enough tension. The shooter must experiment to find the right amount of muscle tightness for optimum reaction time.

At this point it is logical to remind the reader about two drawbacks of negative thinking. First, the shooter's mind is distracted with negative thoughts, making it difficult to think "move." And second, negative thinking causes stress and tension. It's no secret that mental tension leads to muscular tension, and with muscular tightness comes a slowing of reaction time.

Reaction time may also be influenced by the shooter's visual focal point. Having the eyes watching the proper target emergence area will help the shooter move with the target more quickly. For more information on where and how to look, see Chapter 11 — Vision and Sighting.

The shooter who despite a "motor" mind set and a correct point of focus still has a slow reaction time should not consider himself as having limited ability. Another measurable skill is called "movement speed." Movement speed occurs after reaction time has been completed, that is, the actual speed with which the gun is moved during the course of the swing and the pulling of the trigger. Oddly, reaction time and movement speed are not always related in the same athletes. In other words, some shooters may not initiate their movement quickly, but that has little bearing on how fast they can move once the gun swing has begun. Also, the efficiency of the movement will influence gun speed — the smoother and more practiced the movement, the faster it can become.

VISUALIZATION AND IMAGERY

What is probably the most valuable and least practiced tool in the psychology of clay target shooting is "visualization" or "imagery." This training technique might be described as imagination that is put to work for a reason. Imagery can be easily demonstrated: close your eyes for a moment, then ask yourself, "which is redder, a strawberry or a radish?" or "which is darker, a raisin or a prune?" or "if I were to rotate the letter 'N' by 90 degrees to the right, would it make an new letter?"

In order to answer those questions, you probably had to imagine each situation — you created a "picture" in your mind. The same process can be used to mentally see and rehearse shooting clay targets.

Athletes who visualize or imagine performing their skill, in every minute detail, have superior athletic results. The first step in effec-

85

tively using imagery is to include all five senses. Hence, the term "imagery" is usually preferred over the term "visualization," which implies only thinking about what is "seen" during a performance. Effective imagery should be practiced by thinking about or imagining performance from the visual perspective (what is seen), the auditory sense (what is heard), the tactile sense (what is physically felt), the olfactory sense (what is smelled) and the gustatory sense (what is tasted). Imagining "feelings," such as confidence, during a performance can also be included.

The second step in effective imagery is to choose a "perspective" from which to do your imagining. Two perspectives are possible: the Third Person or External Perspective is used by thinking about what is seen from another person's viewpoint. Better put, it is as if you are a spectator or you are looking at a video tape of yourself shooting. The First Person or Internal Perspective involves what you actually see and feel while going through your shooting performance; you see the target emerge and you watch the end of the barrel track toward the target. Although either perspective is "correct," most elite and high-level athletes use the First Person perspective for their imagery training.

Imagery can be practiced anywhere: in your car parked at the shooting fields, while you eat a sandwich at lunch time, while jogging, while sitting in a dark room or while in bed. Find somewhere quiet where you can concentrate without being interrupted for five or ten minutes or more. A word of caution, however, do not do this while driving. Imagery can be such an effective experience that although your eyes are open you may fail to see the road or oncoming vehicles.

To use imagery as a training tool, the shooter must start at the very beginning of the activity and "see" even the smallest details. For example, picture yourself next in line to shoot Station 1 in American Skeet. You see yourself step onto the station and take your proper stance, feeling the concrete beneath your feet. Next you grab two red shells from your right vest pocket and load them in the gun, top barrel first. You hear the over-and-under click shut as you focus out over the center stake, and you feel a light, warm left-to-right breeze on your face. The stock of the gun touches your cheek, you look up slightly for the high house target and say "Pull." You see the target launch out above your barrel, you see the bead touch the target, you feel the squeeze of the trigger, hear the "boom" and feel the recoil as you watch the target shatter and smell the gun smoke. You reset the gun to take the low house target, and so forth. Some shooters rehearse this procedure for four rounds or 100 targets, which takes practice, patience, time and concentration.

Most sport psychology experts agree that you should think positively when you visualize. This means perfect leads and all broken targets. No benefit is gained from the negative reinforcement of watching yourself miss. The point of mental practice is to rehearse what is correct so that the actual task becomes easier and more successful, "perfect practice makes perfect games." Many of the best shooters also "visualize" briefly while on station preparing to shoot. They "see" the gun/target relationship and "watch" the target break, just before they call for the target. This positive rehearsal only takes a few moments and is extremely effective. Not only do you get a mental practice shot at each upcoming target, but it forces the mind to concentrate on the task and not wander or overthink the situation as described in the Concentration section.

Imagery may greatly enhance the scores of the shooter who practices it. Imagery cannot, however, take the place of shooting. It does not train the muscles that perform the functions the mind requires. Muscle memory training is necessary to perform repetitive skills and can be gained only through physical repetition of a task or movement.

Of course, most recreational shooters will not be so committed to their sport that they practice imagery on a regular basis, if at all. But visualization or imagery is an essential element for becoming an elite, national or world-class shooter. Everyone should try it, at least a few times, to see how it works for them.

The psychology of shooting sports takes many forms, but the bottom line is that without a practiced mental management plan, a shooter will not have as enjoyable a recreational experience, and his scores will certainly not be as good.

I will let my long-time friend, Brad Simmons, former captain of the Yale University Skeet and Trap Team and member of the 1976 U.S. Olympic Shotgun Team, tie together the psychology of winning in the shotgun sports. Brad writes:

> There are other things besides the official scores that must be considered when attempting to make a U.S. Team. These are the personal qualities that make up the shooter's edge in a head to head competition such as a United States Team tryout.
>
> One of these qualities is endurance. The person who can not only withstand pressure, but last longer than the others while doing so has an edge not only in a shooting tryout, but in any high-pressure competition.
>
> Another important personal quality in the shooting sports is the ability to concentrate on what you are doing rather than thinking about the kids, your job, or that person walking down the sidewalk behind you. In the fraction of a second it takes for your concentration to drift you've lost another target. But too many shooters try to concentrate all the time during a match. The good shooter is able to direct his concentration totally for the short time he needs it, and to rest in-between.
>
> Also important in gaining a winning edge in shooting is the

87

At some gun clubs, ATV's (all terrain vehicles) create noise and visual distractions.

element of style. Once you learn a style and shoot it well, don't walk into a match and start changing it! You'll only prove two things: that you don't have confidence in your own style and that you are too busy thinking about changing styles to concentrate on the task at hand — breaking all of the targets! Develop your style, put your faith in it, and don't be persuaded to change it in mid-stream.

Another key ingredient in successful competition shooting is to know the rules of the game. Nothing destroys confidence and concentration more than having some rule called on you in a match.

When competing in any match, don't compare scores or keep a record of your place in the standing. Nothing you do will hurt you more in a clay target sport than an overdose of confidence or a "stab" of panic.

A very important key to maintaining a winning edge is being independent. If you listen to what everyone has to say and take everyone's advice, the concentration time involved alone would draw from your attention toward the competition itself. Also, the factor of style comes into play again, for the winners in the game are the ones independent enough to follow their style and not question it. Make winning your priority, and don't let lesser issues get in the way.

The final element of gaining a winning edge in shooting is never quitting, no matter how many targets that you are down in a match. Personal experience has taught me this lesson. In the Olympic trials in 1976 for Skeet Shooting, I was down four targets after the first round of competition! There were 275 left to shoot, and at the end I had caught up (shooting a 292 out of 300). In the ensuing shoot-off with the three other men, factors such as style and concentration were a benefit to my performance. But they would not have helped one bit if I had given up after shooting a 21 in the first round. It goes back to a phrase seen on many junior high and high school football lockers: "Winners Never Quit, and Quitters Never Win!"

NERVOUSNESS AND PHYSIOLOGICAL RESPONSE

Psychological conditions are the topic of extensive research, and psychologists have designed training programs to cope with the stress of competition in most sports. One of the biggest psychological obstacles that a shooter must overcome is pre-match nervousness. In addition to the shooter just thinking he is nervous, nervousness also affects a wide range of undesirable physiological responses. In an article entitled "Psychological Preparation for the Shooter," Dr. J. Montes describes the common physiological symptoms accompanying nervousness of competition:

1. Tachycardia — increase in heart rate
2. Hypertension — high blood pressure
3. Tachypnoea — increased breathing
4. Digestive spasms — excessive intestinal activity and discomfort
5. Polyuria — frequent urination
6. Perspiration — nervous, clammy perspiration not due to heat
7. Vasoconstriction — lessening of blood flow to extremities
8. Muscular tremors — involuntary shaking andmuscle activity
9. Lack of coordination — movements become fumbling and jerky
10. Mydriasis — enlargement of the pupil of the eye
11. Loss of concentration — lack of mental focus
12. Tachypsychiae — increase in speed of the thought process

Dr. Montes advocates a strategy to deal with the nervous tension, which is simply to embrace these feelings as a regular part of competitive shooting. The shooter-athlete is better off accepting the fact that nervousness will always occur in a serious competitor and that coping with nervous tension is as much a skill as correct shooting technique. Relaxation, mental rehearsal and imagery will help refocus the competitor and reduce mental stress.

9. Fitness and Conditioning

Shooters are notoriously among the least fit group of athletes. Yet, it's no secret that many shotgunners perform well without an exercise program. But many don't. How many thousands of times have champion shooters lifted and swung their guns to gain the necessary endurance for long competitions? How much sooner could they have become good shots had they exercised from the start of their shooting career? How many more shoot offs might they have won had they been well conditioned? Will these "good" shooters ever reach their full potential without a conditioning program? Unfortunately, these questions are impossible to answer.

We do know that strength and conditioning plays a vital roll in the mental and physical aspects of all sports. I will attempt to outline the compelling reasons why the shooter-athlete should participate in an exercise program and the proper methods of doing so.

In addition to positioning the bones and muscles at their biomechanically most efficient attitude for ease and speed of movement, the shooter-athlete should also be concerned with developing his or her muscles for strength and endurance. All shoots, whether they are day-, weekend- or week-long, cause fatigue, which in turn hinders performance. By strengthening the major muscle groups involved in shooting, the competitor will not as easily feel the effects of fatigue.

The benefits of physical fitness on shooting performance have become better recognized in the last ten years. However, a strength and conditioning program is not a replacement for shooting, rather it's an addition, which helps provide significant gains with a relatively small investment of time and expense. In addition to general good health, exercise has three major benefits to the shotgunning games: (1) enhances gun hold and swing, (2) helps sustain endurance and (3) develops a relaxed, positive mental attitude.

Overall muscular conditioning will result in an increased ability to steadily hold the weight of a shotgun and swing it smoothly and aggressively at a moving target. A relaxed hold position will be easier, especially for the beginner or female shooter, and reaction time will be faster. Aerobic conditioning will provide a more efficient cardiovascular system. The endurance gained in physical conditioning will make long hours of training on the field less fatiguing. And because fatigue is reduced, training will be more productive. Controversy still surrounds the reasons why exercise provides a more positive mental attitude, but certainly it will help the competitor cope with many of the pre-match nervous conditions (see Physiological Symptoms in Chapter 8 — Sport Psychology). Also, the shooter who invests time and energy toward a goal feels more prepared, more confident and has a higher self-esteem due to this investment.

According to the National Institute of Health (NIH), regular exercise has many health benefits. The reader who studies these benefits will see that they will also help shooting endurance and match stress. The NIH lists the following positive responses to regular physical activity:

- gives you more energy
- helps in coping with stress
- improves self-confidence
- helps counter anxiety
- helps you to relax and feel less tense
- improves sleep
- tones muscles
- helps you maintain your optimum weight

PRINCIPLES OF TRAINING

Any participant, or coach of participants, must follow certain general principles of exercise and conditioning if safety and success are to be met. Of special concern is the coaching of young athletes. The human body will not fully mature until the late teens or early twenties. Growth demands require significant amount of rest and energy. Any training program should be developmental and not physically or mentally destructive. For young or old, exercise routines need to be well researched or designed by a knowledgeable fitness instructor. The following is a list of basic training principles and considerations that are offered as guidelines and should be referenced if creating, participating in or coaching a conditioning program.

Individual Response

There are many reasons why one individual responds better than another when on similar fitness and conditioning programs. Some of these reasons are as follow:

- **Heredity:** some shooter-athletes will respond more favorably to exercise than others due to genetic makeup; however, all can benefit to some degree
- **Maturity:** with regard to instructing youths, some bodies are more physically mature and can handle more training than their peers
- **Rest:** sufficient sleep rejuvenates the body for shooting or conditioning; the successful coach recognizes when to give a day off
- **Fitness Level:** rapid changes will occur in those less fit; observable results come more gradually as fitness level increases
- **Motivation:** one of the biggest challenges facing the participant or coach; goals must be set by the individual, not by an outside influence such as a parent
- **Environment:** stress, heat, cold, altitude, air pollution, humidity and many other factors can influence a shooter-athlete's response to training and conditioning
- **Injury:** those participants with a sore shooting shoulder, sunburn, muscle soreness or injury caused by sports participation may need either more motivation or time off depending on the problem
- **Nutrition:** the participant who misses breakfast, eats a lot of junk food, or drinks too much caffeine or alcohol generally does not perform as well as the individual who eats sensibly and is cautious with alcohol and caffeine (see Chapter 10 — Nutrition for more information)

Adaptation

Small changes occur in the body as it adapts to the demands of exercise. It takes weeks and months of a conscientious fitness program to achieve success. The process should not be forced or rushed. Positive adaptations for shooting sports, as well as general health benefits include the following:

- improved circulation, heart function and respiration (breathing)
- greater muscular endurance and strength

• stronger bones, tendons, ligaments and connective tissue

Overload

Any strength or conditioning program must put a demand on the body's system in order for gains and benefits to occur. As adaptation to increased work occurs, more load should gradually be added. The three main factors that influence the rate of improvement in exercise are frequency (number of workouts per week), intensity (effort involved — number of repetitions and amount of resistance) and duration (length of the session). As the participant becomes proficient with a given workload, at least one of these variables must be changed in order to stimulate more results. Progression should be slow and steady; if the overload is too great too soon then the body will break down rather than respond.

Specificity

The type of exercise undertaken must relate to the desired results. If you are weight lifting specifically to improve your shooting endurance, then heavy "power-type" weight lifting with only a few repetitions per exercise is of little value. Instead, the group of repetitions per exercise or "set" should be higher with lighter weight. Shooting performance will improve most when the training is sport specific.

Variation

As relating to motivation and adaptation, a training program must be varied to avoid boredom and achieve the best results.

Reversibility

It takes three times as long to achieve endurance as it does to lose it. Strength declines more gradually but lack of exercise will cause loss of muscle. Hence, the training regiment needs to be maintained even during the off-season.

Recuperation

Temporary muscle fatigue or soreness is a natural result from an exercise program. Not only are the muscles fatigued, but they may be tired enough to temporarily affect coordination. Consequently, shooter-athletes should avoid strenuous exercise the day before or the day of a competition.

EXERCISE PRESCRIPTIONS

Weight Lifting

Shooters probably need only 20% of their strength to walk and stand, and then repeatedly lift, mount and swing a shotgun. Hence, they do not need massive amounts of strength and power. What they do need is the stability, speed, energy, resistance to recoil and endurance to continue breaking targets through a long contest; weight training will enhance these needs. And, as strength increases, fatigue decreases.

My longtime friend and weight training partner, Jerry Martin, Certified Strength and Conditioning Specialist at the University of Connecticut, endorses the following guidelines for proper resistance (weight) training:

- the basic strength training principles for adults are the same as for youths, however, special care must be given to lifting technique and exercise control when working with young people
- any person, young or old, who wishes to participate in an exercise program, should first check with their doctor for medical clearance
- a fitness area, whether at home or in the gym, should be uncrowded, free of obstructions and have good ventilation and lighting
- resistance training should be preceeded with warm-up and followed by cool-down exercises such as walking, stretching and light weight lifting
- the training program should be designed to increase strength, endurance, flexibility and motor skills that are specific to the participant (shooter)
- all exercises should be done through a full range of motion
- it is unnecessary and often unwise to compete against other lifters or attempt maximum lifts, especially for youths or seniors
- for a training effect, strength and conditioning exercises should be performed for 20-30 minutes a day, three to four times per week
- light weight and high repetitions for each movement are ideal for the shooting sports; the amount of weight chosen should produce "failure" (when the muscle is too fatigued to do more repetitions in that "set" without rest) at between 12 and 15 repetitions
- one to three sets of each exercise should be done
- weight or resistance is increased in 1- to 5-pound increments (depending on the exercise) after 15 or more repetitions can be performed in good form
- don't hold your breath when lifting (inhale when lowering the weight, exhale when lifting it)
- never attempt heavy overhead lifts without a "spotter" (safety assistant)
- mix a cardiovascular or "aerobic" (swimming, walking, jogging, biking) routine with a strength training program for maximum health and shooting-sports benefit
- continue your strength training routine during the off-season

MAJOR MUSCLE GROUPS

A total-body conditioning program is always a sound choice, and the shotgunning games use most of the major muscle groups to some degree. Shotgunning utilizes more of the body's muscles than the other aiming sports, which include riflery, pistol and archery. When the shooting regulations call for an "off-the-shoulder" or low gun mount, as they do in International Skeet, F.I.T.A.S.C. Sporting Clays and several of the novelty shotgunning games, even more muscle action is engaged. The major muscles involved in shotgun shooting, their locations and shooting applications are as follow:

1. Neck — *Location:* front and rear of neck. *Function:* leans the head forward to the gun; back of the neck stretches to let the head come forward. When standing in proper shooting position, the head should be held as upright as is comfortably possible, with the gun stock being raised to the face, instead of the head being lowered to the stock. Because the head and neck should do no more than flow with the rest of the body movements, no major muscle-building exercises are recommended. Many shooters, however, suffer from fatigue in these areas because of tension. Relaxation is the key. Facial muscles should be loose; eyes comfortably open, not squinted. The jaw should be relaxed, without the teeth being clenched. For the neck, stretching exercises are useful.

2. Trapezius — *Location:* between neck and top of the shoulders. *Function:* shrugs or lifts the shoulders, which lift the arms and the gun.

3. Deltoids — *Location:* front and sides of shoulders. *Function:* lift and hold the arms and gun at proper height. The shoulders, a major area of fatigue, support much of the weight of the gun and contribute to the swing and follow-through. The development of the deltoids is especially important to new gunners who tend to hold the gun in position for longer than necessary before calling for the target.

4. Triceps — *Location:* rear of the upper arm. *Function:* extend the arms at the elbow when mounting the gun.

5. Biceps — *Location:* front of upper arm. *Function:* flex the arms at the elbow, hold the gun into the shoulder. The biceps are the muscles opposing the triceps.

6. Flexors & Extensors — *Location:* forearm, underside and topside of lower arm (respectively), between elbow and hand. *Function:* provide the grip strength on the gun. Extend the wrists and hands of both arms. Bear some of the gun's weight. No specific forearm exercises are necessary because the forearms are used as secondary muscle groups in most arm exercises.

7. Pectorals — *Location:* chest. *Function:* The chest muscles are used little during shooting, but they do draw the arms together at the gun.

8. Latissimus Dorsi — *Location:* upper back. *Function:* hold the gun into the body (with the biceps) and bring the gun down off

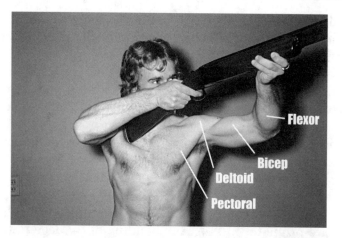

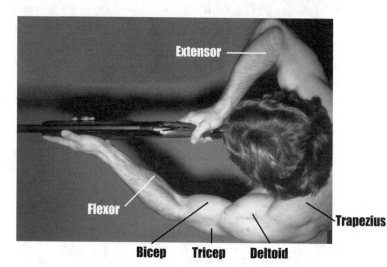

The upper-body muscles used to shoulder, hold and swing a gun are apparent in the well-conditioned shooter-athlete.

shoulder after each shot.

9. Abdominals — *Location:* abdomen. *Function:* stability, keep body bent into the gun at the waist.

10. Obliques — *Location:* sides of waist. *Function:* provide rotation at the waist, especially when tracking crossing targets.

11. Erectors — *Location:* lower back: *Function:* stability, keep body upright at the waist.

12. Quadriceps — *Location:* front thighs. *Function:* support the upper body, especially when shooting with knees bent, provide push into the targets, walking. Straining thighs that are not in condition are a source of fatigue in shooting. People who indulge in squatting, leg spreading, or excessive leaning on the clay target field are prone to fatigue. Any bending of the legs puts tension on the muscles of the front of the upper leg. The shooter's classical stance in clay target shooting is an upright position. Many gunners, however, bend their forward knee or both knees to various degrees, causing quadriceps fatigue and requiring additional leg strength.

13. Biceps Femoris — *Location:* hamstrings, rear of thighs. *Function:* lift lower leg while walking.

14. Gastronemious — *Location:* calves, rear of lower legs. *Function:* leg stability, flex the foot at the ankle, provide push off the toes while walking. The calves should not be used during the shot or follow-through; this would mean that the shooter's heels are being lifted off the ground causing loss of stability (see photos in Chapter 19 — How to Coach).

A Few More Tips

The following exercises are intended for home use; however, they can be more easily performed in a gym.

• At home, select any convenient weight, starting as light as with a box of shotgun shells or a brick if need be. It is best to invest a few dollars and purchase two different sets of dumbbells (found in any sporting goods store), which will allow for more weight on the stronger muscle groups. For less strong individuals, consider buying a set of 5-pound and a set of 10-pound weights. For stronger individuals, try selecting 10-pound and 15-pound dumbbell pairs. Attempt a few repetitions of a couple of exercises in the store to get a feel for the amount of weight needed. Or, fill empty one-gallon plastic containers with water until the desired weight is reached. A gallon of water weighs about seven pounds; filling the container with sand would make the weight even heavier.

EXERCISES

The following exercises have been marked by (1) exercise number, (2) name of muscle worked, (3) a letter — N, H or L: No weight, Heavier weight, Lighter weight, which provide a guideline for the relative strength of the muscle. And, (4) name of the exercise and (5) description of the exercise.

- Exercises should be done through a full range of motion at between 12-15 repetitions, unless otherwise noted.
- Make the speed of each repetition a four count (two up, two down).
- Rest 45-60 seconds between sets.
- Do the exercises in front of a mirror to check your form.
- If you feel any sudden stress or strain, stop immediately and check with your physician.

SUMMARY

Fitness and conditioning, if done properly, can increase your health, longevity and shooting performance. However, it is only one piece of the puzzle. To have a total package of shooting performance enhancement, care should be taken to provide the body with adequate rest, good nutrition and a positive mental management plan.

If you are still convinced that fitness plays such a small part in shooting that it does not matter, then ponder this point: if strength and endurance contributes to only 5% of shooting success, can you afford to miss five targets out of every 100?

Exercise 1. Neck

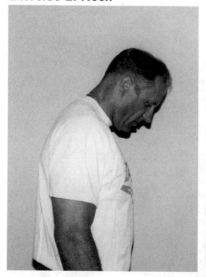 

(N) Neck flexion and extension. While keeping the shoulders square, move the head slowly, tipping it as far forward and backward, then side to side as comfortable. Complete five motions in each direction. Concentrate on keeping facial muscles relaxed. This is also a good warm-up and loosening exercise just prior to shooting. Do not rotate the head as that may cause spinal injury.

Exercise 2. Trapezius

(H) Shoulder Shrugs. Stand and let the dumbbells hang at your sides. Keeping the arms straight, shrug your shoulders as if you were attempting to touch them to your ears. Lower the weights back to your sides.

Exercise 3. Deltoids, front

(L) Front Lateral Raises. Stand holding the weights touching the front of the thighs with thumbs facing away from you. Use alternating arms; lift the weights in front of the body up to eye level, while leading with the thumbs (palms toward each other) or with knuckles up. Keep the elbows "cracked" (not completely straight) and the angle consistent throughout the motion.

Exercise 4. Deltoids, side

(L) Side Lateral Raises. Stand holding the weights at your sides, with your elbows cracked. Simultaneously bring the weights away from your body in a "flying" motion to eye level. Return them to your sides, keeping the elbow angle consistent.

101

Exercise 5. Deltoids, front and middle

(H) Overhead Press. Hold the weights atop the shoulders, palms facing forward. Simultaneously press them overhead to full arm extension, then lower them to the starting position.

Exercise 6. Triceps

(L) Triceps Extensions. Standing or seated, hold the weight in both hands behind your head with elbows fully bent, press the weight overhead by straightening the elbows (while keeping the shoulder joint still).

Exercise 7. Biceps

(L) Biceps Curls. Stand or sit with elbows against the hips. Bend your arms at the elbows and lift the weights up to shoulders. Then slowly lower weight to original position. May be performed using arms alternately or simultaneously.

Exercise 8. Pectorals and Triceps

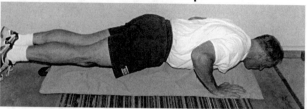

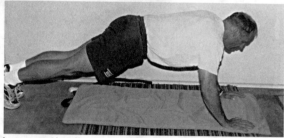

(N) Push Up. Lay face down on the floor, hands palms down and shoulder-width apart beside the chest, toes touching the floor. Press up off the floor to full arm extension while keeping the knees and waist locked. Lower your chest to the floor but do not rest.

Exercise 9. Pectorals and Triceps

(H) (Alternate or supplementary to exercise #8.) Select a flat bench or narrow table (about 12'' wide). Make sure the structure is strong enough to support you and the dumbbells. Lying on your back, start the weights beside the chest at shoulder width. Press the weights toward the ceiling in a semi-circular fashion so that they touch when the arms are extended. Keep the weights over the chest throughout the motion. Lower the weights to their starting position.

Exercise 10. Latissimus Dorsi

(H) Bent Row. Bend at the hips and rest one arm on a sturdy chair or bench (so your back is parallel to the floor). With the opposite hand, hold the weight near the floor. While keeping the wrist straight, pull the dumbbell to the hip and return it near the floor in a slight arc.

Exercise 11. Abdominals

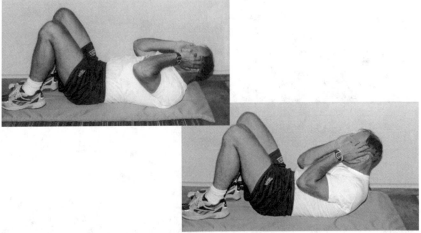

(N) Crunches. Lay with your back on the floor and knees bent, hands at the sides of your head (do not put your hands behind your head, pulling on the head may cause neck injury). "Crunch" upward by lifting your shoulder blades off the floor and squeeze the abdomen without lifting your lower back off the floor. Return to the floor, but keep the tension on the abdomen by not resting the shoulders on the floor. Always hold the elbows out to the sides, not forward (avoid pulling against the neck). Complete up to 50 repetitions per set.

Exercise 12. Erectors

(N) Hip raises. A similar exercise as previously shown (no photos). Lay with your back on the floor and the knees bent, arms along your sides. Rotate or tuck the hips forward (toward the ceiling) and press on the floor with your feet to lift the lower back off the floor. Come up until the back and thighs are in line, hold for a moment and return the hips to the floor. 12-25 repetitions.

Exercise 13. Obliques

(N) Rotary Torso. While seated or standing with your lower back straight, hold a 5'-6' pole (closet pole, dowel, broomstick, old rake handle, etc.) across the shoulders behind the neck by draping your arms around the stick. Rotate the upper body by twisting at the waist as far to each side as comfortable at a moderate speed. Complete 20-30 rotations. Also a good warm-up exercise before you shoot, utilizing your open gun instead of a wooden pole.

Exercise 14. Quadriceps & Biceps Femoris

(H) Squats. Stand erect in front of a chair or bench as if you are about to sit on it. With weights in each hand, and your back held as upright as possible, bend the knees until your buttocks just touch the seat of the chair (thighs parallel to the floor), then stand. Do not take tension off the thighs by sitting down between repetitions, and keep the heels on the floor.

Exercise 15. Calves

 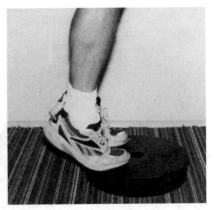

(N) Calf Raises. Stand on the edge of a stair so only the balls of your feet and toes are on the step. Lower your heels as far as comfortable below the level of the step. Press up onto your tiptoes while holding the railing for balance only. Repeat 15-25 repetitions. If this becomes too easy, you may double the body weight by performing them one leg at a time. May work better with bare feet or flexible-soled shoes.

10. Nutrition

SPORTS NUTRITION

"Nutrition" might best be described as the total process involved in the intake and utilization of foods and beverages that provide the body with substances for energy, growth and metabolism. One's nutrition, of course, can be either good or bad (healthy or harmful) depending on the specific foods and fluids that are consumed.

Shooters at all levels of competition, whether elite, Olympic-caliber athletes or members of a local gun club who shoot only occasionally, are always interested in ways to improve their scores. Besides training methods, sports researchers have investigated other means of improving athletic ability. One of the most extensively studied areas has been the effect of proper nutrition on athletic performance. Sound nutrition is an important part of the total training program for the shooter-athlete.

Improper eating or drinking before and during clay target competition may affect a shooter's scores by causing tiredness, lack of endurance, irritability or discomfort on the shooting field. It may also affect a person's ability to handle stress, which inevitably accompanies serious, competitive shooting. Good nutrition will also enhance any fitness program.

The shooter who participates in a day-long competition and believes that nutritional factors are a lot of nonsense should be aware that more energy is expended by a gunner in a day of tournament shooting than by an athlete who participates in an hour of football, basketball, track or swimming.

Nutrition begins playing a role in our lives from the moment we are conceived. The type and amount of food one consumes affects one's ultimate size, strength and stamina. Nutritional research has produced much information concerning the nutrient needs of athletes of different ages and sports. However, we are not concerned here with the science of nutrition as a whole, but simply with what food and beverages may affect shooting.

THE NUTRIENTS

To understand why certain foods and beverages negatively impact shooting performance, it is first necessary to have a concept of nutrition. Knowing what comprises good food will help the shooter select meals not only immediately before and during tournaments, but also year round. Let's start with the basic nutrients.

All foods and beverages must be composed of "nutrients" to one degree or another. Six major categories in human nutrition are classified as nutrients, and they each function in the body in one or more of three ways: (1) provide heat and energy, (2) provide material for growth and repair and (3) regulate body processes. The six nutrient groups are Fats, Carbohydrates, Proteins, Vitamins, Minerals and Water. Of course, volumes have been written about these nutrients and how they function, but our concern is only to give the shooter or shooting coach a brief understanding of them.

Fats: A concentrated source of energy, they contain nine calories (a measure of heat energy) per gram, as opposed to carbohydrates and proteins, which contain only 4 calories per gram. Fats can be broadly classified in two categories: saturated and unsaturated. Unsaturated fats come from plants, examples of which are oils from nuts and vegetables; they are important for some aspects of health. Saturated fats come from animal sources. Examples of saturated fats are butter and lard (the white portions of bacon and meats). Saturated fats are harmful to the health of the body by contributing to excessive weight gain, cancer and artery blockage. The easiest way to tell the two categories apart is that saturated fats are solid at room temperature, while unsaturated fats are liquid. Fats are not metabolized as energy until after 20 minutes of vigorous exercise has occurred. The average shotgun shooter need not worry about insufficient fat sources because the American diet is already too rich in them.

Carbohydrates: Carbohydrates are an immediately available source of energy and usually come from the plant kingdom. They occur in the forms of sugars and starches. Certain carbohydrates are healthier than others and provide more lasting energy; these are called "complex." Complex carbohydrates include fruits, vegetables, nuts, seeds, legumes and whole grains. Complex carbohydrates provide fiber and roughage in the digestive system, and perhaps more important to the athlete, complex carbohydrates provide a "trickle" of energy as they digest. Less healthy carbohydrates are termed "simple." These are sugars and starches that have been commercially processed or refined to their simplest form. Examples of simple carbohydrates include donuts and danish, white flour and white bread, cakes and candy, cookies and cola, pies and pop tarts and sugared cereals and sugared drinks. In other words, any foods composed primarily of white sugar or white flour, or a combination thereof. Because simple carbohydrates have been stripped of their fiber (and other nutrients such as vitamins and minerals), the body absorbs them almost immediately. This rapid absorption causes blood sugar levels to soar, providing a temporary sugar "high." Unfortunately, the energy surge is short-lived. Soon thereafter, blood sugar levels plummet due to a release of insulin into the blood stream (caused by the excessive sugar levels). This metabolic reaction brings on lethargy, drowsiness and fatigue an hour or two after the simple carbohydrates were consumed. This "down feeling" of low blood sugar will necessitate another sugar boost from a candy bar or cola, for example, to swing the energy level back up. A roller coaster effect like this is especially harmful to the competitive shooter. In the middle of a round of tournament shooting the shotgunner may hit a low, thereby creating fatigue, loss of energy and waning concentration. Missed targets are the result.

Proteins: Proteins are the main nutrient for growth and development. Proteins are not readily available sources of energy, but they do provide material for the formation of muscles, skin, hair, bones, cells and hormones. Amino acids are the building blocks of proteins. There are 22 natural amino acids, eight of which are termed "essential," meaning that they cannot be made by the body and must be provided in the diet. Hence, a protein is called "complete" if it contains all eight essential amino acids. Consequently, a food that does not contain all eight amino acids cannot, alone, provide material for growth or rejuvenation. Proteins are usually derived from the animal kingdom. Examples of proteins are meat, poultry, seafood, eggs and milk products. You may have heard that foods such as peanut butter provide protein. The truth is that peanuts, whole grains, corn, beans, potatoes, rice and others are complex carbohydrates. They do have substantial amounts of amino acids, but not all eight — they are not complete proteins. "White" proteins such as chicken, turkey, yogurt, eggs, milk and seafood are preferable to beef, veal, pork or deli meats because they are more easily digested and do not contain much saturated fat.

Vitamins: Vitamins are organic food substances that are found only in living things — plants and animals. This group of nutrients is extremely important to overall health, disease prevention and body functions. Vitamins alone will not improve shooting ability, however, vitamin deficiencies can impair athletic performance. They also play a role in breaking down and releasing energy from food. Vitamins are classified in two groups: "fat soluble" — A, D, E, K and "water soluble" — C and the B complex, which contains about 13 B vitamins. An average-dose multi-vitamin and mineral tablet is safe when consumed on a daily basis and is often recommended by nutritionists. Individual vitamins have dozens of functions in the human body; but of particular interest to the shooter-athlete might be the following vitamins and their applicable functions:

- A — health of the eyes and vision (adaptation to dim light)
- B — assists the body in obtaining energy from foods, anti-stress, health of the eyes and central nervous system
- C — anti-stress, infection resistance (colds), health of connective tissue, inhibits bruising
- E — muscle elasticity, health of nerves, oxygen utilization, endurance

If you take vitamin tablets, some caution is in order. First, large doses of single vitamins should not be taken alone because they may throw other vitamins out of balance. Second, a few of these nutrients are toxic in high quantities, including vitamins A and D and the minerals copper and selenium. If you question the type or dosage of vitamins to take, you should seek the advice of a nutritionist or dietitian. If you eat a varied diet of healthy foods, you may not need vitamin supplementation although many people still take a multi-vitamin as "insurance." The following is a list of common food sources to help you judge your dietary vitamin intake.

Vitamin Sources
- A — dairy products, liver, yellow and orange fruits and vegetables, dark green and leafy vegetables, fish liver oil, eggs
- D — dairy products, mushrooms, eggs, sunlight, bones of fish (from canned or pickled fish)
- E — eggs, wheat germ, expeller or cold pressed (non-processed)

vegetable oils, nuts, seeds, whole grains, legumes
- K — sardines, dark greens, naturally produced by the body in the intestine
- B — molasses, liver, wild game, seafood, poultry, nuts, whole grains, wheat germ, dairy products, legumes, eggs
- C — citrus fruits, dark green and leafy vegetables, strawberries, tomatoes, green peppers, cantaloupe

Vitamin Depleters

Many junk foods reduce vitamins in our bodies. Foods, beverages, medications and substances that deplete vitamins include alcohol, coffee, tea, mineral oil, sugar, tobacco, laxatives, birth control pills, antibiotics, sleeping pills, aspirin, fried foods and foods that are commercially refined or excessively cooked.

Additionally, many activities and conditions will also deplete vitamins in significant amounts. These vitamin reducers include stress, exercise, lack of sleep, sickness, infection, injury, surgery, radiation exposure, sunburn and high fever.

Minerals

Minerals are inorganic food substances. All unrefined and unprocessed foods grown on mineral-rich soil contain these elements; they are mandatory for the health of all life, including plants, animals and humans. Minerals are important to physical and mental well being. They are constituents of muscles, teeth, bones, blood and nerve cells. Minerals maintain a water balance in the body and assist proper central nervous system functioning. Water balance is particularly important to shooters participating in hot, humid conditions where water is lost rapidly.

Minerals can be divided into two main categories: major and trace. Examples of major minerals are calcium, chloride, magnesium, phosphorus, potassium, sodium and sulfur. The trace minerals include chromium, cobalt, fluoride, iodine, iron, manganese, molybdenum, selenium, vanadium and zinc.

Mineral Sources

Good sources of nutritional minerals include dairy products, all vegetables, dried fruits, seafood, wheat germ, whole grains, eggs, nuts, legumes, garlic, onions, mushrooms, organ meats, poultry, seaweed and molasses.

Mineral Depleters

Many junk foods, beverages and medications deplete minerals as they do vitamins. A few of these factors working against minerals are lack of exercise, excessive stress, caffeine, alcohol, white sugar, diuretics, laxatives, commercial food processing and overcooking of foods.

MEALS AND SNACKS

Keeping in mind the above recommendations for foods with adequate energy and health benefits (nutrient content), the shotgunner should then be concerned with how to eat before and during a shooting contest, whether at home or on the road.

Pre-competition Eating

A good principle to follow before competition is to choose foods and drinks that are both physiologically and psychologically pleasing and that your digestive system can tolerate. Generally speaking, a little light food in your stomach is better than too much food or no food, no matter how nervous you get. Most of all, select foods that you are accustomed to eating. The day of the big tournament is not the time to experiment with an exotic breakfast. If you are from Massachusetts and you usually consume waffles topped with fresh fruit and drink tea before a local contest, don't travel to Texas for the World Shoot and try a spicy Mexican-style omelet and black coffee the day of the 12-gauge event.

Breakfast

This is an especially important meal to set the stage for a day of competition — don't skip it! To omit breakfast is to invite hunger, fatigue, low blood sugar and laxness late in the morning. For an active person to be mentally and physically alert, about one-third of the day's food should be taken at breakfast. Coffee and donuts, danish or sugared muffins do not provide a satisfactory breakfast (see the Carbohydrate and Caffeine sections) and will ultimately cause low blood sugar with accompanying fatigue and lack of concentration. Fried eggs and bacon are not recommended before shooting because fats are difficult to digest; they slow the stomach's evacuation time and they don't provide an immediate energy source.

The breakfast menu recommended by sports nutritionists involves a high carbohydrate meal without excessive sugars such as syrup, jelly, soft drinks, donuts, pastries, sugared cereals or sugared coffee. During competition, you need to maintain your blood sugar level with a sustained release of energy. All complex carbohydrates or a combination of simple and complex carbohydrates will help you do that. Satisfactory op-

When the competitor travels, a typical "complimentary continental breakfast" can be found at many motels. It's possible to have a breakfast that will enhance your performance for the morning's shoot. Here, the shooter could have raisin bran or corn flakes with a bagel and juice instead of donuts, danish pastries and coffee.

tions include pancakes or waffles topped with fresh fruit or applesauce, whole grain toast, wheat germ (alone with milk or on top of cereal), grits, oatmeal, bagel with peanut butter, whole grain low-fat muffin, fresh fruit and fruit juices, dried fruit and whole grain cereals. A small amount of easily digested protein will help slow the release of carbohydrates from the stomach and prevent excessive hunger during the late morning. Examples of proteins that could be combined with the above carbohydrates include one or two eggs (not fried), yogurt, cheese, low-fat cottage cheese or low-fat milk. Besides simple carbohydrates, it is also important to avoid oils (fried food), butter, margarine, cream cheese and meats.

These breakfast options are healthy and energy-producing choices for year-round consumption, not just before matches. Yet, a word of caution is in order. If you don't regularly eat high fiber and complex carbohydrate foods you should start gradually and experiment at home first. Some individuals report abdominal gas, bloating, cramps and diarrhea from the sudden intake of excessive roughage if they are unaccustomed to it.

Lunch

It is just common sense not to overload your stomach at lunch if shooting is scheduled for the afternoon, but it is surprising how many shooters under the circumstances will eat two hamburgers and fries or a large bowl of chili and chips and drink two coffees or a large cola. These elements combine some of the worst selections possible: oil from the fries and chips, hard-to-digest protein and saturated fat from the hamburgers and chili, simple carbohydrates from the soda and white bun and caffeine!

Colas and chips make a poor-quality lunch. These shooters caught eating this junk food probably didn't realize it could have a detrimental effect on their performance.

Wise lunch choices include a salad, grilled chicken breast sandwich, sliced turkey on a salad or in whole wheat, peanut butter on wheat bread, soup and crackers, tuna salad or tuna on wheat or rye bread. A light dessert, if needed, could be trail mix, fresh or dried fruit, yogurt or applesauce. For beverage selection, you might consider juices, ice water, sports drinks, caffeine- and sugar-free soda, lightly steeped hot tea or decaffeinated coffee (see the Caffeine section) depending on the weather.

Dinner

If the tournament participant must shoot in the early evening, at a time beyond his usual dinner hour, he should partake in something light, which is carbohydrate and protein based, such as are recommended in the snack and lunch sections. A full dinner just before shooting is unwise.

For dinner before the next day's contest, carbohydrates and white proteins are the best choice. Some dinner component options include soup and salad, grilled or baked chicken or fish, roast turkey, baked or mashed potatoes, pasta, bread, rice, and baked, steamed or stir-fried vegetables. Avoid pork, beef and fried foods. If you must eat junk food, consider pizza with a vegetable topping. Pizza is probably the "healthiest" of the junk foods; the problem arises from eating too many slices. Have a salad with a little light dressing first, so that you do not attack a large pizza on an empty stomach. Beverages could include ice water, juice, low-fat milk, herbal tea, caffeine- and sugar-free soda, lightly-steeped regular tea and decaffeinated coffee. Serious consideration should be given to avoiding alcohol the night before the shoot — to decide, read the upcoming section on alcohol.

114

Large gun clubs usually provide a suitable selection of snacks. The caterers at the National Gun Club in San Antonio, Texas, offered fruit, bottled water, juice and sports drinks in addition to the usual chocolate bars, coffee and chips.

Snacks

An athletic snack should fulfill three goals: (1) take the edge off of your hunger, (2) not over-fill you and (3) help fight fatigue by supplying energy to the body. Once again, complex carbohydrates with a little protein are ideal. The snack should be packable and convenient enough to eat between rounds or events, depending on the type of contest.

Selecting a proper snack depends on where you are, what is available at the gun club and how organized you want to be. If you are driving to the contest from your home on the same day, it is easy to pack yourself a couple of snacks. Some suggestions follow:

- a cup of fruit-flavored yogurt (plain and vanilla have the least added sugar — you can always add your own fruit)
- a peanut butter sandwich (if you are serious about avoiding sugars you need to purchase pure-ground "old fashioned style" peanut butter, 100% stone ground whole wheat bread and all-fruit jelly)
- a protein blender drink made from frozen orange juice concentrate, low-fat milk and yogurt (you can also add fruit or

berries, if you desire)
- a piece of fresh fruit
- wheat cracker or rice cake sandwiches containing peanut butter and/or all-fruit jelly
- a bagel, plain or with peanut butter and all-fruit jelly
- fruit, tomato, V-8 juice or sports drink
- individually packed "no sugar added" applesauce cups
- vegetable sticks

If the contest is away from your house and you are staying in a motel, a few easy-to-pack, non-perishable snacks can be brought from home and carried in your shooting bag. Visit a health-food store; you may be surprised at what you can find:

This shooter probably thought that she would enhance her performance by eating an "energy food" such as a chocolate bar. Instead, a sweet snack causes low blood sugar after the initial "boost."

- trail mix or "gorp" (dried fruit, nuts and granola)
- granola bars
- health-food protein/energy bars
- dried fruit
- dried fruit bars or roll-ups
- thick, whole grain pretzels
- baked, whole grain chips

When selecting snacks at the gun club, avoid sugared drinks, candy, chocolate, donuts, pastries, hot chocolate and sweetened iced tea. Instead, look towards bagels, bran muffins, juices, ice water, toast, fruit, pretzels or crackers.

BEVERAGES

Water

Just about every operation or motion of the body needs water. Digestion and proper utilization of foods cannot take place without water. Nutrients reach the tissues, and waste products are taken away by water. Body temperature is controlled by water through perspiration. Water is more necessary than food is.

Because excessive losses of water due to perspiration lead to fatigue and lower efficiency in shooting, the gunner should be prepared to counteract sweat losses during extended periods of warm-weather competition. The pre-event meal should include sufficient liquid. One to three cups of water or other suitable beverage at mealtime will usually be enough to ensure hydration for

In hot weather, an excellent beverage choice is simply a cold cup of water between rounds

an athlete exercising strenuously for a few hours. Clay target shooters lose water through perspiration much more gradually. Therefore, rather than consuming more water than is comfortable at mealtime, the shooter should take a small cup or a few mouthfuls whenever it is convenient. Water coolers are usually provided at each shooting field at major gun clubs.

A disposable cup of ice cold water between rounds is all a body needs to stay in top shooting form, and it is surprisingly refreshing. Sports-drink squeeze bottles are now in vogue. Filling one of these with diluted fruit juice or sports drink (more on that later) will add a bit of flavor and it will ensure convenient and available fluids.

Milk

Experts in nutrition state that milk is one of the nearly perfect foods, and if not taken for a period of time, the nutrients calcium, phosphorus and riboflavin may be inadequate in the diet. Low-fat milk is an excellent source of protein. Science has not produced any compelling reason for eliminating milk from the athlete's diet as long as the individual can easily digest it. Some people have a lactose (milk sugar) intolerance, which produces gas, bloating, cramps or diarrhea, depending on the severity of the intolerance.

A common misconception about milk is that it dries the mouth. Milk will not produce dryness and discomfort in the mouth or "cotton mouth" experienced by some shooters. Saliva flow and the condition of the saliva are related to the amount of perspiration and reduction of body water content. When it is time for a shooter to appear on the field, his saliva flow may be influenced by his emotional state. Another common fallacy is that if milk is consumed before shooting time it will cause "curdling," resulting in sour stomach. When milk combines with stomach acids, the curdling that results is a natural process of digestion and does not result in stomach disturbance. On the contrary, milk may combat excess stomach acidity by neutralizing the acids, especially when added to coffee. And, it is healthier to add milk to coffee rather than cream.

Carbonated And Sweetened Beverages

These drinks mostly contribute sugar and calories. Some of them, such as colas, contain caffeine in varying amounts and therefore are considered stimulants along with tea and coffee. Caffeine acts as a diuretic; hence, colas and other soft drinks only worsen dehydration (see the Caffeine section). Unless the carbonated beverages are caffeine and sugar free, they should be avoided.

Sports Drinks

I recall Gatorade starting the sports drinks craze by earning popularity in the mid-1970s. Within the past ten years the sports drink wars have exploded on the market with every conceivable color and flavor available from a variety of companies. Even the traditional lime-green Gatorade now also comes in a variety of flavors. With so many products to choose from, the hot-weather gunner may be easily confused. Yet the real question is not which flavor to choose, but are the drinks beneficial, detrimental or simply not necessary?

Grabbing a cola between rounds or before an event adds caffeine and sugar to the competitor's system. But, the combination of caffeine and simple carbohydrate may adversely affect the gunner later in the match.

Most "energy drinks" are about eight percent carbohydrate from various sugars, which is the percentage that most scientists believe is the correct concentration to enhance fluid absorption, power muscles and fight fatigue. You may wish to avoid drinks that list fructose (a sugar) as the first ingredient other than water. Drinks that have large amounts of fructose can slow gastric absorption and cause gastro-intestinal problems in some people.

The major objectives of fluid supplementation during hot weather are to replenish water and to provide carbohydrates. Water, of course, should be your primary concern — especially if you sweat heavily. Studies have demonstrated that if an athlete loses as little as two percent of his or her body weight due to dehydration then performance will be effected. However, if the match is long and the gunner consumes little food during the competition due to nervousness, then a sports drink may be in order. Once consumed, the carbohydrates in energy drinks can be used for supplemental fuel within 15 to 20 minutes. If you wish to avoid too much sweetened fluid, dilute the sports drink 50/50 with water. It will also last longer and save more money for targets!

According to research, if the drink is cool or chilled, it will empty faster from the stomach than warm or room temperature drinks. Cold beverages also taste better, partly because they "feel" more refreshing. And if they taste better, you will drink more fluids, which are what is needed in hot weather. Also, in addition to sodium (salt) the carbohydrates in sports drinks aid the absorption of water from the bloodstream into the intestine.

CAFFEINE

Methylxanthines — xanthines for short — are a group of stimu-

Many shooters don't realize that caffeine is found in a wide variety of foods and beverages. Here is a sampling of some of those products.

lant compounds that include caffeine, theophylline and theobromine. Caffeine is the world's most commonly used and socially accepted drug, and in a pure form it is a bitter, white, odorless powder. Perhaps you don't drink coffee. Did you know that xanthines are found in a wide range of medications and beverages? The strongest of the xanthines, caffeine, occurs in coffee; theophylline is the predominant stimulant in tea, and theobromine is found in chocolate. Tea and chocolate also contain small doses of caffeine.

When ingested, caffeine is absorbed immediately by the body. You will notice its effects within a half hour. Blood level peaks in about an hour and caffeine's stimulating effect lasts for three to five hours, usually declining after three. Caffeine is a central nervous system stimulant and it also releases epinephrine (adrenaline) from the adrenal gland. Because epinephrine is a stimulant, it enhances caffeine's effect. Two parts of the brain are stimulated by caffeine: the cerebral cortex, which governs thought and higher nervous functions, and the medulla, which regulates heart function, breathing and muscle coordination. Blood pressure and pulse rate increase, causing coronary arteries to expand, resulting in greater blood flow to the heart.

Concentration and speed are important skills for the competitive shotgun shooter. In other sports size and strength are crucial, but these elements have less influence on shooting performance. During a long shoot-off, for example, peak concentration is needed the most when it's the hardest to maintain. Caffeine could enhance endurance, speed and concentration. Here's how.

Physical endurance, although not as critical as the mental game, still plays a significant role in shooting performance and results. One study found that 2 1/2 cups of coffee, equal to 300 mg caffeine, taken 60 minutes before exercise significantly increased endurance during exercise. For the first 50 minutes, caffeine stimulated only the central nervous system. Participants experienced a psychological boost: work seemed easier because perception of exertion was lowered and alertness and mood were raised. These effects are beneficial in themselves, but after the first 50 minutes caffeine spared glycogen (carbohydrates that are stored in the body, which are used as a primary energy source during exercise) by increasing the rate that fat was burned. Caffeine reduced muscular fatigue and increased the muscles' capacity to work. Hence, coffee may help shotgunners by increasing physical endurance during prolonged shooting periods.

As an ergogenic aid — a substance that enhances performance — caffeine may have several other properties that are useful to clay target competitors. Caffeine is known to lessen reaction time (see the Psychology chapter) and improve coordination. By stimulating the central nervous system it increases speed and efficiency of mental and physical tasks and helps concentration. Small amounts of caffeine may produce clearer thought patterns and sharpen appreciation of sensory stimuli.

Studies show that after consuming two cups of coffee, driving skills improve and typists type faster with fewer mistakes. Perception and alertness are sharpened. Caffeine is ideal for individuals who must concentrate for prolonged periods — conditions duplicated in shotgun tournaments. If you frequently drink caffeine-containing beverages you will have a tolerance to caffeine but can still benefit from some of its performance enhancements; however, the effects will not be as pronounced as for those who usually abstain from caffeine. Although caffeine's effect is lessened for habitual users, regular coffee drinkers who forego their morning brew could hinder their performance with lethargy and sluggishness — two early symptoms of caffeine withdrawal.

For some shooters, coffee, tea or cola consumption is so important that it becomes a major part of the pre-tournament routine. Eliminating the caffeine may not only take away any ergogenic benefit but it could be detrimental to contest preparation. University of Connecticut Strength and Conditioning Coach, Jerry Martin, noted that: "Drinking coffee before an event becomes a mental factor — like the pregame meal. Steak and eggs are not the best breakfast physiologically, but from a psychological aspect it may be helpful — it becomes a ritual. You must weigh the pros and cons of the dependency."

Caffeine isn't for everyone, and many negative side-effects can result from significant coffee consumption. Some notable drawbacks to consuming caffeine are as follow:

Disqualification. More caffeine is not better. A dose/response curve for caffeine benefits does not exist. Once you have ingested an optimum amount — perhaps one to two cups of coffee for a shooter, more than that does not produce better results and may over stimulate. It could disqualify you from world competition. Some of the most commonly used and abused ergogenic aids are prohibited from international competition, including caffeine. Olympic athletes may consume beverages containing small amounts of caffeine, but its level set by the U.S. Olympic Committee as a banned substance is 12 mcg/ml in urine — the equivalent of 1,200 mg of pure caffeine. A shooter must drink about six to eight cups of strong coffee in a short time to attain that level.

Over-intensity. For some individuals, caffeine used before or during exercise may bring on anxiety, irritability, delirium and hallucinations. Caffeine stimulation increases nervous tensions and agitation prior to a contest. Consuming caffeine products only for competitions may make it difficult to manage the increased mental and physical intensity.

Dehydration. Caffeine is thermogenic. It raises your metabolic rate and internal temperature making you dehydrate and overheat. Used as a main source of liquid, caffeine-containing beverages such as cola are counterproductive, especially during shooting contests in hot weather. Caffeine is a strong diuretic — it makes you lose water through urination. Having to urinate while competing on a distant field is a realistic concern.

Depression and coffee nerves. Persons not accustomed to caffeinated beverages may be unaware of possible depression that follows stimulation. Prolonged coffee consumption may cause headaches, insomnia, nervous irritability and a speeding heart rate. Queasiness or jitters, know as "coffee nerves," imitates the symptoms of anxiety. These feelings of anxiety could increase pre-match nervousness and interfere with concentration and coordination.

Intensifies hangovers. Caffeine can't counteract all the negative effects of alcohol consumed at the pre-shoot party the night before. Drinking coffee the morning of the contest because you are hungover may not be wise. Besides simply "waking you up," caffeine can aggravate some of the effects of a hangover, such as intensifying headaches and multiplying the dehydration process.

Increased hunger. Caffeine can heighten hunger during a shooting contest. It raises basal metabolic rate, known as metabolism, and increases the number of calories burned. It also triggers the release of insulin from the pancreas causing glucose — commonly known as blood sugar — levels to drop, creating hunger. Being a little hungry during a shoot makes you more aggressive, some competitors claim. But too much hunger becomes distracting.

Heartburn. Coffee increases the secretion of acid in

the stomach and may cause heartburn, especially if consumed on an empty stomach. In this case, it's not the caffeine that causes the problem but the various acids found in coffee and tea. Hence, drinking decaffeinated coffee to prevent heartburn before a big shoot won't solve the problem. Adding milk to these beverages helps buffer the responsible acids.

Headaches. Caffeine has a conflicting impact on headaches, depending on the individual and the type of headache. It can cure a headache for some, but prompt a headache for others. Let experience guide you.

Beverage Contents

Only a 6 oz. cup of brewed coffee contains 83 mg of caffeine. And, many shooters don't realize how much caffeine is contained in other popular beverages and medications. Here's a sampling:

- Cold drinks, per 12 oz: Coca-Cola 45 mg; Diet Pepsi 36 mg; Mountain Dew 54 mg; Dr. Pepper 41 mg; instant iced tea 56 mg; Dr. Pepper 41 mg; Surge 52.5 mg and Jolt 71 mg.
- Hot beverages, per 6 oz: Leaf tea 41 mg; instant hot cocoa mix 10 mg; instant coffee 60 mg; decaffeinated coffee 3 mg and, as noted earlier, brewed coffee 83 mg. Of course the average coffee mug holds significantly more than 6 oz of coffee, with proportionately more caffeine, so judge accordingly. Dunkin' Donuts largest coffee cup, for example, holds 20 oz — the equivalent of about 275 mg of caffeine.
- Over-the-counter medications, per tablet: Vivarin 200 mg; No Doz 100 mg; Weight Control Aids 50-200 mg and Anacin and Dristan 30 mg.

Alternatives

Of course you can just quit drinking regular coffee and switch to decaffeinated. But such a sudden change can cause withdrawal symptoms. Caffeine is habit forming. People become dependent on caffeine to maintain their level of work efficiency and performance. As few as three to four cups of coffee a day can cause psychological and physiological dependence on caffeine. Once you are addicted, sudden abstinence from the drug may produce headaches, drowsiness, lethargy, runny nose, yawning, disinterest in work, nervousness and even nausea. You should gradually wean yourself off coffee or cola by reducing the number of cups by one a day every few days until your diet is caffeine-free. Or you can reduce the amount of caffeine in your coffee: new to the market is lite coffee, which contains 50% less caffeine. To replicate lite coffee at a tournament simply ask the restaurant waitress or the gun club food-sever to mix half decaf with half regular coffee. Caffeine-free soda, herbal tea, decaffeinated tea, fruit juice, sports drinks and water make better choices because they replenish fluids and lessen the number of trips to the rest room.

The Caffeine Verdict

Everyone is different and the exact dosage of caffeine needed to increase performance is unknown. My friend and former member of the Yale Skeet and Trap Team, chemist Owen Wallace, Ph.D., stated that: "Clinically, caffeine causes restlessness. It wouldn't do much good if you are in a competition and you are edgy and highly stimulated. It's a trade-off: It's always good to be alert, but you don't want to be pulling the trigger before the target comes out."

If you consume caffeine-containing beverages now, you may want to experiment with varying amounts before practices or minor competitions. Try drinking one or two cups of coffee about a half-hour before the event. Do this periodically with and without coffee and track the results carefully in a shooting diary, making sure to note other factors such as weather temperature and the amount of alcohol and sleep the night before. Don't add much sugar, if any, because it will vary your energy level. To make this a more valid case study, have someone else give you the coffee each time and not tell you until after you shoot if it was decaf or regular.

John Jensen, special instructor to the University of Connecticut Shotgun Team and member of NSSA Hall of Fame, had this to say: "You want to be in control. You don't want to feel panicked — but you want to be aggressive. You need to charge after that target, especially on a shot like high-two or low-six. You must be attentive and sharp, whether it's skeet, trap or Sporting Clays. Caffeine could help you with that. Do I recommend that someone drinks coffee before a shoot? No."

ALCOHOL

Alcohol has been proven to have an extremely negative impact on sports performance. Most people are not noticeably affected the day after one, two or three drinks. However, to the shooter-athlete striving for perfection in a highly coordinated, skilled sport, the effects can be significant. Many shooters disregard most research on alcohol because they are not "alcoholics" or because shooting does not require strenuous physical exertion. Compounding the matter, much of the available information must be extrapolated from other similar sports. Only recently have researchers begun to understand alcohol's effects on fine motor skills such as those required in moving target shooting.

Unfortunately, shooters drink for a variety of reasons the night before a contest. They may believe alcohol will improve their performance. Perhaps they try to relax and quiet pre-match nerves.

Alcohol may be a way into the "in-crowd." Peer pressure is placed upon the shooter to be socially accepted by teammates and competitors. They may think drinking will make them more self-confident. Shooters might believe it helps endurance or that alcohol will relieve frustration and improve psychological well-being.

Sadly, alcohol often becomes a part of the pre-match routine for many shooters. Jerry Martin, Strength Coach at the University of Connecticut said that: "Athletes are one of the most superstitious groups of people. If the athlete, by chance, shoots well the day after a drinking binge, then it could become part of their pre-competition routine. But, of course, in reality that would be very detrimental." Scientifically, alcohol has no value in enhancing the shooter's performance. On the contrary, alcohol is implicated in hindering ability in three critical areas: mental, physical and visual.

The short term psychological effects of alcohol are as important as the physical implications. The mineral magnesium is depleted in the body when alcohol is consumed. Magnesium helps the muscles relax when they are not contracting. Low magnesium in the body causes irritability, nervousness and, in some athletes, increased blood pressure. Although athletes commonly drink to relax, true relaxation is not possible. Alcohol may manifest itself by creating a non-caring attitude.

Alcohol can distort a shooter's image of himself. The psychological aspect of drinking may make shooters think that they are better than they really are: they lose their inhibition. This is a negative effect, because, if performance does not equal expectations, then excuses start. They can use alcohol as an easy way out: "I was drinking last night so I didn't perform up to my potential." It gives competitors a false sense of pride and athletic accomplishment.

Alcohol consumption also has long-term effects on athletic performance:

Unwanted body weight. Excess calories add weight, a detriment in most sports. One 12-ounce beer equals .5 ounces of pure alcohol and 150 calories. An average 150-pound person must run for a full hour to burn the calories of only three and a half beers. Calories from alcohol are not useful during exercise. The amount of oxygen needed to release calories from alcohol is greater than the same amount of carbohydrate or fat. Alcohol's calories are "empty," meaning that they are low in nutrients.

Impaired coordination, concentration, steadiness, balance and the processing of information. The blood's ability to take up oxygen decreases, affecting the

123

brain. It impairs coordination, hinders concentration, affects arm steadiness, body sway and balance, and slows the processing of information.

Fatigue. The increased production of lactic acid, the build-up of waste material in the muscles, accentuates fatigue toward the end of long day of competition.

Increased urination. Alcohol acts as a diuretic. The need for frequent trips to the bathroom will hinder concentration.

The possibility of dehydration. Up to 5% of body weight loss causes strong thirst, discomfort, dry mouth, increased effort in exercise, impatience, apathy and difficulty concentrating. As little as 2% weight loss can influence fine motor skills in athletes.

Impaired judgment, mental activity, memory and learning. Alcohol depresses the central nervous system.

Low body temperature. Hypothermia is a danger during prolonged exposure to cold weather. This is important for shooters competing in winter leagues in cold climates.

124

Small amounts of alcohol have an effect on the body similar to fatigue and hunger. It influences sensory perception, discrimination, reaction time, fine coordination, judgment, alertness and dexterity. All are extremely important factors in the quest to become a champion shooter.

The conversion of alcohol to glucose, commonly called blood sugar, occurs only in the liver and happens very slowly. Muscles can not use alcohol as a direct energy source. Hence the shooter who drinks to enhance his or her energy level is actually depleting it. Heartbeat is quickened and blood pressure is elevated. These are two of the least desirable symptoms a shooter wants during competition. Breathing is affected by alcohol's effect on the brain. Also altered is the shooter's much needed sleep.

Friend of mine and skeet shooter, Michael Gerber, Strength and Conditioning Coach at Syracuse University, said, "Alcohol has a very specific negative effect on restoration and recuperation. It robs your body of rest and impacts the quality of sleep; the athlete wakes up tired and lacking in mental clarity. In an activity like clay target shooting you need reflexes as quick as a cat's. The entire sport is seeing and reacting."

The hangover is the most obvious sign of possible performance impairment. Shooters who drink the night before a match strongly deny any impact on their shooting performance. Standard replies are "I'm not an alcoholic," "I never drink the day of the event," or "all the alcohol is worn off by the next day." However, the shooter who is uneducated about alcohol's retention in the body has little concept of its impact the day after drinking. The physical effects of alcohol-induced hangovers are very damaging to a shooter's performance.

Hangovers can be compounded by jitters, which involve uncontrollable shaking of the hands after a night of drinking. Shooters could have difficulty holding a gun steady or shooting well because of it. A simple headache can be a detriment to the shooter; it is just one other thing that can distract from shooting. It takes away from the task at hand.

And contrary to common belief, there is no quick cure for hangovers. Cold showers, black coffee, aspirin, another drink, "some of the dog that bit you," or exercise, "walking it off," does not help an individual recuperate any faster.

Unfortunately, vision — the most critical aspect of target shooting — is most affected by hangovers. Extremely low levels of alcohol impair the vision and eye coordination of an athlete. A single alcoholic beverage influences eyesight up to 24 hours after all measurable traces of alcohol have left the body. This symptom is called nystagmus. It is the bouncing of the eyes when the head is moved quickly and the eyes try to recover and focus on an object. Strangely, nystagmus does not begin until alcohol has left the body. The amount of visual interference is correlated to the amount of alcohol consumed and can last for several hours.

Other types of visual hindrance occur the day after drinking. Peripheral vision, needed for identifying a target from above, below or from the side of the gun barrel is impaired by alcohol. More time is required to find and track moving objects, which directly increases tracking errors. Focus and depth perception are less accurate. The athlete's field of vision is reduced. Ordinary objects have been shown to be seen as darker and less distinct. Poorly lighted objects, as is the case in late-day shoot-offs, are lost entirely. Reaction time, the time from seeing the stimulus to the time the athlete moves, increases.

The increased chance of missing even one target because of drinking is not worth the risk. Clay target shooting is both an individual and a team sport, so the impact of a lost target may be even greater. Shooters, who have invested thousands of dollars and countless hours to improve their scores, should err on the side of caution and abstain from alcohol before a contest.

For safety reasons, of course, any participant drinking alcohol in any form during a practice or contest should be immediately barred from shooting and ordered to leave the premises.

SALT SUPPLEMENTATION

The gunner need not worry about extra salt during hot-weather shoots to help retain fluids. More than sufficient salt intake is present in the average American diet.

SUMMARY

It is impossible to prescribe a rigid diet for everyone participating in clay target events. Each person's physiological characteristics must be considered. However, all of the preceding information will be of value if it does nothing more than alert the gunner to the fact that nutritional demands are greater than expected when participating in prolonged matches and tournaments. And, that certain foods and beverages can cause fatigue, drowsiness and impact concentration and visual ability. With nutrition, you can be your own test subject. The shooter should analyze his reactions to different foods and beverages at practices and small competitions; record those observations in a shooting diary (see Chapter 17 — Keeping a Shooting Diary). Reread the notes and develop an eating plan before trying something new at the big shoot. Work on developing and maintaining good eating habits, "good habits, like bad ones, are hard to break."

Many interesting, well-written paperbacks, which contain more detailed information on nutrition, are available in any bookstore.

GENERAL FATIGUE

General fatigue during a shoot may be caused simply by poor nutrition. Lack of fitness, mental stress and several other factors can significantly contribute to unnecessary tiredness and loss of concentration. Chapter 12 will deal with the causes of and possible solutions for fatigue, which may occur while participating in the shotgun games.

11. Vision and Sighting

HUMAN VISION

Advice given to new shooters by knowledgeable coaches and instructors is to shoot with both eyes open, if possible. Using both eyes gives the gunner greater peripheral vision, which allows him to pick up the target sooner and judge its direction and speed. Using two eyes provides depth of field or "depth perception," enabling the shooter to view the target and background three dimensionally. Also, the two-eye approach will prevent excessive strain on a single sighting eye. Moreover, the gunner who uses only one eye will be inclined to aim at the clay target rather than point at it. The shotgun is not meant to be aimed like a rifle; it should be pointed.

Some instructors maintain that it is possible to become an expert shotgunner by sighting with one eye, pointing out that some of the great tournament champions employ the one-eye method. It is true that a few of the really outstanding shotgun shooters close one eye voluntarily, but, most of them do so because the master or dominant eye is not the one they use to sight

Inside:

HUMAN VISION

MASTER EYE VISION

BLINKING

SHOOTING GLASSES

EYES AND SMOKE

along the gun barrel. As an example, if a right-handed shooter's left eye is the master eye it must be closed so that the gunner will not be inadvertently sighting with the master eye instead of the one that is actually looking down the barrel. If you have no eye problems, by all means get accustomed to shooting with two eyes open. If your master eye is not the one nearest to the sighting plane of your gun you can still become a good shooter by closing it while on station. Gunners in such a situation find it more comfortable and more effective to permanently cover the eye glass lens. However, this practice invites fatigue in the eye that is doing all the looking. The covered eye could have a "flip-up" covering, so that both eyes can be used for general viewing when the gunner is not on station.

If you are a new right-handed shooter and your left eye is the master, you should switch to left-handed shooting (and vice versa) in order to shoot with both eyes open. But such a change is simply too awkward for established shooters. It is also possible to purchase a gun with a custom cross-over stock, which is "S" shaped to enable the gunner to shoot from his right shoulder if he has a left master eye.

MASTER EYE

As stated, when shooting with both eyes open, one eye usually dominates the actual alignment and coordination of pointing the shotgun. That eye is the "master," or "dominant" eye.

To find your dominant eye, make a small circle with your hands, locate any distant object, and with both eyes open, extend the circle to arms length and put the object in the circle. Here the shooter uses a water-well pipe.

With both eyes open, slowly bring the circle back to your face while keeping the object in view. This should be your dominant eye.

All shotgunners should know which is their master eye. If you are a beginner and you have not been instructed on how to check for your master eye, you can do it yourself. The procedure is simple: with both eyes open extend your arm and point the index finger at a distant object and hold it there. Close your left eye. If the finger remains on that target, it means that your right eye is master. If your finger moves out of alignment with the object, the left eye is master. If your left eye seems to be the dominant eye, you can check the drill by looking at the same object, only this time close the right eye. If your left eye is really your master eye your finger will remain on the object. Another method of checking eye dominance is to form a small circle by putting together the thumb and index finger of both hands. Pick an object and with both eyes open quickly extend your arms, placing the object in the circle. Now slowly bring your hands back to your face, all the while keeping the object within the circle. You should now be sighting through your dominant eye. This same technique works better for some people by cutting a dime-sized hole in a piece of paper rather than forming a circle with the hands. More information on sighting is discussed in Chapter 15 — Learning To Shoot.

VISION

Vision is the process of seeing. The proficiency of a shooter's vision is determined by how and where he or she looks.

Seeing proficiently is a critical part of success in the shotgunning games. "Seeing" or watching the target properly means intensely focusing on it, thereby creating or enhancing concentration (for more on concentration see Chapter 8 — Sport Psychology). But "seeing well" means the physical function or ability of the eye to pick up and track moving targets. "Seeing well" requires good vision through eye function, proper shooting technique, good corrective lenses, and knowing where to look. Both elements of seeing a target properly — mental and physical — will be discussed. Let's start with the mental aspect of seeing.

Visual Concentration

Visual concentration does not mean staring at the target. Staring is just a form of distraction. When staring, the eyes do not focus on the target even though they are looking at it. The eyes are dissociated from the target and the result is loss of concentration with little awareness of what is really happening. Have you ever driven for a short time and then not been able to remember driving that stretch of roadway? You were staring at the road, but not concentrating on it.

How often has an experienced shooter missed an easy shot? It happens when taking the "easy" target for granted by lapsing in visual concentration. The shooter must learn to never move his eyes ahead of the visual stimulus, breaking visual concentration and misjudging the target. To be consistently successful, the shotgunner must determine a target's flight path by intently looking at it and not letting go of that visual lock until the body has responded and the target is shattered. Concentration is based on visual centering and our movements are coordinated by our eyes. When we lose visual mastery, poor shooting performance results. Leon Revien, O.D., author of *Sportsvision* wrote: "The secret to good concentration is keeping both eyes on the ball, or any stimulus [clay target], without being distracted by background, peripheral images, shadows, color changes, and extraneous sounds and movements."

According to Revien, the skills and functions that are necessary in good sports vision are trainable. With practice the athlete can develop rapid responses to visual stimuli, plus enhance concentration, accurate spatial judgment, confidence and reduce eye fatigue — a vital factor in performing well under stressful conditions. These skills can be developed over time by intently watching hundreds of moving clay targets and by doing exercises at home.

"Cord-ball" is an excellent at-home exercise designed to develop accommodation and convergence (see definitions below), which are two highly desirable visual skills for the shotgunner. For this exercise you will need three beads, buttons or similar objects of approximately 1/2- to 3/4-inch in diameter in different colors, a 10-foot-long piece of thin string or fishing line and a thumbtack. String the three beads and attach one end of the line to a well-lit, bare wall or other plain surface using a thumbtack. Whether you sit or stand, make sure the string is at eye level. Center the beads on the string 2 1/2 feet apart and 2 1/2 feet away from each end.

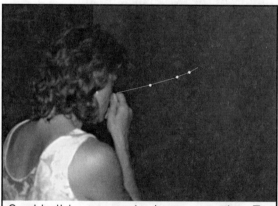

Cord-ball is an easy-to-do eye exercise. Ten feet of line, three beads and a thumbtack are all that is needed to create the exercise at home. Spread and tie the beads apart at 2 1/2' intervals, attach one end of the line to the wall with the thumbtack and hold the other end against your nose. Now you can focus from bead to bead to develop your shooting vision.

To perform the exercise, hold the loose end of the string against your nose and focus on the first bead until you can see it sharply — the other two beads will be seen as "blurred doubles." Now move your focus to the middle bead until it is in sharp focus and the near and far beads are blurred doubles. Do the same for the third bead. Rapidly repeat this procedure, moving your focus from far to near and near to far. Continue this exercise for three to four minutes, but less if you feel eye strain. As the days go by, you'll notice that the eye fatigue does not occur as soon. When you become good at this exercise, challenge yourself by moving the beads to different distances.

Another simple exercise is to watch a swinging ball. This activity will help train your eyes to track and concentrate on a moving target and ignore background distractions. Simply get a small, tennis-size ball or other suitable object, a child's wooden block for example, and attach fishing line, a narrow cord or thin rope to it — you may have to tape the line or cord to the ball if the ball proves too slippery to tie to. Hang the cord from an overhead fixture or tack it in a doorway at eye level (basements make good places for this exercise because you can leave the ball in place from day to day). Stand an arm's length away from the ball and give it a moderate push so that the ball swings in uneven elliptical patterns. Focus intently on the moving object through its travel while trying not to "see" any of the surrounding background. Do not move your head to track the ball. As the ball slows, push it again in another direction. Stay with this drill for three minutes. Try moving your position in the room so that you do not get accustomed to the background. To further develop a focal point (see the Psychology chapter), write dime-size letters around the circumference of the ball with a magic-marker. While watching the swinging ball, pick a letter and try to stay focused on it.

A variation of this exercise can be used to enhance eye-hand coordination. Give the ball a shove as before, but then quickly step back two arm lengths away, or about five feet. Using the same hand that you use to swing your gun, track the moving ball with your index finger, arm extended. To further develop muscle memory, simulate the gun hand-hold placement and arm position that you would use when shooting; in other words, make sure the knuckles on your pointing hand are turned to the side, not up, and that your elbow is slightly bent and elevated. Try tilting your head forward a bit so that your eyes track the target while rotated upward, as if your head was on the stock.

More detailed information on athletic vision, visual performance and eye exercises can be found in several books, including *An Insight To Sports — Featuring Trapshooting and Golf* by Wayne Martin, O.D., and *Sportsvision* by Leon Revien, O.D. & Mark Gabor.

The following skills (with brief definitions) compose good shooting vision:

accommodation: adjusting the eyes' focus to see targets clearly at varying distances

acuity: the ability to discern objects; also called pursuit movement — centering the eyes to keep them aligned with the target; works with hand coordination; does not find moving objects but locks onto the target once peripheral vision has located it; visual clearness

convergence: having two eyes fixed on a target at the same time to maintain a single image

depth perception: depth of field; the ability to see objects as three-dimensional and thus judge distance precisely

span of recognition: saccadic movement (see below); peripheral or side vision; area of the retina away from the focal point (acuity area); recognizes, locates, interprets, and then reacts to the target, but does not center or align on it

speed of recognition: how fast the eye can identify the target

Pursuit movement (see "acuity") and saccadic movement (see "span of recognition") are critical in moving target shooting. Saccadic movement locates direction, speed and distance of a moving object. This is a function of what is loosely referred to as "peripheral vision." Saccadic is the primary eye movement to a traveling target.

After the moving target has been located and the speed and direction have been determined, then pursuit movement centers on the object. Pursuit movement keeps the eye aligned with the traveling target. The saccadic movement and the pursuit movement work independently of each other — saccadic can not center and pursuit can not locate. But each must complement the other.

When the shooter lets his eyes drift off the focal point of the target and back to the field of motion, in other words switches from pursuit to saccadic movement, visual confusion occurs. By making this switch the shooter delays his shot or flinches and the target is lost. Once the target is located with peripheral vision and the shooter's eyes then lock onto it, he must visually concentrate hard enough to prevent any other movements or objects from the field of vision from distracting his attention. A good example of this occurs when a hunter flushes a covey of quail. Instead of picking out and staying with one bird, he sees the entire group and "pack shoots." Unless purely lucky the result is no hit birds, and the hunter wonders how he could have missed such an easy shot.

Restated, saccadic and pursuit movements are equally important but separate in their functions. Any occasional or intermittent distractions will likely cause flinching, delayed shooting and missed targets. The shotgunner must work hard to develop these visual skills, permit them to assist each other yet keep them distinctly separate in their function.

It is important not to stay trained on a focal point all the time; this practice quickly causes fatigue. One way to begin practicing "relaxed" and "focal point" looking is to imagine your eyes as having four zoom-focus settings, like a video camera. Let's choose Station 1 low house in skeet an easy example. (1) After you drop the shell into your gun, focus out in a broad area. You will see the low house, the grass, the sky, the center stake (target crossing point) and the protective fence to the right of the house. As you put the gun to your face, zoom in one notch. (2) Now you are looking at the house, you no longer "see" the fence, the grass, or the center stake. You focus to the spot where you first expect to see the target emerge. (3) As the target emerges it will go from an orange blur to a solid object (saccadic movement) as you begin your swing. (4) With the gun moving, your eyes click down to the final zoom (pursuit movement) setting and "see" your target focal point. Hold this intense focus as the target crosses the field and through your shot. Immediately after you follow-through, relax your vision back to "wide angle" as you take the gun off your shoulder.

Champion trapshooter Dan Bonillas once put it this way: "I keep my eyes at all times in the target area [beyond the trap house]. Once I see the direction of the target [saccadic movement] I attempt to narrow my vision as if pulling a drawstring on a dufflebag and move to the target [pursuit movement]."

BLINKING

On average, the human eye blinks 15 to 20 times a minute. Blinking is an automatic and controlled skill, which we do to protect, cleanse and moisten the eyes. To shoot well, it is critical that the shotgunner refrain from blinking during the entire process of gun swing, shot and follow-through. A blink takes about 1/5 of a second to complete. In one of the shotgunning games (International Trap), clay targets can travel at up to 65 miles per hour and will cover a distance of 18 feet during 1/5 of a second — the time of a blink. Hence, if you blink in the process of tracking a target, you may not see six yards of its flight.

133

SHOOTING GLASSES

Every clay target shooter should wear protective glasses. The primary reason, of course, is because of the chance of being hit in the eye with a jagged, speeding piece of clay target. Even in shotgunning games where the likelihood of getting hit by a piece of clay target is remote — trap for instance — it is still possible to get gunpowder residue or dust blown into the face. Shooting glasses also protect the eyes from glare and ultraviolet (UV) radiation from the sun. And, most shooters believe that certain lens colorations help them locate and track moving targets against various backgrounds under different lighting conditions, thereby enhancing performance.

The problem, especially for the beginner, is that a dizzying selection of styles, lens colorations and tints is available in shooting eyewear. Let's start by explaining the design (shape, size and style) of shooting glasses rims and lenses.

Small, circular, wire-rimmed frames and small, heavy, black horn-rimmed frames interfere with sideways eye movements and peripheral vision. On a skeet shot like Station 2 high house, for example, the shooter with these type of frames will look back toward the window (target opening) and have his vision blocked. Or, his right eye will be looking through the large gap between the lenses — a most distracting situation. Also, when putting one's head down to the stock the wearer of these small, low riding glasses will be looking

Glasses whose lenses are small and far apart are not preferable shooting glasses.

Ideal shooting glasses. A light tint with wide lenses that ride high on the face are perfect for maximum vision on the shooting field. This pair was made by Decot Hy-Wyd (see Appendix C).

at the frames or over the top of the glasses.

Proper shooting eyewear frames should be wide, thin and made of wire. Many shooters use gold rims, but some find the gold distracting. In this case, matt-black frames are available. Likewise, the lenses must be wide, high and distortion free. Make sure you select break-resistant lenses. Good sports glasses are, of course, shatter resistant.

Another feature to look for in shooting glasses is "UV protection." Ultraviolet radiation is undetectable by people because it is not visible to the human eye. Shooters spend many hours in the bright sun. Unfortunately, prolonged exposure to UV rays causes damage to the cells of the cornea (front protective covering of the eye) resulting in corneal ulcers and cataracts. A hat or cap helps, but to prevent permanent eye damage, the lens must provide UV protection. Further, because the dark lenses dilate the pupil, they let more harmful UV radiation into the eye. In other words, dark "shades" made popular by the sunglass industry may cause unnecessary harm to the eyes. Therefore, the most protective lense is a lightly tinted one designed with UV protection. Also, do not confuse UV protection with polarization; polarized glasses are what fishermen use to reduce glare so they can see into the water better.

Shooting eyewear should have thin, flexible wrap-around ear pieces. Wrap-arounds prevent the glasses from falling off the shooter's face when bending over to pick up dropped shells, hulls or other objects. The thinness of the wire adds comfort, which is critical if the shooter wears earmuffs instead of earplugs; earmuffs squeeze thick ear pieces against the head and discomfort results. Nose pieces on good shooting glasses are placed low on the lenses, this keeps the glasses riding almost comically high on the face. The advantage here is the ability to look through the lenses, not above them, when the head is down on the stock. High-riding lenses also prevent them from hitting the gun stock. Over the years, some of the best shooting-style eye glass manufacturers have been American Optical, Bausch-Lomb, Zeiss and the very popular Decot Hy-Wyd. For these and other fine eyewear manufacturers, see *Black's Wing & Clay*, listed in Appendix C.

The lenses themselves, besides being high, wide and close together should have the proper shading. Determining correct tint and coloration for each shooter is a difficult task, and in most cases it is strictly individual preference. Because of the way people see color differently, the color or shade that is suitable for you may be distracting to someone else. Consequently, don't give a new shooter a colored or tinted pair of glasses that you "swear by" — that color may be wrong for them.

The stimulus to the eye is light. Like a camera, depth of field, or "depth perception" and sharpness is increased with a constricted aperture. The pupil should be as small as possible, hence, the more light that the shooter can comfortably tolerate by wearing lighter lenses, the better his or her vision will be. Therefore, the worst possible lens coloration is found in the typical, popular dark green or dark gray sunglasses. The best tint is no tint unless absolutely demanded for comfort, and then it should be as light a tint as possible.

Although you may think that dark glasses make you look "cool" or "dashing," they are a poor choice for shooting eyewear.

Using tinted or color-absorptive lenses shifts the color wavelengths of light entering the eye, which can affect perception time and visual recognition. Hence, colored and tinted lenses must be selected with care. According to research, the relative visibility for lens colors, in order from best to worst, is as follows: clear, yellow, fluorescent yellow, fluorescent orange, orange, fluorescent red, red, blue and green. Added to the mix is the fact that some lens manufacturers offer different combinations of these colors. Still, the research is not conclusive on the best single color.

One study by Heinson (1958) found that: "The visibility varies with the background but yellow was the easiest to see in every background." Yet another study cited in *Shooting Sports Research* by the NRA (1988), stated:

> Yellow lenses have been rumored to have advantages for shooters, especially in low light, outdoor conditions (fog or cloudy skies). Yellow lenses absorb light waves in the short end of the color spectrum and can darken shadows on hazy days. There is no evidence that this acts to improve marksmanship performance. The effect of lenses seems to be primarily a matter of preference.
>
> Whether shooting skeet, trap or live game in the field, distance vision to locate and track the target is of prime importance. Prescription glasses need to provide sharp visual acuity with adequate vision for close range tasks (identifying shell, loading, etc.).

Decot Hy-Wyd, one of the top-selling shooting glass manufacturers, emphasizes light tint. They write: "Once again, the single most important feature of your glasses, other than proper prescription, should be having them as light a tint as you can stand." Decot has this to say about the color lenses they offer and target sighting conditions:

Lens Color	Conditions
Rose	Good when shooting orange, lime green, black, and white targets against all backgrounds.
Purple	A combination of gray and vermilion. Excellent when shooting against a green background as it dampens the color green and enhances an orange target against the green background
Orange	Works well when shooting at orange targets against an open or varied background
Bronze	Good all-purpose lens for clay target shooting
Red	(Vermilion) Used when shooting against a green background and can work well for those who have a red/green color deficiency
Yellow Gold & Clear	Recommended for low light conditions. These colors will give you a high percentage of light transmission. The gold and yellow lenses will give you a brightening effect and better definition of your target.
Green & Gray	Neither of these colors do anything to enhance the target. The green will enhance a green background and actually disguise the target. Decot makes these colors because we get orders from shooters and eye doctors who don't know the difference between sunglasses and shooting glasses.

EYES AND SMOKE

Eyes not only work best when they have had adequate rest through sleep, but they also require clean air. Late-night card games, where people are smoking, will add greatly to eye strain in the next day's shooting. Similarly, shooters who go from a smoky clubhouse directly to the shooting fields are expecting too much from their eyes. Under such conditions the eyes will not perform at their best and the shooter's scores may drop. (For more information, see Ocular Fatigue in Chapter 12).

12. Fatigue

The physiological element that most influences the shooting accuracy of experienced shotgun competitors is fatigue, and it can involve any or all of the human elements discussed in this section (Part II). I am not referring to total exhaustion or the type of fatigue that a shooter may experience after a long day of work or a night of carousing, but to the more subtle yet not less important element of hidden fatigue, the kind that is hardly noticeable and that is often ignored by the great majority of shooters, especially the veterans.

Fatigue may creep up on the gunner in the course of shooting in one or more of the following forms: muscular, mental, ocular, acoustical, thermal and nutritive, all of which are capable of draining some of the energy and concentration that is required for "top-form" shooting.

MUSCULAR FATIGUE

The most common and most pronounced fatigue is muscular, the kind that affects the whole body, and is suffered by those who force themselves into exagger-

Inside:

MUSCULAR FATIGUE

MENTAL FATIGUE

OCULAR FATIGUE

ACOUSTICAL FATIGUE

CLIMATIC THERMAL FATIGUE

PHYSICAL CONDITION

A crouch with excessive leaning at the waist is sure to cause fatigue later in the match. Also note the right heel lifting off the station, which indicates further problems with this shooter's form.

ated squatting, leaning, and leg-spreading positions while on station. Loss of energy by such muscular strain occurs slowly, sapping the shooter's energy until, as the shooting progresses into another round, his or her scores begin to drop.

When any part of the muscular body tires, it affects the responses of the entire system, including eyesight, which needs to be keen at all times for good shooting. Body reflexes and eyesight may be only slightly affected by loss of energy through muscle strain, but the effect may still cause targets to be missed and consequently make the difference between a good score and an excellent one, or winning or not winning a championship.

A strained stance is easily corrected. The gunner simply assumes a more upright relaxed position (see Chapter 15 — Learning to Shoot). The correct position may feel awkward at first, and the shooter's scores may initially suffer, but once the stance is developed, his or her scores will be higher than they were originally. Another common, creeping malady not recognized by many shooters is arm weariness. During shoots, when the gunner is not actually shooting, the gun should be held or rested in such a way that its weight is not borne entirely by the arms.

On station, pointing the gun for too long before calling for the target is a common cause of fatigue, especially among new shooters.

With the gun open, this is an acceptable way to rest between shots, thereby lessening fatigue of the arms and shoulders.

Any serious shotgun enthusiast who wishes to improve his shooting should engage in a strength and conditioning program. During actual shooting, the benefits of such exercise will go a long way towards eliminating muscular fatigue. Chapter 9 — Fitness and Conditioning contains guidelines and photographs identifying the muscles involved in shotgunning and the suggested exercises to strengthen them.

MENTAL FATIGUE

Some shooters can combat mental fatigue better than others. Of course the degree of mental fatigue depends upon the individual's personality and his competitive experience. Mental stress can affect scores, especially when participating in tournaments away from the shooter's home grounds, when he has to think about motel accommodations, car rental, registration, practices, food, ammo and so forth. The common-sense approach to alleviating mental fatigue in such circumstances is to make all arrangements well in advance and not wait until the last moment. Another type of mental fatigue may be brought on by psychological responses and can be reduced or avoided with proper mental focus (see Chapter 8 — Sport Psychology).

OCULAR FATIGUE

Tired eyes and good shooting are simply not compatible. A shooter's eyes may be strained or irritated to a point that will subtly affect his shooting ability without the shooter being aware of it. If reaching the shooting grounds requires a drive of several hours, a short nap will help rest tired eyes. Sitting in a clubhouse full of cigarette, cigar, or pipe smoke will irritate eyes.

Something as obvious as the need for a cap as a protection from bright sunlight should not have to be mentioned, yet I constantly see shooters who disregard this imperative, even after the coach's recommendation. Not only does direct sunlight produce eye strain caused by constant squinting, but the targets themselves cannot be seen as well. Exposure to glare accelerates body fatigue and contributes to headaches.

Our eyes use energy, and when pushed — as in clay target shooting — they draw even more body fuel. Shooters, who believe that watching several rounds of targets shot by others will help their concentration are making a mistake. It will only produce eye fatigue, especially on bright days. Most good shooters like to watch a few targets at the field on which they are about to compete, and rightly so. But intently watching dozens of targets should not be done immediately before a gunner expects to shoot because his eyes may not recoup in time for his own shooting.

Excessive reading immediately before going out to the clay target field may be a hindrance to some shooters. During intercollegiate competitions I often see students sitting in cars or in the clubhouse deeply engrossed in their studies. Perhaps they are feeling pressured to get classroom assignments done. But it stands to reason that eyes that have been focused for an hour or more on small print may prematurely tire. Young eyes generally adjust quite quickly, but I believe it would help the shooter if he ended

Even after the coach's urging, this shooter still "doesn't like hats." Note that the coach's eyes are shaded, but the shooter's are not. Bright light tires the eyes and causes squinting and fatigue. The wise gunner will always wear a cap or visor when shooting.

his book or lap-top reading at least a half hour before shooting.

Are eye drops useful in soothing or removing irritation? Yes, the drops may feel good, but such medication may hinder the focusing of the eyes. Serious tournament competitors who use eye drops should consult an oculist concerning the specific eye medication in question.

ACOUSTICAL FATIGUE

The human ear's reaction or objection to too much noise is not outwardly apparent. However, an abused inner ear may well make its objections felt, causing gun swing hesitancy, flinching, and other subtle faults that are not easily detectable. None of these imperfections may be permanent, but they may occur frequently enough to be reflected in the shooter's scores.

Of course, everyone but a fool wears hearing protectors while shooting. But many gunners remove their hearing protectors the moment they finish shooting and do not use them again until they are back on the shooting field. It is not uncommon to see a group of participants sitting on a bench close to the firing stations, either watching the other shooters or waiting to shoot. Not one person in the squad will have his ear device in place. Ignoring gun blast in such situations, especially in day-long tournaments, can be harmful to the ears, not only by causing immediate miscues in shooting or headaches, but also by contributing to permanent ear damage. Prevention, of course, is simple; wear protective ear devices at all times when you are close enough to gun report to feel the slightest discomfort.

CLIMATIC THERMAL FATIGUE

Hot weather fatigue, that is, loss of energy through overheating, is a summertime hazard caused by excessive loss of water due to perspiration. This condition lowers general physical efficiency, leads to fatigue and increases the chance of missing targets. It can be a serious handicap to clay target shooters, especially for those traveling to

Hopefully, this competitor is done with the day's shooting. Lying in the hot sun will contribute to dehydrationtion and fatigue. If you must nap, do so in the shade.

southern tournaments where the climate is distinctly warmer than the one they came from. Precautions are simple but necessary: wear a lightweight hat that has a brim to shade the eyes and a peak or crown that permits ventilation. A wide-brim straw hat is fine, but don't wear a heat-retaining felt cowboy hat, no matter how dashing it makes you look. Keep eyes unstrained by wearing appropriately tinted glasses (see Chapter 11 — Vision and Sighting). Clothing should be light-colored, lightweight cotton, and consider a lightweight long-sleeve shirt and long pants if you are susceptible to sunburn. Wear sunblock on all exposed skin. Drink plenty of cool liquids to avoid fatigue and overheating from dehydration. Avoid caffeinated beverages, as they act as diuretics and will speed dehydration (more on that in Chapter 10 — Nutrition). When traveling south, try to arrive a day ahead of time so that your system can start to acclimate to the hot conditions. Rest in the shade or in an air-conditioned clubhouse or vehicle at every opportunity. And, skin cancer threat aside, don't lay out in the sun unless you have completed all shooting.

PHYSICAL CONDITION

Naturally, in a squad of shooters of equal ability, those who are physically fit will likely outscore those who are not. To be in good physical condition for shooting, one may need to go to a gymnasium, jog, swim or do the simple at-home exercises prescribed in the Conditioning chapter to prevent muscle fatigue. If you are overweight or elderly and that sounds too strenuous, walk whenever possible. I do not mean you have to go long distances; a comfortably vigorous walk daily during your lunch hour will be beneficial. Walk to different shops. Do some window shopping. Walk, stop, stand and continue again. This is exactly the kind of activity you encounter on the shotgunning fields. From the moment you enter the clubhouse to wait to be registered for a squad until you leave the last shooting station you are walking, stopping and standing — activity that might best be called "disruptive endurance." Many clay target shooters are also hunters. Being in good physical condition going from the clays season to the bird season will not only make your hunting more pleasurable, it will also make it safer.

13. Flinching

According to Webster's dictionary, the word flinch means "to shrink from as if from physical pain; wince; to tense the muscles involuntarily in fear."

CAUSES OF FLINCHING

Flinching is an affliction that suddenly develops, adversely affecting the capabilities of clay target shooting veterans as well as newcomers. Flinching prevents a smooth or continuous swing. It may cause only a slight hesitancy, or it could be responsible for stopping gun swing completely or yanking the gun downward at the moment the trigger is pulled. Obviously, flinching is highly detrimental to the attainment of perfect or near perfect scores. It is an important discovery when a shooter finds that flinching has become a problem. But what causes the problem? One definition of flinching offered by my father, Ed Migdalski, author of the book *Clay Target Games*, may lead to an answer: "Flinching is an involuntary physical or mental reaction brought about by the anticipation of pain or discomfort." If the

143

The coach or instructor may spot the shooter reacting to a shot just before pulling the trigger. Lifting the head off the stock and closing the eyes are two symptoms of flinching.

shooter consciously or unconsciously expects bodily inconvenience it is impossible for him to concentrate fully on shooting the target. In order to put the mind at ease it is necessary to discover the cause of the flinching.

It is a simple matter for a beginner to get nervous trying to remember all the do's and don'ts of shotgunning fundamentals and get so confused that he flinches. The instructor can stress that the new shooter concentrate on a single key thought, such as "keep your head on the gun" or "follow-through." By concentrating on one thought, it will push out the clutter that the beginner has on his or her mind. After a while, the basics of the game will become natural, such as the process of shouldering the gun, calling for a target, seeing the target, establishing a lead, smoothly pulling the trigger and following through.

When beginners flinch from pain, they usually close their eyes momentarily in anticipation of the recoil. When the eyes close, the gun stops and the target zips past. One method of checking to see if a new shooter is closing his or her eyes is to ask (when they hit a target) if they saw it break.

To correct a flinch in the new shooter, the instructor should check for proper gun fit; a gun that is too long will force the stock to be held farther out on the shoulder muscle. Also, look for correct gun butt placement in the shoulder pocket. Raising the trigger-hand elbow may rectify the problem. Also, the gun butt should be equipped with a recoil pad. The instructor can switch the beginner to a smaller gauge gun or an automatic (if using a pump or over-and-under), which will have less kick. Another cause of flinching is ill-fitting ear protectors that do not shield the inner ear from the gun blast. In some cases, flinching will be caused by the gun stock hitting the bottom of the earmuffs, thus dislodging them enough to let the loud noise be less muffled. Or, perhaps the new shooter has not inserted his earplugs correctly; after all, how is he supposed to know how loud the gun should sound?

When flinching suddenly becomes a problem with experienced shooters, diagnosis is not so simple. Most professional gun writers suggest that the shooter examine his equipment thoroughly. Is the gun stock too high? Does the gun fit properly? Is the recoil pad right for the gun? Have you changed from light to heavy clothes, or the other way around? Did you change guns? If so, is the trigger pull heavier than on your other gun? Any one of these factors could be the reason for the veteran shooter to suddenly start flinching. Elite shooters sometimes develop flinches from the shear number of targets that they shoot. These high-level competitors may be firing up to 20 boxes (500 shots) per week. The obvious solution is to significantly reduce the number of shots taken. Other options might include having a gunsmith install a recoil reducer inside the stock, switching to super-lite ammo or practicing with a smaller gauge shotgun.

Another common cause of occasional flinching occurs when a shooter is accustomed to shooting at a target in a specific point along its flight path. If for some reason the target gets a jump on the shooter or the gun/target relationship is not quite right, the subconscious mind still says: "Pull the trigger now!" and yet the sight picture (gun/target relationship) is not correct, a discrepancy between mind and body exists. The result is a flinch, with the gun barrel often being yanked downward considerably. Because this is caused by the subconscious mind, the shooter will know that he flinched but will have no idea why. I've seen it happen dozens of times with shooters who are experienced. My solution is to teach them to "look harder," (see Visual Concentration in Chapter 11) which usually clears the problem by forcing them not to shoot until the sight picture is correct.

But another possibility exists — one that I have never seen discussed in any periodical: that flinching can be the result of fatigue. Fatigue can have a significant affect on the normal capabilities of a shooter. Therefore, when trying to help a shooter affected by flinching, the first thing I do is check for symptoms of fatigue. I look for arm fatigue, which, in my estimation, is a prime cause of flinching. If the arms have had no meaningful exercise in the couple of months before shooting, then are suddenly put to work holding the gun and swinging it during a couple of rounds of trap or skeet, they will rebel and actually tremble. A sure sign of arm fatigue occurs when the shooter shifts his weight onto the back leg and thrusts his forward hip out in an attempt to counter-balance the gun's weight. Tired muscles commonly occur among inexperienced shooters, women, youngsters and seniors, although no shooter is immune to flinching caused by muscle fatigue.

Eyestrain, improper shooting glasses, excessive alcohol consumption the night before shooting or too much coffee drinking are but a few more of the likely causes of flinching. See the appropriate chapters on Fitness, Vision or Nutrition if you think any of these problems pertain to you or a shooter that you coach.

RELEASE TRIGGERS

A release trigger could be a solution for some types of flinching. A release trigger is, as the name implies, one that fires the gun when let out rather than pulled, hence avoiding the jerking motion associated with a pull trigger. It usually takes between 300 to 500 shots to become fully accustomed to a release trigger — they fire a little sooner than pull triggers and the shot ends up being behind the target until the shooter adjusts for it.

I recommend closely analyzing all other possible causes and solutions for a flinch before running out and spending money on a mechanism that you may not like and that may not solve the problem (or only temporarily solve the problem). If you do buy one, be sure that it is of top quality and that you keep the mechanism clean — they have more moving parts than a pull trigger. It is also wise to inform the referee that you are shooting a release trigger in case of a gun malfunction.

PART III:
Mastering the Techniques

14. Safety and Etiquette

Because potentially lethal firearms are involved in recreational shooting, the conduct of those participating is a matter of concern to everyone present. Safety rules must be rigidly obeyed and enforced. Some behavior patterns are set by the regulations of trap, skeet and Sporting Clays, while common sense and good manners govern others. Basically, the rules of etiquette fall into three categories: safety, courtesy and sportsmanship.

SAFETY

No compromise exists where safety is concerned. New clay target shooters should be thoroughly familiar with the ATA, NSSA, NSCA or USA Shooting rulebook(s) (see Rules and Regulations later in this chapter) and should pay special attention to those sections dealing with safety, before attempting their first round of shooting. Also, a newcomer should not be permitted to join a squad unless an arrangement has been made with a veteran shooter or instructor to be at his

Inside:
SAFETY
COURTESY
SPORTSMANSHIP
RULES AND
REGULATIONS

This shooter's gun is open, but it is not the safest way to hold a firearm.

150

side at each station to observe and coach him on matters of safety.

Safe target-shooting routines differ from hunting practices in several respects. First, in target shooting, the gun's mechanical safety is never used, as strange as that may seem. The reason is to prevent the safety from being accidentally left on after calling for a target. In this case, the shooter would pull the trigger and the gun would not fire — the target is ruled "lost" because of human error, not gun malfunction. Second, in hunting, the gun is loaded when you step into the hunting area and it is carried that way through the activity. In clay target games, the gun is not loaded until the very moment you are on station and about to call for the target, and the gun is carried empty the rest of the time. Third, in hunting, it is often acceptable to carry the gun — loaded or not — pointing off to your side because you are either alone or your partner is on your opposite side. But in target shooting, many people are often around you, therefore, the gun can only be carried pointing up or down. Fourth, when hunting with a semi-auto or pump gun, a third shell is usually loaded, but with clay target shooting the third shot is never needed and never loaded.

Gun safety begins before you reach the shooting field. As soon as you remove your gun from its case, whether at your car or at the clubhouse, the action (the moving mechanism, which loads and unloads the gun) should be opened immediately. The gun should be carried with its action open until you are on station and ready to shoot. Never place a shell in the gun until you are on the shooting post and it's your turn to fire. The loaded gun must be kept pointed in a direction that will not threaten injury to you, other shooters, field personnel or spectators. An important safety rule concerns both the shooter whose gun is loaded and ready to shoot but who then faces a delay, such as equipment breakdown, and the shooter who arrives at the station out of turn. The gun must be pointed outward and the shells must be extracted before the gunner turns to walk off the station.

Every gun club should have the following rules posted in large letters and in a conspicuous spot:

The author's wife, Carol Migdalski, leaves the trap field with her over-and-under carried in an ideal fashion — comfortable yet safe.

• TREAT EVERY GUN AS IF IT WERE LOADED
• KEEP THE MUZZLE POINTING IN A SAFE DIRECTION AT ALL TIMES

- DO NOT LOAD YOUR GUN UNTIL READY TO SHOOT
- MAKE SURE AMMO GAUGE AND GUN GAUGE ARE THE SAME
- KEEP THE ACTION OPEN WHEN NOT SHOOTING
- ALL SHOOTERS MUST WEAR EYE AND EAR PROTECTION

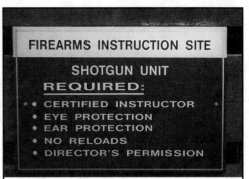

This sign is posted at the Yale University trap and skeet fields primarily because of liability concerns

One pointedly worded sign that is posted at many gun clubs simply states, "OPEN OR OUT!" In other words, keep your gun open at all times — except when firing — or you are out of the competition.

Again, I warn the newcomer. Your mistakes or omissions, like forgetting to put a second shell in the gun when shooting pairs or pointing at the low house for a high house target, are expected and accepted. But ignorance or casual disregard of safety rules will not be tolerated by fellow gunners. Read the rule book(s) concerning gun safety and shooting procedures before going out on the field for the first time. Better to be safe than sorry.

By the way, it is acceptable, and in fact necessary, to close over-and-unders, side-by-sides (double barrels) and single-shot guns in order to stand them in a gun rack. However, open these guns *immediately* upon lifting them off the rack. Pump-action and autoloaders must remain open while racked.

When picking up or shouldering your shotgun, resist the natural urge to put your finger on the trigger. This is a common fault that I find with the beginning shooters. The finger should be kept off the trigger until the shotgun is in the gun-ready position (at the shoulder, beneath the armpit or at the hip, depending on the game) and the shooter is about to call for a target. Until then, the finger can be rested on the trigger guard or alongside the receiver. If the target is delayed for some reason after calling for it, the finger should be removed from the trigger before dismounting the gun.

A carelessly placed over-and-under is not only closed, but it is pointing at the driver's seat.

Although more common in hunting situations, the shotgunner must take extreme care to never let the muzzle become clogged with snow or mud. This unfortunate condition will go unnoticed by the gunner and fellow participants. Contrary to novices' common belief, the shot charge will not simply push out the blockage. Instead, sudden backpressure is created and the barrel explodes

151

and sends pieces of deadly shrapnel in all directions. If the groundcover is mud or snow, keep the barrel well elevated and check the muzzle for blockage before shooting. If blockage does occur, keep the gun open and immediately acquire a ramrod from your cleaning kit and push out the barrel obstruction. The same danger of obstruction occurs when a shotshell wad does not clear the barrel due to faulty reloaded ammunition. Again, clear the muzzle immediately. Never put the gun aside to clear at a later time — you may forget; or, someone else may pick it up and shoot it.

Dents or slight bends in the barrel are also dangerous. Initially, the gun may shoot satisfactorily, but the shot repeatedly abrading against the bend or dent will wear the barrel in that location and it may eventually burst. Seek a competent gunsmith to evaluate the barrel imperfection before shooting the gun.

Be sure that gun and ammo gauges are identical. A smaller gauge shell, such as a 20, placed in a 12-gauge gun, would slide part way down the barrel and become lodged. When followed by a 12-gauge shell, either immediately or at a later time (after the shooter forgot to dislodge the wrong shell), and then fired, results in a sideways-blown barrel. Making matters worse, the area where the gunner's hand rests along the forearm is about where the explosion will occur. Emptying your pockets of shells after you shoot will help avoid mixing them with another gauge the next time on the range. Also, you will note that manufacturers clearly label each shell and shell box with the gauge, and color-code them to help avoid mistaken identity.

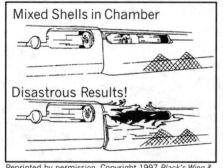

Mixed Shells in Chamber

Disastrous Results!

Pay close attention when reloading to insure that no weak hulls or double powder charges are used. Most modern firearms should withstand the pressure of an improperly loaded shell. But repeated double charges or an old or weakened barrel may cause a life-threaten accident.

And, of course, never mix shooting with alcohol or drugs. No excuses. No exceptions.

COURTESY

Courtesy in the shotgunning games involves nothing more than good manners and concern for other participants. Starting at the clubhouse, don't touch another person's gun or gear without the owner's permission. Don't place your gun on a table — especially in the eating area; racks are always provided. Don't clean your shotgun in the clubhouse unless a specific area has been set aside to do so. Don't dry-fire at or follow another shooter's targets with your gun at any time on the field or on the walks behind the shooting field. Don't talk in a loud voice, and don't talk at all when a member of your squad is on station ready to shoot. Some shooters are extremely sensitive to distractions while they are concentrating on the forthcoming target. Do not offer advice. Comments like, "you were behind the target," or "you shot above the target," are not usually appreciated and may do more harm than good; after all, your critique might be wrong. Only experienced instructors should coach, and only when asked to do so.

Because you are a new shooter does not mean that you have the right to take more time than is required at the shooting station. Don't hold your gun to the shoulder for longer than is necessary. It wastes time and contributes to fatigue. Also, don't swing your gun back and forth along the anticipated target flight path before calling for the target. This action tires your arms, makes you look ridiculous, and the other shooters in the squad will be annoyed at you for taking too long on station. Fifteen seconds is the maximum amount of time needed to load and mount your gun, establish a hold position and call for the target. And, don't delay calling for a target because of a wind gust. Simply proceed as normal and concentrate a bit harder — you can still hit the target.

When you miss a shot, don't stand on station groaning or leave the station kicking hulls (spent shotshells), muttering, swearing or shaking your head. A squad member should not be able to tell if you hit or missed the target by your actions. And certainly don't tell the next person coming up on station why you missed. Not only is such conduct objectionable, but it makes you appear immature. When you miss, be a sport. Step off the station smartly, keep your mouth shut and your thoughts to yourself. Also obnoxious is the shooter who smokes while waiting his turn to shoot, and then casually flips his live butt onto the field or grinds it under his shoe on the station before mounting his gun.

Be careful when asking other competitors about their scores. For example, "Well, how did you hit 'em?" is usually considered friendly and non-offensive; it requires no definitive reply. However, asking, "What was your score on that round?" is too direct and invasive; it requires a specific number in a reply. Some shooters don't like to talk about their performance — especially if they shot poorly. All scores are posted on a scoreboard. If you really need to know someone's results, check the board. Better yet, just worry about your own scores.

Other common courtesies may be less obvious to the beginner. Take, for example, the new trapshooter with his powerfully ejecting autoloader. It may throw hulls at the person on station beside him. This is extremely distracting to the shooter who is about to call for a target. A simple solution is to install a shell-catcher across the action of the gun.

SPORTSMANSHIP

Sportsmanship in shotgunning is no different than in any other sport. The chief example of poor behavior is the shooter who disputes

153

First-time shooters have little control over where their empties fly, sometimes even hitting themselves in the face. But experienced shooters can be poor sports by intentionally directing their ejected hulls at a competitor.

the referee's call, either on his own shots or those of another squad member. Even worse is the shooter who tries to browbeat the puller or referee into changing his decision from a "miss" to a "hit." Another type of poor sport is the shooter who misses and then hotly demands that the machines and the target flight be checked in the middle of a shoot. Legal target flight is determined before the competition, usually early in the day when wind influence is at a minimum; the targets remain at that setting for the duration of the contest. A sudden gust of wind may or may not be the reason for a miss, but it is no reason to call for a target check, thereby disrupting the rest of the squad's shooting. If the target-throwing machine is malfunctioning it will be obvious to everyone, including the referee.

Even at national championships I have witnessed other blatant examples of poor sportsmanship. Take, for example, one shooter who didn't like the puller's releases during a trap practice — he turned and threw a hull at him. And, during a skeet shoot-off, one gunner stepped off the station and intentionally ejected the empties from his over-and-under against the chest of the next man on station (with the intent to irritate him so much that he'd miss his next target). Such displays of poor sportsmanship are improper and shouldn't be tolerated by competitors or referees.

RULES AND REGULATIONS

All official clay target games held locally, nationally or internationally follow specific rules and regulations designed by organizations and associations. The Amateur Trapshooting Association guides American Trap. The National Skeet Shooting Association directs American Skeet. The National Sporting Clays Association oversees Sporting Clays. And, International Trap and Skeet are governed by USA Shooting. The addresses of these organizations can be found in Appendix B.

Consider joining one or more of these organizations. As a member you will receive their fine monthly publication (except the ATA; its official magazine, *Trap and Field*, is sold separately) and a copy of their rulebook. Read the rulebook cover-to-cover. A most distracting situation occurs when a new shotgunner is shooting his best score and he loses a target because he broke a rule that he was unaware of.

15. Learning To Shoot

TO SHOOT WELL ... YOU MUST FIRST LEARN TO SHOOT PROPERLY

Congratulations! You want to learn how to shoot. The shotgunning games can be extremely challenging at times; so first, you need a little self-confidence. You must remember that if you can see the target clearly, and have average coordination, you can learn to shoot moving targets with a shotgun. All that's needed to get started is knowledge of the fundamentals, some concentration and a little determination. If you have these three elements, then you can — and will — hit targets. However, be sure to study Chapter 14 — Safety and Etiquette thoroughly before picking up a gun.

What are the fundamentals? The six most important things to learn in shooting at moving targets are:
• The Master Eye
• Proper Stance
• Correct Gun Mounting
• The Right Sight Alignment
• The Need To Lead The Target
• The Importance Of Swing And Follow-through

Let's take them in order, beginning with:

DETERMINE MASTER EYE

If you can learn to shoot with both eyes open, by all means do so. Although it may seem unnatural to point a gun with both eyes, it is easier to learn the proper way now than to try and change later. Shooting with both eyes open will greatly increase your peripheral vision and depth perception (see the Vision and Sighting chapter), which will enable you to see the target sooner and focus on its flight path more precisely. With both eyes open, one eye usually governs the actual alignment and coordination of sighting a shotgun — or pointing a finger for that matter; very few people have equal eye ability. The eye that prevails over the other is called the "master" or "dominant eye."

To find out which is your dominant eye, do the following: with both eyes open extend your arm that you think would hold the gun (usually your non-dominant hand) and point your index finger at an object across the room or in the distance. Close your left eye. If the finger remains on the target, it means that your right eye is master. If your finger moves out of alignment with the object (to the left), the left eye is master.

Your dominant eye is on the same side of the body from which you should shoot. For example, if you are left-handed but right-eye dominant, you should place the gunstock against the right shoulder. This way, you will be learning to shoot right-handed with both eyes open. The gun will naturally point at the target, instead of several feet to the side of the target as it would if you shot left-handed with both eyes open. More information on eye dominance is discussed in the "Vision and Sighting" and "How to Instruct" chapters.

Take time to observe a good shooter's form. The gun is brought up to the face (not the face down to the gun), the elbows are held high, the body is leaning slightly into the gun and the forward knee is "cracked." Feet are shoulder-width apart and placed to put the body in a comfortable attitude in relation to the target breaking area.

PROPER STANCE

At this point, it will be most clear to use the right-handed, right-eye dominant shooter as an example. Left-handed shooters need only to reverse the directions.

A comfortable stance is one that permits your body to be under control at all times, not tense, but alert and expectant. The body must be able to flow without restriction in the direction in which the target is traveling and be in balance at the instant that you wish to hit the target. A good shooting stance has been compared to a boxer's stance: hands up, feet slightly spread, the left foot leading, balanced and relaxed, but leaning forward and aggressive.

Proper stance means that your body is in a comfortable attitude in relation to the target breaking area. The feet should be shoulder-width apart and parallel to each other. If you drew a line across your toes from foot to foot, this line should neither be parallel nor perpendicular to the flight line of the target, but in between.

Once foot placement has been established, shift more of your weight to the

An easy, general way for the right-handed beginner to remember proper foot placement is to split his stance with the front right corner of the shooting station. Left-handed shooters would face the front left corner.

left foot. Do not permit the left hip to thrust forward, this causes the weight to be placed on the back or right hip, which will cause you to shoot over targets. Rather, lean the shoulders and trunk of body slightly forward. Slightly bend or "crack" the left knee. In this position, you will be able to pivot at the waist while leaning into the gun. Experienced shooters set their feet relative to the spot where they wish to hit the target and then turn back to their hold position (the spot where you point the gun when expecting a target) to call for a target. The body then "unwinds" while tracking the target to the target breaking area (usually at about the mid-point of the target's flight). The need to pivot is more pronounced in skeet and Sporting Clays where the targets are frequently crossing, as opposed to going away as they do in trap.

Broadly speaking, in skeet and trap, the stance of a right-handed shooter should be facing the front right-hand corner of the station. As the shooter progresses through the stations, the feet are turned slightly more to the right (relative to the stations) on each successive station. To achieve this simplistically: in skeet, align your stance on the station so that your belly button is always facing the low house window. In trap, start on Station 1 facing the forward right-hand corner of the station. Turn slightly right on each of the following four stations until your stance is parallel with the right hand side of Station 5. For more information see Chapter 20 — Fundamentals of Skeet, Trap and Sporting Clays.

CORRECT GUN MOUNTING

The basic premise in mounting the gun is that you bring it up to the face, not the face down to the gun. To do this, grip the forearm of the gun a comfortable distance out, with the angle of the elbow approximately 135 degrees. The trigger hand should be wrapped

157

Instructor Carol Migdalski has dropped her right arm to better demonstrate the proper gun butt placement in the shoulder pocket. The top of the stock should be about in line with the top of the shoulder. The head is then lowered to the stock until the eye is aligned with the sighting plan.

158

firmly, but not tightly, around the pistol grip (see the Gunology chapter for gun part nomenclature).

Lift the stock to the face, and nestle the gun butt in the "pocket" between the collar bone and shoulder bone. The pocket is developed when lifting the trigger-hand elbow up to nearly parallel with the ground. The gun butt-pad should be placed in the shoulder pocket in such a way that the top of it is level with the top of the shoulder. In some cases, the top of the butt may be an inch or so higher than the shoulder — this is O.K. too.

Keep the side of the stock as near to the neck as possible. Now lean your head forward until your cheek rests on top of the stock. When the stock is of proper length, the tip of your nose should be about an inch from your trigger-hand thumb. Keep your face square, in other words, eyes level with the ground. If the stock fits you correctly, your dominant eye will be looking down the sights of the barrel. With the cheek laid firmly against the top of the stock, the right shoulder should be raised and pushed forward into the shotgun. If your face is in proper position, but you are looking below the sights at the receiver (the sloped metal part just forward of the pistol grip), then the comb of the stock is too low for your facial structure. I believe that standard-size shotguns will satisfactorily fit about 70% of the beginners. If you are short or tall, or if you can only see the receiver when looking down the barrel, then you should see a gunsmith or qualified instructor to have the stock modified or to change guns. More on this subject can be found in Chapter 18 — Methods of Instruction.

Skeet shooter Richard Wick demonstrates one method of approximately fitting a shotgun. When holding the gun butt in the crook of the elbow, the first joint of the trigger finger should reach the trigger. A qualified instructor or gunsmith can be consulted for a more precise gun fit.

THE RIGHT SIGHT ALIGNMENT

A shotgun must be mounted properly in order to hit flying targets consistently. When the gun is brought up in correct position to your shoulder, face and eye, it will shoot exactly where you are looking. With both eyes open and your focus on a distant object you will see two barrels — the real one and a "ghost barrel" — this is normal (see Chapter 11 — Vision and Sighting for more details). With practice, you will mount your gun and merely look at the spot where you choose to have the shot charge go. This is especially important in the shotgunning games that require a low-gun mount (off the shoulder until the target is seen). The gun must then come up to the face smoothly, quickly and be aligned precisely with the dominant eye. A good way to practice shouldering and sight alignment is to hold the gun at hip level, close both eyes, bring the gun to the face, then open your eyes while focusing out. Your dominant eye should be looking down the sights. The sights on a shotgun serve only to initially align the barrel with the eyes. Once this occurs, the focus should always be out at the target area.

Sighting At A Target

Your eyes cannot focus both in the distance and up close at the same time. When you pick up a gun, point it at a stationary object in a safe direction. You will note that if your eyes are concentrated on the target, only about the front one-third of your gun barrel is in focus. In other words the portion closest to your eyes is blurred or out of focus, but the tip of the forward sight is clearly seen.

Now, to get to the real nub of "pointing" a shotgun. Use only the sighting plane of your gun that is clearly defined and ignore everything else that is out of focus or blurry. This is the reason why the expert clay target shooters do not use the rear bead of the shotgun for sighting at the target. The trick is to ignore the rear bead, and sight off the tip of the gun, that is, the forward bead. This method of sighting brings your natural binocular vision more easily into use. By ignoring the rear, the left eye is put into action. Because the vision of the left eye is not blocked by the gun barrel hoisted to your right shoulder, it has an unobstructed initial viewing of the target; it therefore assists in seeing the target sooner and estimating the speed and angle of its flight. The rear bead of a shotgun should never be used for pointing the gun at target. If the beginner uses it for anything besides checking the initial alignment for gun canting and proper shouldering, he is ruining his chances of learning the easy method of "pointing" a shotgun.

The next technique is to avoid looking at the gun barrel at all. For example, when you point to an object in the sky, such as a star or a bird, you are looking at the object, not your fingertip. Yet, you are pointing directly at it. The same method is employed when

Your eye should be in line with the sights on the gun, but your focus must be out at the target area. Note that the shooter's head and gun are level, elbows are elevated and the index finger of the left hand is pointing alongside the gun's fore-end. All comprise excellent form.

pointing a shotgun, there is simply not enough time to focus in to the sights and back out to the target, in fact, doing so will give you a very hesitant gun swing. You should never look back to the sights as you might in riflery. Hence, the reason you "point" a shotgun but "aim" a rifle. More detailed information on the eyes can be found in Chapter 11 — Vision and Sighting.

THE NEED TO LEAD THE TARGET

Lead, or forward allowance, is the compensation that must be made in order to hit a moving target. Imagine trying to direct the stream of water from a garden hose at a youngster running across your lawn. If he were some distance from you, and traveling fast, you would have to swing the hose nozzle ahead of him, and keep it swinging, in order to douse him. Though a clay target moves a lot faster than a youngster, and a shot charge outraces a stream of water, the principle is similar.

Depending on the particular shotgunning game that you choose to pursue, all targets, except those going straight away from you, must be lead to one degree or another. Factors determining lead include speed, flight angle and distance of the target. Some shooting sports, like skeet, have no variation in the target's flight path or speed. The shooter moving to different firing positions or "stations" creates the angles. Here it is possible to have approximate lead "formulas" for hitting the targets. In other shotgunning games, like Sporting Clays, angle, speed and distance must be calculated when the target is thrown, hence, the similarity to hunting conditions.

THE IMPORTANCE OF SWING AND FOLLOW-THROUGH

Simply moving the gun to a point ahead of the target and stopping as you fire is not enough. Think back to the garden hose. As you swung the nozzle out ahead of the running youngster, you had to continue swinging — maintaining your lead — at a constant speed to keep the stream of water hitting him. So, too, must the shotgun be kept swinging as the trigger is pulled. Imagine that the garden hose, instead of shooting a steady stream, were equipped with a trigger that released but a short burst of water; similarly, the pellets fly in a short string, not in a ball or a long stream. Now you have a rough idea of how the shot charge behaves on its way to the target. After the shot is taken, the gun swing must be continued for a moment. This "follow-through" contributes to good shooting fundamentals by maintaining the lead on the target.

COORDINATION OF MIND AND BODY

In shooting, as in most worthwhile endeavors, achievement of perfect coordination of mind and body is the result of continued practice. To the new shooter, the smooth, fast, precision displayed by the expert may seem beyond normal ability. It is not. Through application of the fundamental principles, development of proper form and consistency of technique, the expert has established a pattern of well-conditioned mental and physical reflexes only by practice. Your first few times out on the shooting field will find you somewhat lacking in the full coordination that you will attain later. Don't worry about it; simply resolve to improve with practice.

Having familiarized yourself with the fundamentals, you are ready to put the basics to work. To do this, read the many other applicable chapters in this book. And, to greatly enhance your skills and reduce learning time, seek a qualified coach or instructor.

FINDING AN INSTRUCTOR

Most newcomers to clay target shooting usually become interested in the sport through friends who are gunning enthusiasts. Many have also been drawn to it when presented with the opportunity in school or college, either through physical education courses or club sport programs. Rod and gun clubs naturally draw portions of their memberships into the shotgunning games. And, some people were exposed to shotgunning through parents who belonged to a sportsmen's club or who hunted.

If you are interested in becoming a clay target shooter but haven't had the benefit of any of the above situations, you have four avenues open to you. You can join a club that offers clay target shooting as a regular activity, pay a professional instructor, join a class or do it yourself.

If you join a club, you will soon discover that many shooters welcome the chance to instruct or coach you. Beware! All shooters, even the ones with only a few weeks experience, like to give their opinions and teach new shooters. Whether the club has certain regulars who do the instructing, or the opportunities for learning are informal, I suggest that you do the following: if there is an instructional program, and you have a choice of instructors, observe them in action or seek recommendations. If instructors are not available, watch the veteran club members who have reputations for being good shooters. Take note of those who shoot with an easy, relaxed form, who do not squat, lean forward in a strained manner, or spread their feet wide apart. The shooter who uses an exaggerated stance may also call for a target by shouting "Yaaa!" or "Nowww!" or some other noise resembling a bear's growl or a pig's grunt. A few such extremists may shoot good scores, but only because they have been participating in clay target shooting for years, with the result that they find it practically impossible to change their idiosyncratic styles. These shooters will have good intentions, but they will teach you their way of shooting — a style that has been developed through poor fundamentals or for the benefit of the audience rather than for purpose of shooting efficiency. When you have located an experienced shooter with good form and a calm style, approach him after he has finished shooting. Ask

One-on-one instruction will give you the best results when learning to shoot.

him if he could spare the time to instruct you in a "round" (one game consisting of 25 shots) of skeet or trap, which is easier than starting off on the more challenging Sporting Clays course. The best way to learn is to begin at the easier stations, but this may not be practical because the club may have imposed time restrictions on regularly scheduled squad shooting.

Unquestionably, the most productive way of learning clay target shooting, if you can afford it, is to hire a "pro." Pros are usually available at large gun clubs. The pro approach has many advantages, including access to a field where no one else is shooting and one-on-one instruction. Here again, if more than one instructor is available choose the one who is relaxed and calm; he will have more patience with you. Also, seek recommendations. Rates for qualified instructors can range from $25 to $100 or more per hour, depending on their status and reputation. Still, paying $50 or $60 per hour to learn a lifetime skill is not a bad deal — it is about the same rate a mechanic charges to fix your car. Another method of finding an instructor is to contact the National Rifle Association. They can provide names of certified instructors and coaches who live in your area and who may be available to teach you individually or through an NRA sponsored class (see Appendix B).

Classes, courses or clinics are a convenient and legitimate way to learn shotgunning. You will not receive total one-on-one instruction, but you will usually have more instruction time for your money. In most cases, eye and ear protection, loaner guns, ammo and targets are provided. After the class is finished, you may still wish to contact a personal instructor to further develop your skills.

FINDING CLUBS, CLASSES, CLINICS AND EQUIPMENT

An ultimate guide to finding shotgun instruction and shooting clubs is now available — buy a copy of *Black's Wing & Clay — Shotgunner's Handbook*. This amazing annual book includes listings for 64 shotgun shooting schools and hundreds of shotgunning clinics nationwide; 1,694 Skeet, Trap and Sporting Clays clubs state-by-state; and, 1,292 companies providing shotgun related products and services worldwide. It also contains dozens of charts, graphs, indexes and "How-To" articles for the beginning shotgunner, as well as 1,279 hunting destinations. Send $14.95 plus $4.00 for shipping and handling to: Black's Sporting Directories, P.O. Box 2029, 43 W. Front St., Suite 11, Red Bank, NJ 07701. Phone: (908) 224-8700. Or, contact Masters Press (see inside cover of *The Complete Book of Shotgunning Games*). *Black's Wing & Clay* is an excellent shotgunning reference and is a worthwhile investment.

DOING IT YOURSELF

In the "do it yourself" approach, the learner can go a long way towards becoming a competent clay target shooter, although eventually the help of an experienced shooter may be necessary. These are some suggestions, ideas and procedures to take into consideration:

- Read this book from cover to cover.
- Call or write the National Rifle Association and National Shooting Sports Foundation (NSSF). Ask them to send you their brochures describing methods of shooting or ways to receive help getting started in the shooting sports (see Appendix B).
- Buy a "How To" video on skeet, trap or Sporting Clays (depending on your interest and type of shotgun fields available near you). Professional videos can be found through monthly shotgun magazines, *Black's Wing & Clay Handbook* (see Finding Clubs above) and in some well-outfitted outdoor shops. Become a member of one or more of the major shotgun sports governing bodies: the National Skeet Shooting Association, the American Trapshooting Association and the National Sporting Clays Association. All offer excellent shotgunning publications, which contain "How To" articles and advice columns. These organizations also provide information on dates and locations of their competitions nationwide (see Appendix B).
- Subscribe to a monthly shotgunning magazine. One particularly fine one is *Shotgun Sports* magazine (see Appendix C). Study the magazine(s) thoroughly; they contain many valuable "How To" and informational pieces.
- Check the new Internet Web Site "Where To Shoot" at http://www.wheretoshoot.org.
- Visit the trap and skeet fields. Observe the shooting procedures and watch how the gunners position themselves in shooting order. Note how they hold their guns open when not shooting and how no gun is loaded until the shooter steps on station, ready to shoot. Be aware that the loaded gun is always pointed to the open field. Also, notice that no talking takes place when a person is on station ready to call for a target.
- Study the stances the shooters assume when at station. Disregard the squatters, leaners, and leg spreaders. Be sure to observe foot position. The principle point here is that although the gun is pointed towards the target house the feet are comfortably aligned in the direction toward which the target is expected to break. Note that the good shooters will invariably hold their elbows high when the gun is shouldered. (This helps to place the gun butt in the hollow of the shoulder pocket and facilitates gun swing and follow-through.)
- When the squad is through with a round of shooting, ask the person reloading the target machines to show you the machines and

how they work.

- Now to the gun and ammunition. The ammunition is no problem. Trap or skeet shells or "ammo" can be bought at most gun clubs and outdoor sports shops. Later, when you become experienced, you can learn to load your own shells and save money. But don't buy a gun until you learn to shoot and become familiar with guns. Clay target shooting requires special types of guns. They can be rented for a nominal fee at gun clubs, or your instructor will loan you one. When you become proficient, you will want to buy your own. Aside from the satisfaction of owning your own shotgun, your scores will be better if you always shoot with the same gun. The most popular clay target model for the beginner is the autoloader (also called semi-automatic) because the gun is one of the least expensive and has less recoil than an over-and-under or pump shotgun (Chapter 21 — Gunology). Refer to the section of this book that describes the types of shotguns. Also, you would be wise to review the portions that deal with gun fit and safety.

If you are a hunter, you have obviously passed the gun safety test before you obtained a license. Therefore, it is possible that by following the above directions you can actually "do it yourself." But I strongly suggest that you make every effort to have an experienced shooter next to you on the field for the first couple or three times that you shoot.

Buying a gun.

16. Shooting Gear and Attire

When the new shooter first enters a clubhouse or walks onto a skeet or trap field, one of the first things that he or she will notice is the other shooters' attire. More specifically, pieces of gear that shooters wear to assist them in breaking clay targets. These items include strange looking eye glasses that ride high on the face and have unusually colored lenses (such as yellow, orange, purple or red), funny looking earmuffs and ear plugs, pouches slung across the hips and vests with leather patches and letters stitched on them.

As in any sport offering a choice of gear types, shooters use a wide range of quality and styles of the above mentioned items. Eyewear, for example, may range from $3.99 per pair of clear polycarbonate safety goggles to $150.00 or more per pair of fine shooting glasses with sets of interchangeable, tinted prescription lenses. Ear protection can range from $1.99 per pack of 12 disposable plugs to $120.00 per pair of battery operated, noise-activated earmuffs. Let's examine why this paraphernalia and certain

Eye and ear protection are essential equipment for *anyone* on or near a shooting field. The author's daughter, Maggie, age three, traveled to the National Gun Club in San Antonio, Texas, with coaches Mom and Dad and the Yale Shotgun Team to attend the Intercollegiate Clay Target Championships.

clothing items are needed.

EYE PROTECTION

It is absolutely imperative that eyeglasses be worn during shooting, primarily as a safety precaution and secondarily as an aid to shooting during varying light conditions. At times, the sharp, dispersing fragments from broken clay targets pose a danger to the unprotected eye. The incoming targets at skeet Stations 1, 7, and 8 present the greatest risk of a piece of the target hitting the shooter or another squad member. Also, it is possible to have gunpowder residue blown back into the face by the wind, which causes eye irritation. Regular prescription glasses and ordinary sunglasses will serve the purpose, although specially designed shooting glasses are highly recommended (see Chapter 11 — Vision and Sighting for shooting glasses selection). No shooter, whether a beginner or an expert, should ever venture onto a shooting field without eye protection.

EAR PROTECTION

Ear protection is just as necessary as eye protection, though the injury is cumulative and not as sudden and dramatic as having a piece of the clay target hit the eye. Noise pollution may affect the hearing so gradually that a shooter may not realize that permanent impairment of his hearing is occurring. Some young shooters, teenagers especially, believe that they are tough enough to disregard protective ear devices while shooting, but they are mistaken. Many shooters have suffered partial hearing loss because they failed to wear ear protectors; some brag about it. But once the thin membrane of the eardrum is damaged by repetitive gun blasts, it will never return to normal. It is also important to wear ear protectors when you are a spectator standing close enough to shotgun firing to feel noise discomfort. In a pinch, if you lose your ear protectors, a piece of rolled cotton will help; it is better than nothing, but it does not provide sufficient long-term protection.

Ear protection manufacturers put a "Noise Reduction Rating" (NRR) on all packages of ear protectors. The NRR is indicated in decibels ranging from the lowest protection of 0 to the highest protection of 30. As you might suspect, a direct correlation usually exists between the cost of the ear protectors and the NRR. Here is a sampling:

	Cost	Decibels (NRR)
Ear Muffs	$11.99	17
	$16.99	21
	$19.99	27
	$24.99	29
Disposable Earplugs	$ 1.99 (per 12-pack)	25
Molded Disposable Earplugs	$ 2.99 (per 12-pack)	29

Ear protection can be classified as either inner or outer earwear. The four standard types of ear protectors are as follow:

Inner Earwear

A popular, inexpensive and disposable earplug is simply constructed of a sponge-like substance. When squeezed, it fits into the ear and moments later expands to fill the ear canal. These can be found in outdoor sports shops, sporting goods stores and building supply stores.

They cost between .50 and $1.00 per pair at gun shops, and can be purchased for considerably less at large sporting good stores. If kept clean between uses they can be reused several times. To place earplugs, it may be helpful to reach around behind the head with the hand opposite the ear being fitted and pull backward and upward on the outer ear while inserting the plug. This helps straighten the ear canal for easier insertion.

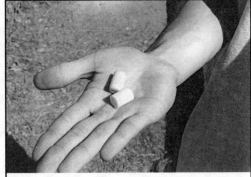

Disposable foam earplugs are inexpensive, small and light weight. They can be purchased in pairs or by the dozen.

Special, individually molded earplugs, usually obtainable from hearing-aid specialists, are preferred by some shooters. These plugs are formed when a dough-like substance placed in the ear, solidifies into a flexible, rubbery agent that retains its shape. It adopts the exact form of the ear canal. They have one drawback: through extended use they may slightly expand the ear canal, occasionally necessitating that a new pair be remolded to the shooter's ears.

Another plug type, known as "Sonic Ear Valves," are widely used by shotgunners. They are of a flexible, rubber-like composition and are designed to fit anyone's ears. Inside they contain a

Disposable plugs are rolled or squeezed prior to insertion in the ear canal. Once inserted, they gradually expand to a comfortable fit.

167

mechanical diaphragm, which is activated by the noise level. The advantage is that low-level noise, such as talking, is audible but the blast or the shotgun is muffled. None of these inner ear pieces should be shared due to hygiene considerations.

Some shooters prefer earmuffs to earplugs. Muffs are ideal as "loaner" ear protection for shooting classes and clinics.

Outer Earwear

Earmuffs are cup-like devices that cover the entire ear and are lined with noise-absorbing foam. They are held in place by a metal or plastic band that reaches over the head from ear to ear. They are available in various designs. Some shooters object to this type of ear covering because, with their head on the gun, the upper edge of the stock hits the lower part of the muff when the gun is shouldered. This is particularly a problem with shooters who use a gun with a Monte Carlo (raised) stock. Shooters with long hair or dangling earrings may also have difficulty with earmuffs, as do shooters who like to wear high-crowned hats. Muffs are also hot to wear in the summer. However, earmuffs have some advantages too: they are good for winter wear because they shield the outer ear from frosty wind chills, and they can be shared or reused endlessly (ideal for shooting classes) because no part touches the inner ear. And, some people simply don't feel comfortable with foam or rubber plugs shoved into their ears. Some shooters who wish to block out noise distractions wear earplugs in addition to earmuffs.

HEADWEAR

Young gunners often shun headwear. They disregard, or do not recognize, the fact that a wide-brim hat or a baseball-style cap is a benefit in several ways. Caps help to shield the eyes and glasses from sun glare, they protect the face from target pieces, they shield the surface of the shooting glasses from rain, and they reduce chances of heat fatigue in the summer. In winter, a hat or cap helps retain body heat. Some shooters state, "I don't like to wear a cap." Suppose a football player said, "I don't like to wear a helmet"? Like a football player, you'll acclimate to the headgear and be glad that you did.

VESTS AND POUCHES

The prominent features of a shooting vest are a shoulder pad and large pockets. The shoulder pad can be made of cloth, or real or synthetic leather backed with thin foam-rubber padding; its purpose is to prevent gun butt slippage and help cushion gun recoil. International Skeet- and Sporting Clays-style vests have a pad that extends from the hip to the shoulder to facilitate mounting a gun from the low-gun or off-the-shoulder position. The large pockets are for conveniently carrying shells and hulls (spent shells).

Shooting vests come in a wide variety of styles and colors. Most notably, summer vests are made of mesh and trimmed with lightweight cloth, whereas winter vests are solid cloth. A vest also gives a shooter a place to stitch on the name of his team (usually across the upper back), an embroidered patch from his gun club or his own name. Vests range in price from between $50.00 and $100.00, depending on style, quality and brand.

The shell pouch rides around the lower waist and therefore does not drag on the shoulders, as do the shell-stuffed pockets of the shooting vest. The pouch is held in place over a hip by a wide belt — but not the same one that is used to secure your pants.

The more expensive pouches are made of leather or suede, are divided into two compartments and come with a belt. If you cannot immediately afford a vest or fancy pouch, just buy a synthetic shell pouch for about $12.00; any old belt will do to hold it in place.

All clay target shooters should wear a shooting vest or a shell pouch. Few things are as distracting and frustrating as having to wait while a fellow shooter goes digging for a shell in the tight pockets of snug-fitting denim jeans. Also, if you choose to reload your hulls, they can be retrieved from the gun and carried in the vest or pouch. A general gun club rule is that if your hull hits the ground it becomes club property.

The shooting vest features lightweight material, a shoulder pad, large pockets and spare shell holders; this one was made by Bob Allen (see Appendix C). Also note the shooter's long hair, which is tied back to look professional and be functional.

169

The shell pouch is divided into two sections or pockets, one for loaded shells and the other for "empties."

HAIR CONTROL

Exasperating to the participant as well as to the other members of the squad is the frequent need of both male and female shooters to brush long hair out of their eyes before every shot, especially when the gun is loaded. If you have long hair and don't want to cut it, wear a hat, use a bandana or a sweatband or anything else that will keep your hair under control and out of your face.

Sandals make poor shooting footwear; they provide little support or cushioning and the tops of the feet are exposed to sunburn and large chunks of flying clay targets.

FOOTWEAR

Beginners, but also many experienced shooters, often give little thought to the type of shoes they wear on the shooting field. Use common sense. Wear shoes that have support and cushioning in the soles to reduce fatigue, backache and provide a stable shooting base.

In the summer, do not wear sandals, clogs, loafers, moccasins, deck shoes or go barefoot. Sun heat, absorbed by concrete or asphalt walks, will penetrate thin soles and contribute to heat fatigue. Topless shoes will not protect the feet from large chunks of flying clay targets or sunburn. Most moccasins, clogs and deck shoes provide little cushioning and support. Going barefoot looks unprofessional and is foolish because of multitudes of sharp clay target pieces scattered on the shooting stations and walks.

High-heeled shoes, like cowboy boots, however popular in the south and west, are not conducive to good shooting. Boots have slippery soles, no support and no cushioning. Worse, lifting the heel causes the legs to tilt forward, which puts the body off balance. Running shoes offer support and cushioning, but they are thin and upturned beneath the toes, hence, they may not provide a complete base or "footprint." The best footwear choices for long periods of warm-weather shooting are cross-trainers, walking shoes or light hikers worn over lightweight 100% cotton socks.

For chilly or soggy conditions in fall or spring shooting in the north, or winter in the south, you might try the new breed of high-tech "hikers," some of which are insulated and waterproof. Many hikers are made by brand-name sports shoe manufacturers and are offered with "air-sole" cushioning. A wide variety of handsome, leather outdoors shoes are also available; Cabela's, for example, offers a "Sporting Clays Chukka" for only $59.95. These lightweight, all-leather shoes are waterproof and insulated with 400 grams of Thinsulate. A pair of middleweight, wool-blend socks completes this footwear package.

In cold and wet, freezing or snowy winter conditions wear heavy wool socks under substantial, insulated boots. Wool socks are preferred over cotton because they retain most of their insulation properties when damp or wet. For maximum weather protection, look toward hunting or pac boots with rubber lowers and leather or nylon uppers and Gore-Tex or Thinsulate insulation. The discomfort of cold feet becomes a nagging distrac-

Cross-trainers with air soles are ideal footwear for long, warm-weather shooting sessions on concrete or asphalt.

tion and will hinder your shooting performance. The aforementioned footwear products may be found at large sporting goods stores or through outdoors catalogs such as Cabela's or L.L. Bean (see Appendix C).

COLD WEATHER CLOTHING

Warm and comfortable clothes that allow free movement, especially of the arms and shoulders, are the basic requirements for enjoyable winter shooting. A gunner whose mind is on his cold feet or freezing hands will not shoot well. Long underwear such as those worn by skiers is a necessity. A turtleneck sweater is a blessing when the wind breezes over snow. A down, wool or pullover hat should be used because much body heat is lost through the head. And a pair of warm boots (see above Footwear section) must be worn. In very cold weather the jacket could be one of the many nylon, insulated types. Stay clear of the bulky, slippery surface kind unless a non-slip shoulder pad has been sewn on. Some shooters wear a shooting vest over their winter jackets, but a larger size is usually required. For the bitter weather of northern winter-league shooting, insulated, pullover pants are helpful. A pair of thin, insulated gloves completes the outfit.

SHOOTING GLOVES

Many experienced, warm-weather shooters wear a thin, golf- or driving-style leather glove on the hand that holds the forearm of the gun, or sometimes on both hands. The primary reasons are for comfort and grip. Some gun forearms and pistol grips are heavily "checkered" (the wood is etched for design and to help the shooter's grasp), however, this checkering digs at the hands of some individuals during recoil and eventually causes blisters. When palms are sweaty, the finish on the gun can become slippery; thin leather gloves improve the grip.

Shooting and hunting gloves and mittens are available with the four fingers, or just the trigger finger, exposed. Some shooters simply take off the trigger-hand glove when ready to load and fire. A thickly-gloved trigger finger makes it difficult to feel the trigger, causing early or late shots and safety concerns.

HOW MUCH DOES IT COST?

The general opinion among non-shooters is that clay target shooting is a rich man's sport. That may have been the case years ago, but not today. The options available, in terms of financial outlay, run from inexpensive hand-trap shooting, to the moderate cost of a couple of rounds of trap or skeet per week, to the large amounts of money that highly competitive gunners spend on custom guns, shells, registration, food, travel and lodging.

The least expensive, and in many cases the most enjoyable, type of

171

clay target shooting, involves parent-and-son, parent-and-daughter, or the entire family, on a day's outing, for which they may be equipped with a 20-gauge, single-shot shotgun, ammunition that has been loaded at home, a case of clay targets, and either a hand trap or a portable target-throwing mechanism.

A case of targets and a couple boxes of hand-loaded shells cost less than taking the family to the movies or to a restaurant. A plastic hand thrower that will serve for years costs about the same as a pound of ground coffee. Earmuffs cost less than a tank of gas for a car. And shell pouches can be homemade from discarded women's pocketbooks, appropriately modified and equipped with an old belt. A second-hand 20-gauge shotgun can be an inexpensive holiday gift for someone in the family, and everyone can use it!

If the newcomer to the clay target games wants to shoot recreationally and enter low-key competition on weekends, the original financial requirement for gun, glasses, ear muffs and vest or pouch are insignificant in proportion to the many years of service they will give. At today's (1997) prices, a trap or skeet gun is obtainable for about $800. Second-hand guns can be purchased for much less. The great majority of weekend trap and skeet shooters load their own shells for about one-half the cost of a store-bought box. Also, most regular gunners join a club, thereby becoming eligible for reduced rates in target fees and bulk ammo purchases. Some clubs also buy the shell components (for reloading) in huge lots and sell them to members at discount prices. With these methods, a round of skeet (shells and targets) costs less than the price of a movie. From then on, the cost depends on how intensely the shooter pursues competitive shooting, how much time he can give to traveling and how much he can spend. The top shooters earn back their investment, and more, in cash-award winnings.

17. Keeping A Shooting Diary

Your shooting performance is closely linked to a series of variables that change from day to day, month to month and year to year. The more you can control these variables — instead of letting them control you — the more consistent your scores will be. Such variables can be broadly grouped into three categories: physical, mental and external. Physical conditions might include energy level, soreness, stance, sighting, hold positions, swing and the effects of food and drink. Mental conditions could encompass stress, imagery, negative and positive thinking, key thoughts, attitude and concentration. External variables may involve a wide range of factors such as guns, ammo, clothing, field layout, weather, sunlight, distractions, location, referees, background and season.

The only way to accurately remember all these variables and use this information to your advantage is to write them down. After many written entries, or sometimes after only a few, you will see patterns develop that help or hinder your performance. You will also

Inside:

CONDITIONS AND LOCATION

PSYCHOLOGICAL STATE

PHYSICAL FACTORS

NUTRITION

EQUIPMENT, CLOTHING AND ACCESORIES

CREATING A DIARY

SHOOTING DIARY FORMAT

Even before cleaning his gun, this skeet shooter takes a few moments to record his performance in a shooting diary while his recollections are still fresh.

notice what conditions are unique to each shooting location and you can then adjust or plan accordingly. The best way to write all this "stuff" in an organized manner is in a shooting diary. Here's what you need to know about diaries.

CONDITIONS AND LOCATION

In the shooting sports, practice and money are almost never as plentiful as you need or would like. To accentuate the investments spent on clay target shooting, every serious shotgunner should keep a shooting diary. It's not hard to do, and it doesn't take much time, but you must be conscientious about it.

Keeping a shooting diary can be compared to attending school: students take notes during class and then bring the notes home and study them for the exam. So too should you record events from every contest, take your notes home, and review them before the next shoot. If you are a new shooter, or one that practices and competes only occasionally, then you can record your practice sessions as well.

The diary can be started with generic information about each contest: where it was held, the date, the weather conditions, and your score. Although some of this may seem unimportant to the novice, things like wind, temperature and sun can make the difference between a winning score and second place. For example, you may compete extensively but only get to shoot at a few locations every other year. Maybe the first time you were at a specific field the sun was directly in your eyes at Stations 1 and 2 on the 8:00 AM flight. Or, on a different range, prevailing southwest winds may always come in hard between noon and 3:00 PM. By entering that information in your diary, and reviewing it before your next shoot at those locations, you will be able to avoid the 8:00 AM flight at one range and the early afternoon squad at the other.

PSYCHOLOGICAL STATE

Your psychological state is one of the more influential conditions on your shooting performance. Some shooters score best when they are a little angry or irritated, others find irritation distracting. Parts of your normal life like home, school, work or personal relationships influence your state of mind the day of the shoot. If you think you can completely block out these variables you are kidding yourself. The diary is the best way to remember how you dealt with distracting thoughts at contest time.

"Key thoughts" and "imagery" encompass items that you mentally rehearse just prior to calling for the target. Key thoughts or a mental "checklist" includes examples like "watch the target," "follow-through" or "keep my head down." Imagery involves mental rehearsal of what you are expecting to see and feel. Recording the mental processes that worked for you under certain conditions, as well as those that didn't, are noteworthy.

Confidence, a winning attitude and avoidance of negative thinking belong to another category of mental variables that can be recorded and studied for future use. For more information on mental discipline, see Chapter 8 — Sport Psychology.

PHYSICAL FACTORS

Physical factors can be divided into two sub-categories: physical condition and physical techniques. Examples of physical conditions include how you felt — was your energy level up, or were you dragging? What activities had you recently been involved in — were you working out with weights for the last two months or has your running been consistent? And, soreness — did you have a bad sunburn, were your feet extremely cold or was your shoulder or cheek bruised from all the shooting the day before?

Physical positions and techniques include your stance, hold position modifications, place in the squad that you shot, grip on the forearm of the gun, follow-through and others. Any of these that worked or didn't work, or were new or experimental, should be recorded. You can also mention other gunners who shot in your squad, how their timing, pace and actions influenced you, and how you can adjust in the future if you expect to shoot with them again.

NUTRITION

Eating habits the day before and the day of the shoot can have a profound effect on your shooting performance. Items to especially look for are foods you consumed before and during the shoot that helped maintain or drain your energy level. Beverages with caffeine that enhanced your concentration or made you too jittery, or the amount of alcohol the night before the shoot and how it made you feel the next day should be noted. For more information on food and beverages, see Chapter 10 — Nutrition.

EQUIPMENT, CLOTHING AND ACCESSORIES

If you have several guns, try different ammo or change chokes or gauges, then these variables are likely to influence scores. Carefully record this information in your diary.

Have you ever had on too much clothing, or not enough? Have you found that wearing a heavy down coat and then taking it off just before you shot worked best in winter league? What about gloves for hot weather — did you find them distracting or helpful? Or, perhaps you haven't shot with gloves on and you want to remember to do so next time the temperature exceeds 70 degrees. Do you shoot better in the heat with a vest on, or when using an ammo pouch? How about in the winter, can you fit your vest over your clothing without restricting movement?

What footwear worked best for you? Do you think that the cowboy boots contributed to your fatigue and that cross-trainers might be a solution in the future?

These and many other variables in gear can impact your comfort and performance. When noteworthy, record them in your diary. Of course, all the writing in the world will not help you much if you don't remember to look back in your diary and review the conditions and make changes that you recommended to yourself. The diary also won't work as effectively if you only write in it periodically.

Keeping a diary has the advantage of forcing you to review your shooting performance, which is a type of mental rehearsal. It helps you dwell on positive outcomes yet forces you not to simply dismiss poor performances as being "off that day." Being "off" has a reason behind it. The diary will help you discover that reason.

CREATING A DIARY

For the shooter who just wants to jot down notes, many generic diaries, bound hardcover notepads, spiral-bound notebooks and daily planner-style booklets are commercially manufactured and can be found in any stationary supply store. For the shooter who prefers a more regimented and detailed diary, I suggest that you sit down at a personal computer and design your own sample page. Once this page (or half-page) is to your liking, print it and bring it to a copy center and have it reproduced, stapled, bound or covered, depending on need and preference. Your only limit is your own creativity!

To develop useful information over time, you should record every shoot, no matter how insignificant. Try not to think of only the highlights or of minimum information — the smallest detail might end up being the one that makes a difference in your performance.

To assist the shooter in designing a diary, I offer the following detailed model. Of course any items can be added or deleted to suit your needs.

SHOOTING DIARY FORMAT

Shoot and Location_____ Date _____

Background _____ Score _____

Light (visibility) _____ Glasses (type/tint) _____

Weather _____ Target Color _____

Wind (speed & direction) _____ Time _____

Mental Condition (stress, distractions, confidence, imagery, etc.)

_____

_____

Mental Checklist (key thoughts) _____

Physical Condition (prior workouts, practices, activities, weight,
energy, etc.) _____

Positioning (stance, hold positions, arms, etc.) _____

_____

Food and Drink before Match _____

Effect _____

Food and Drink during Match _____

Effect _____

Firearm(s) (make, model, gauge and chokes) _____

Ammo (brand, type, shot size, powder load) _____

Clothing and Accessories _____

Summary and Comments _____

_____

_____

Future Plans (lessons learned) _____

_____

_____

_____

18. Methods of Instruction

This chapter is geared toward the new instructor. Yet, the certified or "expert" instructor will likely find some tips or techniques that he or she was previously unaware of. Besides, almost everyone can benefit from a "refresher" now and then.

WHO IS INSTRUCTING?

Clay target shooting can be instructed in at least three ways, depending on the qualifications of the instructor and the needs of the participant. The first is a formal class, course or clinic taught by a certified instructor. The second type is informal instruction given by a parent, friend or local gun club member who is a "pretty good shot." And the third type is a one-on-one or small group lesson taught by a shotgun "expert" who is not necessarily certified, but who has much personal experience, success and an outstanding reputation. All of these methods can be beneficial and educational if done properly. However, the parent or "regular" at the local gun club is not as likely to have the teaching skills, experience and finesse of the certified instructor or expert.

BECOMING AN INSTRUCTOR

Anyone with adequate shooting and safety experience can teach skeet, trap or Sporting Clays to newcomers at a local gun club, though I urge that person to consider becoming a certified instructor. By doing so, he or she will be able to present shotgunning in a more organized, competent and safe manner. Legal liability is also a concern for the gun club owner or program manager who permits someone to teach shooting. If an accident occurs, the club or the program will usually fare better legally if a certified instructor was supervising the shooting.

The National Rifle Association has a fine instructor certification program, which is well worth a prospective instructor's time and effort. To qualify as an NRA Shotgun Instructor, you must do the following:

• Possess and demonstrate a solid background in firearm safety and shooting skills acquired through previous firearm training (such as completion of an NRA Basic Shotgun Training Course) and/or previous shooting experience.
• Meet the following age requirements for each rating: Certified — 21 years of age or older; Assistant — 18 years of age or older; Apprentice — 13-17 years of age.
• Satisfactorily complete an NRA Basic Shotgun Instructor Training Course, and receive the endorsement of the NRA Training Counselor in charge.
• Successfully complete the NRA Shotgun Instructor Exam, with the following percentages for each rating: Certified — 90% or higher; Assistant — 85% or higher; Apprentice — 85% or higher.
• Submit your application with the appropriate certification fee. Membership in the NRA is not required, but is strongly recommended.

Responsibilities as an NRA Certified Shotgun Instructor include the following:

• Conducting NRA Basic Shotgun Courses annually in accordance with policies and procedures outlined by the NRA.
• Upholding the quality and integrity of national firearms safety and training standards established by the NRA.
• Promoting firearm safety and shooting.
• Reporting training data to the NRA.

For more information on becoming an instructor, contact the NRA at: Training Department, National Rifle Association, 11250 Waples Mill Road, Fairfax, Virginia 22030, phone 703-267-1430, (Internet — http://www.nra.org). For information on gun safety, guidelines for youth shooting, home firearm safety, or to acquire videos and handouts for your program, contact the NRA Safety and Education Division at the address above, phone 800-336-7402. And, the NSSF at: National Shooting Sports Foundation, Flintlock Ridge Office Center, 11 Mile Hill Road, Newtown, Connecticut 06470, phone: 203-426-1320.

BASIC FIRST-AID

There is no excuse for not having a first-aid kit in the clubhouse or at the shooting site. Simple Band-Aids go a long way in treating small cuts inflicted by pieces of flying targets, or fingers nicked by gun actions. A cold-compress is a good remedy for the bruised shoulder or cheek of the beginner. Eye wash solution is helpful if target dust or gunpowder residue eludes eye protection on a windy day.

In case of an extreme shooting accident, as unlikely as it is, a telephone must be available nearby. If shooting instruction occurs at a remote site without a clubhouse, or if the clubhouse has no phone, the instructor must have a charged, cellular phone handy.

To further enhance safety, and to help legally protect yourself, the gun club and the sponsoring program, it is wise to become certified in basic first-aid and CPR (Cardio-Pulmonary Resuscitation). Being knowledgeable in first-aid will give you peace of mind and add to your instructing credentials.

HOW TO PRESENT CLAY TARGET SHOOTING

New shooters should not be handed a gun and led onto the fields to shoot until they know what clay target shooting involves. Progressive instruction will be much easier if students are first made aware of the basics.

Use the information found later in this chapter to organize a lesson plan. Type the outline and double space between lines so that it can be easily read. Leave a wide right-hand margin to accommodate additional notes. If writing with a personal computer, use some of the program's features to highlight your outline: numbers, asterisks, bullets, bold, italics, size and underlining can all accentuate aspects of your outline, making delivery from your notes smoother and more stimulating. Review the lesson plan before your presentation. The depth and length of your discussion will depend upon the age and interests of the audience, as well as the purpose of the class.

The first part of the introduction to shotgunning should take place indoors, if possible. Seek a schoolroom, meeting room, cafeteria, gymnasium, clubhouse, or wherever a chalkboard, charts and TV-VCR can be used effectively, and where participants do not have distractions. You will also need a table on which to lay the shotguns and other visual aids. Guns should always have their actions open and muzzle pointed away from the audience. Actually, disassembled guns are more effective for demonstrating firearm parts, and will help emphasize safety.

The second part of the introduction will be on the range to demonstrate the facilities. Whether instruction is intended for one person, a dozen, or a class of 20 or more, each novice should first observe a round of skeet and trap or Sporting Clays. A "mini match" could be arranged between two experienced shooters for an exhibition. Using a one- or two-man squad saves time and better holds the group's attention. It is probably best if the instructor does not shoot in these demonstrations; he could be perceived as "showing off" or he could have a bad day and not look like such an expert after all. Also, someone needs to oversee the group during the exhibition.

Next, each group should be shown the interior of the houses and the target-throwing machinery while the instructor explains how the traps work and how the clay targets are loaded. For safety, the power must be shut off and the trap arm released while the students are inside the house. During this introductory lesson the instructor need not take time to explain the composition of the clay target, its speed in flight, how many are packed in a case, etc. Such details are reserved for the classroom. Move the group to Station 1 or 7 on the skeet field, and a few targets can be released to show the target's line of flight. Targets could then be released when the group is on a middle station. In this way, the students will realize that although the target flight is constant, different shots are available at the different stations.

The instructor should plan this first lesson so that enough time is allocated to visit the trap field and demonstrate the difference between trap and skeet. While the group peers into the trap house, explain how the machine would oscillate, causing the target to fly out at angles unknown to the shooter. Be sure to indicate that the machine can be set so that all targets fly out directly ahead, since that is the way the machine set during the first shooting session.

If the class will be learning to shoot NSCA 5-Stand Sporting, watching a shooting demonstration is fun and useful but sometimes extremely confusing. Therefore, it is helpful to tour each of the (uncocked) target launch sites, explain the nature of the machine and how and where it throws the target. Also, note any differences in target composition, such as the "rabbit,"

The multi-faceted NSCA 5-Stand Sporting may appear overwhelming to the novice.

and explain their special functions. Then, point out the menu cards, one by one, and indicate how they correlate to the hidden target throwers that were just toured.

Important as it is to show new shooters the physical aspects of the fields — houses, traps and target flight — it is equally important for the instructor not to dwell in any length on any portion of this introduction, because too much talking will simply bore the newcomers. The potential shooter should be left looking forward to the next lesson.

I have instructed numerous shooting courses, classes and clinics over the past 20 years, and have always written two variations of the same lesson plan — one in detail for the instructor(s) and one in outline form for the students. Currently, I team-teach a non-credit physical education shooting class with my wife, Carol Migdalski, who is also an NRA Certified Instructor. The Athletic Department at Yale University offers the course, which is simply called "Introduction to Trap and Skeet Shooting." The following is the detailed outline that we use to instruct our participants, who range from freshmen students and Ph.D. candidates to faculty and staff. However, few, if any, have ever held a gun before, and some comprehend English only as a second language. Hence, we start at the most elementary level, just as if we were teaching junior high school students; but we're also always careful not to "talk down" to the group. Besides promoting recreational use of firearms, we have found, as have many other schools, that this course is a feeder for recruits into our club sport shotgun team, which I coach. Here is how we give our course:

- Three Saturday sessions, four hours per session.
- The class is limited to only 10 participants, five per instructor (the class is offered in February in New England, so we keep the class small to enhance safety and learning in cold weather).
- The first session is "lecture only" in our outdoor-education class-room on campus, complete with refreshment breaks with muffins, juice and coffee (which are worked into the class cost). This lecture is mandatory to participate in the other two classes at the fields.
- The second session is half lecture in the clubhouse and demonstration on the field followed by student shooting.
- The third session is about one-third lecture and two-thirds student shooting.
- Targets, ammo, earplugs and transportation to the range are covered by the class cost, however, guns are borrowed from the club sport shotgun program.
- In other courses, instructors teach safety early in the first lecture. We do it as the last thing before shooting so that safety is foremost in the beginners' minds.

Course Outline
Introduction to Trap and Skeet Shooting
Session One — Classroom Only

1. Introduction
- Instructor introductions and credentials
- Student introductions: "please tell the class your name, three things about yourself and about any shooting experience"
- Purpose of the course
- Course format
- View five-minute collegiate shotgun shooting video (Intercollegiate Clay Target Championships)

2. Clay Target Shooting Review
- Brief history: how it all began
- Statistics: number of shooters participating, female participation and accomplishments in the shotgun sports, reference NSSF (see Appendix B)
- Recommend some available books or publications (such as *Shotgun Sports*, *Skeet Shooting Review*, *Sporting Clays* and *Trap and Field* magazines, see Appendix C)

3. Benefits to the Shooter
- Challenging individual or team lifetime sport
- No senior age restrictions
- Social aspects and travel opportunities

4. Guns: Rifle versus Shotguns
- Bullet vs. pellets (show samples)
- Barrel differences (show chart)
- Differences in purpose

5. Uses of the Shotgun
- Clay target shooting
- Hunting
- Law enforcement
- What you see in the movies (sawed-off shotguns, buckshot blasting through a door, etc.)

6. Types of Shotguns (show actual guns — pump, semi-auto and over/under, and also show gun-types chart) and their advantages and disadvantages.
- Over-and-under
- Side-by-side
- Pump
- Semi-automatic
- Single shot

184

- Bolt action

7. The Shotgun Shell and its Components (pry open a shotgun shell, show chart and pass around shotshell components)
- Hull
- Primer
- Wad
- Powder
- Shot
- How to buy shells
- Explain "Hieroglyphics" on a shell box (for example: 2 3/4", 1 1/8 oz., 3 dram equiv., # 7 1/2, 12 ga.)
- Shell length and chamber capacity

8. Reloading
- Basic concept and routine
- Why reload?
- How does one get started?
- Safety precautions

9. Popular Shot Sizes, their Applications, Advantages and Disadvantages (show samples in small, clear vials)
- Clay target games (9, 8, 7 1/2)
- Upland game, small game, waterfowl (7 1/2, 6, 5, 4, 3, 2, 1, BB)
- Big game (buckshot, rifled slug)

10. Gauges and their Uses (show sample shell of each)
- 10, 12, 20, 16, 28, .410-bore
- Dangers of mixing ammo

11. Parts of a Shotgun (demonstrate with a gun)
- Butt, stock, pistol grip, action, chamber, trigger, trigger guard
- Barrel, forearm, ventilated rib, sights, muzzle

12. Chokes
- Description and purpose
- Full, improved modified, modified, improved, cylinder bore
- Applications

13. Clothing and Accessories (show samples)
- Shooting glasses (styles, lens tint)
- Ear protection (plugs, muffs)
- Hats and caps
- Vests and pouches
- Footwear
- Gloves and clothing (summer & winter)
- Long hair control and problems with large or dangling earrings

14. Targets
• Pass around a few clay targets
• Composition, color and speed of flight
• Break (crush) a target on a board or on the table
• Emphasize eye protection
• Briefly explain scoring

15. The Shotgunning Games (show charts and diagrams)
• Skeet
• Trap
• Sporting Clays
• Hand and portable trap uses (show a hand thrower)

16. The "Eyes Problem"
• One eye versus two eye shooting; advantages and disadvantages
• Determining the master eye (demonstration and class exercise)
• Options for cross-eye dominance

Session Two —
Lecture in the Clubhouse and Field Work

1. Concerns of the Beginner
• Noise
• Recoil
• Gun weight
• Flinching

2. How to Hold and Fit a Shotgun
• Brief discussion about holding a gun and how and why it should fit (instructor demonstrations)
• Class exercise (class is divided in half by size, and each group meets with an instructor to be fit to appropriate length guns; the goal is to keep the number of guns needed to a minimum, hence, the shorter people and the taller people stay divided for the duration of the actual shooting)

3. Shooting Techniques: The "Four S's"
• View shotgun shooting fundamentals video
• Discuss and demonstrate Stance, Shouldering, Sighting and Swing
• Class exercise (groups again meet with instructors and take turns trying proper stance, shouldering and sighting; instructor checks and adjusts body positions accordingly)

4. Gun Safety
• View gun safety video
• Discussion: how accidents happen (hunting versus target shooting)
• Carrying a gun

- When to load and unload
- Other safety issues and concerns
- Shotgunning etiquette

5. Move Group to Fields
- Distribute eye protection and ear protection
- Watch demonstration "match" between two experienced shooters (Yale Shotgun Team members), one round each of skeet and trap
- Brief tour of ranges

6. Student Shooting
- Distribute guns and one box of shells each
- One group shoots 12 shots on skeet and one group shoots 12 on trap (the first or "25th" shell is not shot at a target) and then the group and instructors rotate

7. Field Clean Up (students pick up hulls, instructors reload and close houses)
- Instructors clean guns after class dismissal

Session Three —
Shooting First, Followed by Discussion at the Clubhouse

1. Student Shooting — two boxes of shells (students and instructors rotate disciplines after one box on each field)

2. Field Clean Up

3. Caring For a Shotgun (at clubhouse)
- Disassembling demonstration (over-and-under and automatic)
- Cleaning, oiling and reassembling demonstration
- Proper storage
- Travelling with a shotgun

4. What's Next?
- Taking the next step: finding places to shoot, instructors, classes, clinics or clubs (refer to *Black's Wing & Clay — Shotgunner's Handbook*, see Appendix C)
- Purchasing a "first gun"
- What will your new sport cost?
- Helpful organizations: NRA, NSSF, NSSA, ATA, NSCA, USA Shooting (provide handout with brief descriptions of each, addresses and phones)

5. Recap and Reflections
- Sit in a circle and briefly discuss "before and after" (fears, feelings, thoughts, changes in attitudes, etc.)

EXAMINATIONS AND AWARDS

Oral or written exams lend a tone of organization and seriousness to any class, as well as helping to keep students alert. We do not give exams in our class (above), but it is not a certification class either. The instructor may use this publication as a textbook with assigned readings and draw questions from those section, provided that the answers are covered in class. The instructor can purchase generic "certification of accomplishment" awards or design them himself on a personal computer. If certified by the National Rifle Association, the shotgun instructor can acquire lesson plans, study booklets and standardized exams from the NRA and teach a registered course, complete with certifications. Or, something such as a copy of this book or *Black's Wing & Clay — Shotgunner's Handbook*, could be given to each participant as a "graduation" award.

GROUP OUTDOORS APPROACH

A plan should be followed when introducing trap and skeet to students or others who want to try shotguns and the shotgun games, but who do not initially care to become shooters. Usually, time is limited. Interest must be stimulated. Basics must be given. Each student should shoot a few shots (preferably at least six or nine) at a moving target. Major corporations, for instance, have been recently using clay target shooting, instead of golf or tennis, as a means of developing teamwork, equality and camaraderie among their executives. Such a group is probably not interested in trap, skeet or Sporting Clays history, statistics, why the .410 is measured in bore, why some trapshooters prefer a single barrel and dozens of other details. The participants want to know what clay target shooting is, be able to say they fired a gun (and maybe even hit a few targets) and then get together for refreshments and talk about the experience. The instructor's lesson must be abbreviated but meaningful. It should emphasize gun safety and should include a brief tour of the fields and a peek at the interior of the houses. The basics of stance and gun hold need to be covered. And, above all, the instructor must design a plan by which 20 or more shooters fire at least a half-dozen shots each. At the same time the instructor must prevent boredom among those waiting to shoot. One method of doing this is to frequently speak to the group, rather than to only the current shooter. For example, if a participant drops a shell, turn to the group and explain that a competitive shooter would temporarily kick the live shell aside and reach in his pocket for another, rather than disrupt his concentration by bending over to pick it up. The group can also be told to determine where their colleagues' shots are hitting the target by the way it breaks. Or, have those waiting take turns being your "assistant" by pulling and scoring. If a second field and instructor are available, ask the instructor to help, thus reducing the group size by half.

HOW TO INSTRUCT

The best place to teach new shooters is directly behind the house on the trapshooting field. The gun, shells, earmuffs and puller's cord can be conveniently placed on the roof when necessary. A piece of cardboard or carpet remnant placed on top of the house will prevent damage to the gun. The trap machine must be set to throw straight-away targets. Always start the new shooter with a skeet or open-choked gun behind the trap house. A trap gun with its elevated stock, long barrel and tight choke will make it difficult to hit this close straight-away. If the facility does not have a trap field, take the participant(s) to Station 7 on the skeet field. Station 7 low house is an excellent starting position, but I prefer the trap field because I can move behind and to the right of the right-handed shooters without interference from the building or target opening.

A portable trap can also be used for teaching, provided it is secured to a base or to the ground and throws targets consistently straight ahead. Use a hand trap as a last resort, because the new shooter will be under enough stress without worrying where the target is going to fly. And use it only if you are capable of throwing straight-away targets consistently while standing to the rear of the shooter, yet close enough to control his actions. The autoloader is an appropriate firearm to use when teaching shotgunning; it is easy to load,

A youngster can start learning to shoot moving clay targets at about age 10, depending upon maturity level. The late Jim Dee, former director of Winchester's "father and son" programs, instructs the author, young Tom Migdalski, from behind the trap house. Duncan Barnes (far left), currently the editor of *Field & Stream* magazine, and Bob Goss assist.

unloads automatically, has less recoil than other types of shotguns and will likely be the novice's first gun. The gun butt should be equipped with a rubber pad to lessen recoil and slipping. Selection of gauge depends upon the age and physical structure of the learner. Smaller males in their mid-teens and most females are strong enough to start with a 12-gauge. However, many beginners in these categories will have a more pleasurable experience if they start with a 20-gauge gun. The trade-off, of course, is that the smaller gauge guns make target hitting more difficult. A single-barrel 20-gauge "youth gun" works well for younger or smaller boys and girls. The instructor must use common sense when fitting gun and gauge to shooter.

TEACHING THE FUNDAMENTALS OF TRAP AND SKEET

Assuming that the new shooter had gun handling and gun safety lessons, instructors could follow the outline below as an orderly and progressive plan for teaching moving-target shooting. However, a few of these steps may have already been covered in the classroom presentation.

Check And Adjust For Dominant Eye

To check for the dominant eye, have each member of the class point his or her finger at your dominant eye while they keep both eyes open. You will quickly be able to determine which eye the student is sighting with because the finger will align with the master eye. For more information, see Chapter 11 — Vision and Sighting.

Cross-eye dominance occurs when, for example, a right-handed person's left eye is master (and vise versa). If the lesson is a one-time experience (see the Group Outdoor Approach earlier), or if the person has had some shooting experience and can only shoot right-handed, then he could shoot with the dominant eye closed. Closing one eye, however, is tiring, and it reduces peripheral vision and depth perception; it also causes squinting of the open eye. A solution is to block the sight of the barrel by the dominant eye by placing a small patch on the eyewear lens of that eye. By only blocking part of the dominant eye's vision, the shooter can keep both eyes open and use peripheral vision. The patch can be made of semi-transparent tape or an adhesive dot, which are available in packs at stationary stores. The patch should be as small as possible, perhaps starting with dime size — it can be made smaller if the shooter wears well-fitting glasses. Take the following steps to place the patch: First, make sure the gun fits. Second, ensure that the shooter's glasses are snug and properly seated. Third, be positive that the gun is unloaded, and with the shooter's finger off the trigger, have him place the gun to the face, keeping the dominant eye closed. Fourth, stand in front of the shooter and look down the barrel, thereby checking the position of the non-dominant eye, which should be seen in line with the gun sights. Fifth, with the patch held delicately in your fingers, instruct the shooter to open his other eye without moving his face. Sixth, lean forward and place

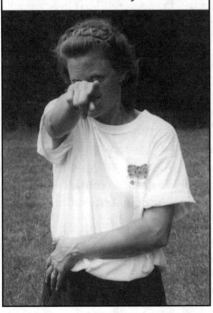

The instructor can quickly determine that the shooter above is right-eye dominant and that the shooter below is left eye dominant.

the dot on the lens so that it blocks the dominant eye from seeing the barrel. Although this process only takes a minute, the instructor may need to support the weight of the barrel because the new shooter's arm will tire quickly.

The alternative to this process is simply having the right-handed person shoot left-handed and vice versa. The instructor should attempt this long-term solution if the person desires future shotgunning. It is always best to start the newcomer shooting with both eyes open.

Target-pointing Practice

Have the group (or individual) stand in an appropriate "shooting" position and point toward the expected target flight for a straight-away target. The instructor says "Pull" and then releases a target. The shooter(s) track the target with their index finger and say "bang" when they have the target aligned. This exercise develops hand-eye coordination and timing.

Position The Shooter

The extended hand should grip the gun's forearm near its midpoint with the elbow at about a 135-degree angle. Elbows should be held high — just below parallel with the ground.

Emphasize a relaxed, well-balanced posture. For a right-handed shooter, the left foot should be forward and slightly bent at the knee with slightly more weight on it, and vice versa for left handers. (See Chapter 15 — Learning to Shoot, for more details.)

Check For Proper Eye Alignment And Seating Of Gun Butt

One of the best methods of introducing the newcomer to correct gun positioning, especially those with less arm strength, is to start by placing the gun vertically on top of the shooter's shoulder, thus pointing the barrel skyward. With left hand by

A novice gunner who is cross-eye dominant and shooting with both eyes open will cant the head. In this case, a right-handed shooter is trying to sight with the dominant left eye.

A gunner who is same-eye dominant will have his or her eye properly aligned with the barrel when shooting with both eyes open.

191

Teach the beginner to point at and lead a target with the index finger while keeping both eyes open. You must explain that it is natural to see two fingers — the real one and a "ghost" finger — which may appear blurred; the target, however, should be in sharp focus.

One of the easiest ways to teach correct gun shouldering is to have the beginner, using only the trigger-hand, set the gun atop the shoulder pointing upward. Step two is to sight down the barrel. Step three is to grasp the fore-end with the other hand and lower the gun into proper shooting position.

his side (for the right-hander) and right hand holding the pistol grip, the shooter then places his cheek on the stock and sights along the upright barrel. Raising his left hand to grasp the forearm of the gun, and without changing angle of his head or arms he then lowers the gun to shooting position. As a result, the gun butt will be placed where it should be — high, but completely in and against the hollow of the shoulder. The eyes will then be correctly aligned with the gun barrel and directed toward the target.

Take A Rest

The instructor must realize that a new shooter who is otherwise non-athletic will quickly fatigue. Stressing about this new sport may also drain energy. In either case, be sure to rotate shooters frequently or provide sufficient rest periods, which the instructor can use to discuss other points.

Load The Gun

During the first lesson, the instructor should carry all the shells and load the gun, thereby increasing safety and giving the new shooter less to worry about. While the beginner holds the gun with barrel pointed down and out, the instructor slips the shell into the chamber and closes the breech while telling the new shooter what to expect.

The First Shot

I have the student take his or her first shot at a distant tree, bush, cloud or other object before shooting at a target. This acclimates the new shooter to the experience of the noise and the recoil before trying to hit a moving target.

The placement of the supporting hand is critical to shooting efficiency. Only three fingers should be used to support the fore-end of the gun. The index finger should be alongside the thumb, pointing with the barrel. There are two reasons for learning this technique: first, the elbow can be raised more easily because the strain is taken off the wrist. Second, the shooter simply points his finger at the target — where the finger points, the gun points!

Dry Fire

After the beginner has taken his first shot at a stationary object, place a snap-cap or hull in the gun and have the shooter take a couple of practice "shots" at a straight-away target. It is helpful to both the student and the instructor for the trigger to be pulled and the "click" to be heard (it will be necessary to re-cock the gun if more than one dry fire is taken). This exercise gives the instructor an indication of the student's timing, gun/target relationship and lets the student concentrate on the target rather than the noise or recoil.

Shot Intervals

The average beginner should not fire more than five shots without taking a rest. This is important for the learning process, the shooter's comfort and for safety. If two or more pupils are involved, then they should, of course, each fire five shells in rotation. I have found that three shots per person are ideal with larger groups to reduce the wait. Three-shot rotations also prove better with weaker individuals who tire rapidly.

Swing And Follow-through

When a shooter becomes proficient at hitting the straight-away targets (perhaps 50% of them), he can be taken about 15 feet to the left of the trap house and given instructions on stance, hold position, gun swing and follow-through. He should be told to point the gun ten to 15 feet ahead of the house at shoulder height, and as the target flies out he should swing with it and fire the moment he sees that the gun is slightly ahead of the target. The next series of shots can be taken at an increased distance of about 25 feet from the left side of the trap house. Continue the same exercises on the right side of the house. When the instructor is convinced that the shooter can load and handle the gun safely, and swing, lead, and follow-through, he is ready for the 16-yard trap stations (after switching to a trap gun) or the skeet field, though these options are best reserved for a later lesson.

At The Trap Field

If the beginner is interested in trapshooting, the machine remains on straight-away, and the shooter begins at the center position (Station 3). Once the shooter hits these targets fairly consistently he or she can be moved to Stations 2 and 4, and then again to 1 and 5. During the next lesson, the trap machine can be set to throw just right targets and then just left targets with the above sta-

Start the novice trap shooter on Station 3 with the machine locked on straight-away. Using a stack of targets is an effective way to demonstrate both the vertical and horizontal hold positions on the house.

tion sequence repeated. The student's progress will determine when the machine should be readjusted to oscillate in regular trap routine. How many lessons or shots are required before, and if, the beginner is introduced to his first full round of trap will depend upon the individual, ability of the instructor and purpose of the class.

The above teaching procedure is a long, detailed and gradual one; it is by far the best way to build fundamentals and develop a good shooter with few, if any, bad habits. Unfortunately, in a large group setting with only one or two sessions (and when skeet must be covered as well), you may need to offer a "crash course" and never reach the oscillating targets.

At The Skeet Field

Station 7 is the place to start a beginner at the skeet field, unless there are extenuating circumstances like late-afternoon sun in the eyes. The low house target will be easy for the beginner if first instructed behind the trap house. The high house or incoming target is excellent for teaching the newcomer to swing because plenty of time is available and little lead is needed.

Instruction should progress at a rate commensurate with the shooter's ability. After the beginner has become familiar with Station 7, take him to Station 1, where the incoming target is similar to Station 7. This is another excellent place to practice swing. Station 2 low house and then 6 high house should be next because a more significant lead is required, which will impress the gunner that leads are different at each station. Instruction can then continue on incomers at Stations 3 and 5, followed by both shots on 4. For the next lesson, I have the shooter repeat a few of the easy shots as a refresher, then move to the outgoing targets, starting at Station 4 and progressively moving closer to the houses, eventually ending on 8. Because of the skill diversity found when teaching more than one shooter, it is necessary to move the group back and forth between easier and more challenging stations.

TIPS FOR SUCCESSFUL INSTRUCTION

- Keep it simple. Simplification is the mark of skill in an instructor. The beginner can only learn if he or she understands. Highly technical information and language does not impress and should be avoided.
- Repeat it. Repetition and simplicity go hand-in-hand. Repeating certain information, especially if said differently the second time, will enhance learning. Regardless of how many times the instructor has heard it said, it is all new and fresh to the beginner.
- Use nametags. The instructor will find it beneficial to call students by name, especially because safety is so critical. Also, in a noisy, outdoor environment where hearing is muffled by ear protection, a specific name gets attention more quickly than "you." A good

nametag system is to cut two strips of masking tape per participant and ask them to boldly print their name on both pieces using a thick, indelible magic-marker. The idea is to place one nametag on the front of the shooter and the other nametag behind the participant's shooting shoulder. This will be the instructor's perspective — from *behind* the shooter, not in front!

- Know the individual. Although you may be giving group instruction, try to get to know and remember each student after the first session. This process should start with student introductions at the beginning of the first class. Each student may need a slightly different teaching approach or style to help him or her succeed.

- Make it visual. Visual aids go far beyond words. Professionally designed charts are beneficial, but videos are better, and "the real thing" is a step above videos. The talented instructor will use many visual resources in a practical and stimulating fashion.

- Make a materials list. Few things are as frustrating as getting up in front of the class and realizing that you have forgotten a critical visual aid. Write a list when designing your lesson plan and double-check it when preparing for the class.

- Discuss physical contact. It is much more efficient to position a shooter by lifting an elbow, pushing a hip, adjusting the gun stock on the shoulder, pushing the head forward or gently kicking a poorly placed foot. After all, does your barber say: "Joe, please tilt your head slightly forward and to the left side a bit," or does he just gently push your head? However, some people are not comfortable being touched. If this is your teaching style — and it is a good one — mention it to the class (or individual) beforehand and ask for anyone who is uncomfortable with this method to speak to you aside from the group.

- Ear and eye protection. The student(s) must always wear ear and eye protectors on the field, even when waiting their turn to shoot.

- Gun placement. Check frequently to see that the gun is in the shoulder pocket; this will prevent muscle bruises.

- Watch jewelry. Large or dangling earrings may be pressed against the gunner's neck by earmuffs or be torn from the ear by gun recoil.

- Reduce fatigue. Space the shooting and do not rush the teaching. If the weather is hot or cold, stop at the session's midpoint and return to the clubhouse for a beverage break.

- Shooting doubles. Do not attempt doubles until the beginner is comfortable with singles and all gun-handling procedures. Advise the gunner what to do in the event of a broken target or gun malfunction. Dry fire at a pair or two first to help the shooter adjust to the timing.

- Praise a hit. Sound enthusiastic! "Warm fuzzies" encourage progress and love of the sport. Discount the student's misses as unimportant and compliment other aspects of their shooting, like stance or follow-through. An occasional pat on the shoulder or back is a good technique and is positive feedback for the shooter. The male instructor should be careful, however, with this method when working with female students, especially in a school-sponsored shooting class.

• Don't coach by saying "you were behind it" or "you were above it." Instead, say something like, "you were close, now let's move your hold position out a bit on the next shot," or "good job, just remember to keep your face on the stock." In other words, gently and positively create a cure rather than simply stating the negative-sounding cause of the miss.

• Stay alongside. The instructor should be at the beginner's side at each station until the shooter is proficient in safe gun handling, and is thoroughly acquainted with the rules and regulations of clay target shooting.

• Watch the swing. If the shooter's gun swing is hesitant or "stop-and-go," he or she is most likely trying to "aim," that is, focusing from the target to the gun sights and back to the target. Tell the novice to disregard the barrel and look only at the target. In extreme cases you may need to digress — have the shooter put the gun in the rack and finger point at a half-dozen targets before resuming shooting.

• Watch the head. If the shooter is lifting his or her head off the gun, the stock (comb) may be too low and the shooting eye is being buried beneath the gun's sight plane. The more you say, "keep your head down" the worse the problem becomes. Switch guns or temporarily tape some 4" x 6" pieces of corrugated cardboard on top of the stock to "build it up," thus elevating the cheekbone and eye.

This is the view that the instructor would see if the gun stock is too low for the shooter. Notice that the right eye is buried beneath the sight-plane. Make sure that the gun is empty, the safety is on and the finger is off the triger before attempting this sight-alignment check.

• Shoulder pain. If a female shooter is wincing or flinching and complains of sharp shoulder pain from recoil, first check the gun fit, the stock may be too long resulting in slippage of the butt out onto the shoulder joint. If the gun placement is okay, the problem may be that the recoil is digging the small plastic buckle on her bra strap into her shoulder. The male instructor, of course, should approach this subject tactfully.

A quick solution might be to suggest wrapping Band-Aids around the buckle or, in the future, wearing a sports bra. If neither of these aforementioned situations are the problem, switch the shooter to a lighter gauge gun and/or have the shooter strap on a shoulder recoil pad; the best ones are gel-filled.

- Watch for gun stopping. If the shooter stops the gun on each shot, tell him or her to lead the target (or the broken pieces) until they can no longer be seen. This will force the fundamentals of face-to-gun and follow-through.
- Insufficient lead. If the shooter can not keep enough lead on a specific target, and your other standard techniques fail, try visualization. For example, if the shooter is on Station 4 on the skeet field, tell him or her to visualize placing four garbage can lids on edge, in a row (at the distance of the target), and drag them through the air with the gun muzzle. The target should be "seen" trailing or touching the last lid. When explained correctly, you'd be surprised how often this technique works! (For more information on "Visualization," see Chapter 8 — Sport Psychology.)

UNCOMMON GUN SAFETY EXAMPLES

The most important subject that the instructor must emphasize to his group is gun safety. And one of the most dramatic ways of doing this is to place a one-gallon plastic jug, filled with red-dyed water, on a post or the ground (the jug could be set before the group arrives to the spot). Then (with ear and eye protection on all participants), from a short distance, the instructor shoots directly at the jug. It bursts in an ugly way. The instructor then picks up the shredded remains of the jug and displays it to the group while saying: "this torn jug provides a graphic illustration of what could happen to somebody's abdomen if a shooter gets careless. Never point a gun in another person's direction!" Such a demonstration will often be followed by silence.

Gun safety is uniquely jeopardized when loose-fitting glasses/ear-muffs slip, when a hat is in the way, or when the wind blows long hair into the novice's eyes. Often the shooter suddenly and unexpectedly lets go of the gun with his extended arm (supporting the gun's weight) to correct the problem, while leaving the trigger hand in place. This action causes the muzzle to drop dangerously low and applies pressure to the trigger. Even after the instructor cautions the shooter, the instinct to use the extended hand remains. Be especially watchful of the cross-eye dominant shooter who is a lefty shooting right-handed (and vice versa) — he will have his master hand on the gun's forearm. Because of these safety concerns, the instructor should require long hair and dangling earrings te be kept in check, provide properly fitting gear and never leave the beginner's side.

TEACHING CHILDREN

The principles that pertain to teaching teenagers and adults apply to youngsters. Be patient and encouraging with their progress and instruct in gradual and well-planned steps. The only differences are that lighter guns and easier targets are used and work sessions are kept shorter. I also like their first target to be stationary; I do this by

Father and son. Rich Haigh instructs son Richie, age 8, with a 20-gauge, single barrel "youth gun." This day, his first time out, young Richie shot only stationary clay targets, which were hung on the target crossing stake.

placing one on top of the center stake (target crossing point). However, the process of teaching children to shoot involves several basic factors that must be considered and applied intelligently.

First, there is the question of age. When is the proper time to start learning to shoot? A husky, "mature" boy of 8 or 9 can probably handle a single-shot, 20-gauge "youth gun." Generally, about the earliest a child should begin taking lessons with a shotgun is between the ages of ten and 12.

I was exposed to shooting at the age of six when brought to the skeet fields by my Dad. I didn't realize that I was being introduced to the shotgunning games. He made no attempt at showing me how the people were shooting. If I wanted to watch or had questions, okay; if not, that was okay too. We wouldn't stay too long. But he was always sure that I could enjoy juice and a blueberry muffin at the clubhouse, and occasionally wet a line in the fishing pond. In other words, this experience was a fun outing, and I began pestering my Dad days in advance to "go to the club." That was good!

After several trips to the club grounds, my Dad brought a .22 rifle and placed it on the rifle shooting bench because I was too small to hold it. With eye and ear protection in place he let me snap off a few .22 shorts, just to let me hear the "bang." It wasn't many weeks later that I was shooting tin cans and enjoying it greatly. Young children have little interest in paper target "bullseye" shooting, but they love to see tin cans topple off a perch.

Two years later, when I was eight, which is too young for some children, Dad presented me with a single-shot 20-gauge shotgun (I note that my father is a qualified shotgun instructor and coach). My first lessons were nothing more than shooting at the bottom end of a bucket (with permission of the club's management); I loved inspecting the pellet holes afterward. From then on it was a matter of holding me down. Perhaps he

The author instructs a group of summer sports camp children. Keep the group size to a minimum, use a light, small-gauge gun, fire only three shots per rotation and never leave the shooter's side. When working with children, the instructor should always hold all the shells in his vest or pouch.

started me too well, because today some of my main interests in life are clay target shooting and waterfowl hunting! And now, my own daughter, three-year-old Maggie, has already been to three National Collegiate Clay Target Championships with my wife, the Yale Shotgun Team and me. The plane flights, airport shuttle buses, hotels, restaurants and "the guys" (her friends on the team) made the trip exciting (she had already been exposed to a few practices and local shoots so that the noise wasn't startling; and she always wore eye and ear protection near the fields).

Make it fun! While attending the Intercollegiate Clay Target Championships, the author's daughter, Maggie, age three, pretends to drive a big tractor used to maintain the grounds of the National Gun Club in San Antonio, Texas.

In my experiences above I have tried to indicate that with children the teaching process must be gradual, and above all it must be fun. Boredom from technicalities and over talking will kill interest. And I emphasize that children vary greatly in size, strength and maturity. Some kids may not be responsible enough to shoot until they have reached their teens.

Other points to note: never try to teach beyond the child's attention span, which generally runs about 20 to 25 minutes. Start the youngster shooting with a .410-bore or 20-gauge, single-shot gun. You will have to load the gun, and cock the hammer after he has put it to his shoulders. Be sure that the gun butt is equipped with a recoil pad, and that it is firmly bedded in the hollow of the shoulder. Purchase the lightest loads possible, even if you have to pay a little extra for them — this is not the time to burn up heavy 20-gauge loads left over from the hunting season. There is nothing that will discourage a young shooter as much as a bruised shoulder. Constantly check to see that the elbows are held high, which will help keep the butt in place. Encourage and praise the youngster at every opportunity. Watch for signs of fatigue. All of the activity, besides the actual shooting, can quickly tire a young boy or girl. And try to incorporate something else fun into the trip, like stopping at the frozen yogurt shop on the way home. Besides being enjoyable for the youngster, the experience will help the bond the parent(s) and child.

During the beginning of a child's shooting program, do not dwell extensively on safety rules. You should never leave his or her side during the preliminaries. There will be plenty of opportunity to teach rules of safety and conduct when you start the child shooting clay targets. The parent should read the portions of this sections (Part III — Mastering the Techniques) pertaining to instructing and coaching and apply those principles when appropriate.

199

AGE TO QUIT

Lessons in shooting can begin at almost any age over eight. But when is it time to quit? One of the wonderful features of clay target shooting is that a person can enjoy the sport throughout life. Many national championships have been won by persons in their 60's and 70's. And, I have witnessed individuals shooting proficiently in their mid-80's. Staying active helps slow the aging process, and clay target shooting is an excellent sport for seniors to participate in. Shooting involves gentle use of many of the major muscle groups, and it keeps the mind, reflexes and eyes sharp. The gun club also provides an ideal social setting for seniors and retirees who have outdoor interests in common.

PHYSICALLY CHALLENGED

Clay target shooting is a great equalizer. The physically challenged individual can participate from a wheelchair equally against other shooters. The shooting sports will help give the challenged individual self-worth and an active, lifelong hobby where they can mainstream without feeling at a disadvantage. Any instructor can apply the basics learned in this chapter to the new shooter in a wheelchair. Most skeet and trap fields are on fairly level ground and parking lots are usually nearby. Instructors should encourage physically challenged shooters to learn and participate at every opportunity.

19. How To Coach

The new shooting teacher might suspect that those chapters on "Coaching" and "Instructing" are best treated as one. Actually, coaching differs from instructing in several ways. The instructor is the technician who meets with his students on a limited basis and grinds out the fundamentals of clay target shooting: history, safety, guns, shells, targets, shooting procedures, field layouts, gear, attire and costs. Although the same person may fill the roles of instructor and coach, the coach's duties are different from those of the instructor.

The coach is an analyst and an advisor who trains his students over long periods. His primary responsibility is to observe the shooter, examine his style and scoring, and then draw conclusions and make recommendations that enhance the athlete's performance. But he has other responsibilities. He listens sympathetically to alibis and acts as psychologist, parent and disciplinarian. He arranges budgets, practices, matches, travel and other team activities. In the college setting, the coach is also the liaison between the shooting team and the administration.

The purpose of this chapter is to use my 25 years of shotgun coaching experience to introduce effective methods of guiding new shooters and coaxing that extra target from advanced competitors. Unfortunately, one chapter can't cover everything; after all, entire volumes have been written about "how to coach." The astute coach, therefore, will read the other pertinent chapters in this book, extract the appropriate information and integrate it into his coaching routine. Particularly important is Part II — Body and Mind, which covers Psychology, Fitness, Nutrition, Vision, Fatigue and Flinching. Depending on the experience of your shooters, other chapters in this section (Part III — Mastering the Techniques) can also be applied, including Etiquette, Shooting Gear, Keeping a Shooting Diary, Methods of Instruction and Fundamentals of Skeet, Trap and Sporting Clays. In other words, this "How to Coach" chapter will provide insights into effective coaching, but it will require a thorough grasp and application of many other parts of this book, as well as other resources, to bring athletes to the elite level.

BECOMING A CERTIFIED COACH

Becoming a certified coach adds credibility to your skills and helps protect you and the program from liability. The National Rifle Association has a coach certification program in all the shooting disciplines, in which three coach levels exist: *Appointed Coach*. This is a coach who teaches "grassroots" programs at the local level only; *Certified Coach*. This person can coach at schools, camps and programs at the national level; *International Coach*. This person works in conjunction with USA Shooting and coaches advanced shooter-athletes at the national and international level to reach the U.S. Development or National Team.

1. Appointed Coach

To be eligible to become an NRA Appointed Shotgun Coach, you must do the following:
• Be at least 18 years old.
• Successfully complete the NRA Coach School and exam — prerequisites:
 √ Complete an NRA Basic Shotgun Shooting Course or have a current Classification Card, or
 √ Meet 4-H or other marksmanship training program requirements, or
 √ Apply for a waiver because of experience and background in shooting.
 √ Pay a $25.00 fee, which is valid for three years.

2. Certified Coach

To be eligible to become an NRA Certified Shotgun Coach, you must

do the following:
- Be an NRA Appointed Coach.
- Be at least 22 years old.
- Be certified as an American Sport Education Program (ASEP) Coach.
- Hold, or have held, an NRA Shotgun Classification Card.
- Hold a current American Red Cross Standard First Aid certification (or equivalent).
- Pay a $25.00 fee, which is valid for three years.

3. International Coach

To be eligible to become an NRA International Shotgun Coach, you must do the following:
- Have all of the above qualifications of an NRA Certified Coach.
- Attend an International Coach School.
- Pay a $25.00 fee, which is valid for three years.

H.Q. Moody, the NRA's National Coach Trainer, is quick to say that the purpose of the current program is to maintain a qualified and active pool of certified coaches, not simply "patch collectors." A large part of this reason is because of liability. Once certified, you must do the following to maintain your certification every three years:
- Be actively coaching.
- Keep a coach log showing 20 credits earned per year (credits are earned by coaching athletes at various competitive levels, see below).
- Maintain first-aid certification.
- Send in your $25.00 renewal fee.

NRA COACH CREDITS

Level	Credits
International Championship (per match)	15
National Championship (per match)	10
Sectional/Regional (per match)	7
State Championship (per match)	5
Local (approved matches, per event)	3
Qualification Program (per program)	1
Annually Coach an NRA Club or other program	1

The NRA Coach Program is still evolving. For the latest information on NRA Shotgun Coach certification, contact: H.Q. Moody, National Coach Trainer, National Rifle Association, 11250 Waples Mill Road, Fairfax, Virginia 22030, phone 703-267-1401.

APPROACH TO COACHING

"Behind it!" "Above it!" "Below it!" If that is your approach to coaching you are proceeding incorrectly. Many shooters who break 18 of 25 targets become instant "coaches" and use that technique to advise other shooters. I have watched veteran shooters and instructors coach the same way. Such a coaching method does little to improve the shooter. And worse, the so-called "coach" is not always correct in his assessment.

Instead of only diagnosing where the shot pattern was in relation to the target, the coach must also analyze the shooter. If, for example, the gunner's shot was behind the target there was reason for it. To only inform the shooter that he was "behind it" is negative and almost meaningless. Instead, perhaps the shooter needs to move his hold position out. Or, maybe he stopped his gun. Or, his lead was insufficient. These are intelligent and constructive solutions. But, the way that the coach phrases his suggestions is important; "pointers" should be presented in a positive form. For example, saying, "Increase your follow-through," is far better than saying, "You stopped your gun." Both comments address the same problem; however, the former gives the gunner's mind a positive action to take, while the latter does little but reinforce the error.

When developing a coaching style, the coach should set some ground rules for the team, perhaps after meeting with the team captain. These policies can be printed and distributed at practice or they can be discussed at a team meeting. Team rules vary, but a few examples include alcohol consumption (such as the night before a contest), travel with guns, attendance at practices, methods for determining squads, funding, reloading, safety and etiquette, attire, field clean up, captain's responsibilities and others. One more point that must be stressed is that there is only one coach (or one coach and one assistant, as the case may be). Otherwise, some team members will give advice to their teammates who miss targets; and, it is usually the same old "You were behind it, or "You were ahead of it." This is especially true if the shooter who is missing the targets is a beginner. Sometimes, two or three reasons are suggested by one squad! Not all team members will agree with the coach. But that doesn't alter the policy — one person coaches, and that person is the coach.

One particularly helpful volume on all aspects of coaching is entitled: *Coaching Young Athletes*, by R. Martens, R. Christina, J. Harvey Jr. and B. Sharkey, published by Human Kinetics Publishers, Inc., Champaign, Illinois, 1-800-747-4457.

COACHING NEW SHOOTERS

If the beginner still can't hit a target after being instructed in the fundamentals, the coach must do some analyzing. Of first concern is eyesight. Are you sure about the dominant eye? Is the shooter losing sight of the target under the barrel? Does the learner normally wear prescription glasses but leaves them off while shooting? How long ago did he have an eye examination? If no problem exists with sighting the coach should check, one at a time, five other common reasons why new shooters miss targets.

Sighting Along The Barrel

Most new shooters "aim" the gun by trying to fix the sights on the target. It is a natural thing to do. Although it is the most common fault of newcomers, and an important factor in shotgunning, it is surprising how few coaches diagnose this problem. The usual instruction is "Don't aim, point the gun." Of course, that is good advice to someone who knows the difference between aiming and pointing. Most beginners however, will nod their head as if they understand, but they don't. The better approach is to say, "After you shoulder the gun and align your eye along the barrel, forget the sights. Focus and concentrate on the target, never on the gun!"

Pulling Face Away From Stock

Another natural tendency for a newcomer is to pull the face from the stock. Either the gunner is anxious to see whether he has hit the target, or he follows it with his eyes and leaves the gun behind, or he is afraid of the recoil. This fault is simple to diagnose by watching the shooter's head.

Not Following Through

If the shooter is not following through, it is easy to detect because he stops his gun upon pulling the trigger. The fact that the target was missed because his swing stopped must be explained to the beginner. Emphasis on complete swing and follow-through will eventually eliminate the problem. Some shooters automatically stop their swing when the target is hit, but the coach must emphasize that the follow-through continues whether the target is hit or missed. Telling the shooter to lead the target, or the broken pieces, until they can no longer be seen is an effective method to train follow-through and face-on-the-stock fundamentals.

Gun Butt Shifting From Shoulder Pocket

Another common fault with beginners is letting the gun butt slide from the hollow of the shoul-

After making sure the gun is empty, the coach can check for proper sighting along the barrel. The gun stock is too low for this shooter, causing his eye to be below the sight-plane. Switch guns or increase the stock height. A quick, temporary solution is to build the comb up with corrugated cardboard and cover it with moleskin, which can be found at any pharmacy. A permanent solution is to have a gunsmith install an adjustable comb device.

205

The coach's view shows a properly fitted stock. The shooter's eye should be visible and in line with the sight-plane.

The astute coach will quickly recognize these common shooting mistakes — straightening the body and lifting the head off the stock.

Poor foot position. The shooter's feet are too far to the right for a Station 2 low house. This causes the body to work against itself as evidenced by the twist in the waist and legs. As a result, the gun was forced off the face prematurely in the follow-through.

Poor foot position. The shooter's feet are parallel to the front of the station (note the shooter's feet on the right). On a straight-away or right-angle target, the body works against itself and the face comes off the gun.

Poor foot position. Station 2 low house, left-handed shooter. The shooter's feet are at a 90-degree angle to each other: note the twist in the waist and the stock leaving the face as a result. The coach should turn the right foot to make it parallel with the left foot.

der; this can happen downward or outward. (Also, too short a stock will slip down, whereas too long a stock will slide out.) If the butt slips down, the gunner strains his head forward so that it remains on the stock, and if it happens after the first shot in doubles, the second shot will be over the target. If the butt slips outward, the recoil may hurt the shoulder muscle or joint. An ache in the shoulder caused by bad seating of the gun butt may cause flinching, squinting and eye closing.

Foot Position

Although foot position is one of the first fundamentals taught, it is one that must be watched because the tendency is to direct the feet toward the target starting point — toward the trap — rather than where the target will be hit. Such a stance causes the shot to be behind the target because the muscles and bones restrict the gun swing. It is not sufficient to only instruct the shooter in correct stance; he must be told why his feet should be positioned that way, "to enhance swing and follow-through, and to be in a natural, comfortable position at the point where you shoot the target." The position of the body in its most comfortable attitude to the target breaking area is called the natural point-of-aim. In other words, set the shooter's feet to where he should break the target, then "coil" him back to the target's point of origin. Some experienced shooters prefer to position their feet *slightly* past the natural point-of-aim to assist follow-through.

IMPROVING PRACTICE SESSIONS

Simply having the shooter-athlete bang away full rounds, always starting on the first station and ending on the last, is not as constructive a practice as the new coach might suspect. You may think, "If a match consists of four rounds of 25 shots, how could practice be more perfect than shooting four rounds?" Pause and reflect upon any other sport. Take football for example. Does the head football coach have his team play a 60-minute game each day, all week, in preparation for Saturday's game? Of course not! The squad is divided into offense and defense (the same way you might separate skeet and trap shooters), and the players work on plays, drills and conditioning within their discipline. Only the day or two before the game might they get together for a non-contact scrimmage.

How about track? Does the 400-meter runner train exclusively by running 400 meter races in practice? Rarely. And when he does, it is usually only to check his time against his goals and to determine which segments of the race need attention. Instead of 400 meters, the runner may work on 200- and 300-meter dashes to help develop speed and explosiveness. During other practices he may only perform 600- and 800-meter runs to develop endurance and pacing. In other words, by breaking down the whole and working on its components, the total will become stronger when reassembled.

SHOOTING DRILLS

Every shooter I have ever coached prefers shooting full rounds to drills. And why not? Full rounds are fun — they offer variation, challenge and the chance to keep score. Scoring is interesting, and at the right time it is the most reliable tool for gauging progress. But there is plenty of time for scoring on match day. The challenge of the shooting coach is to develop meaningful practices involving partial rounds and countless repetitive shots while keeping the athlete's intensity high. The drills must be sport specific; for example, there is little sense having your American-style skeet competitors shoot off-the-hip (low gun-ready position) on American targets because that skill will never be used. In fact, such selection of practice technique, though it may be fun and challenging, may affect stance, timing, rhythm and hold positions.

I offer a series of tips and suggestions to practice the shotgunning games, which you can modify or expand upon, as needed, and apply to your shooters. In some examples, I give consideration to practice at gun clubs where shooting is only permitted in rounds. For coaches and athletes who have access to a private field, or can shoot whatever they want, the drills, of course, can be more creative.

Skeet
- Shoot tougher targets — Your shooter(s) will cause little disruption to the rest of the squad by skipping the easier shots, such as Low 1, Low 2 and all of Station 7 and repeating targets on Stations 3, 4 and 5.
- Double the doubles — On Stations 1, 2, 6 and 7, rather than shooting singles, have your athlete(s) shoot a second set of doubles.
- Increase the difficulty — If the club permits only full rounds, switch

the gun(s) to a smaller gauge, shoot 1-ounce instead of 1 1/8-ounce loads or screw in tighter chokes to train precision.

- Repeat stations — Entire boxes can be shot on only one or two stations, perhaps focusing on different stations every week. A full round could occasionally follow this exercise to "tie it all together."

- Work backwards — Start on Station 8 low house and work your team in a clockwise rotation so that their final shot is Station 1 high house. This stimulates concentration and prevents "coasting" through the last few stations. In other words, if a shooter is straight through Stations 5 or 6 the tendency is to think, "I've got my 25-straight in the bag." However, I caution against mixing order within the station. Don't have your students shoot single low houses before single high houses, or doubles before singles; they may confuse the order during a match.

- Shoot one-direction targets — A very effective drill is to have your team skip doubles and shoot rounds of all incomers, all outgoers, all high houses or all low houses. Each exercise has its advantages and works on solving different problems.

- Shoot half-stations — Instead of shooting from the regulation positions, have the team shoot *between* the stations, such as half-way between Stations 1 and 2, then between 2 and 3, and so forth. The purpose is to stimulate concentration and adjust to varying target angles, which is good practice for windy days.

- Practice quick 8's — Have your shooters take several strides off Station 8 towards the house. By practicing quicker shots, the normal shot will be slower and easier when they return to it. A miss-and-out contest can be made of this drill by determining which shooter can get the closest to the house before missing. The same rule that applies on Station 8 applies here — they must shoot before the target passes their body.

The correct low-gun hold position for International Skeet. The body is balanced, yet aggressive, and the gun muzzle is in line with the eyes and the target flight path. The gun butt is touching the top of the hip.

International Skeet

Most of the above practice ideas for American Skeet work equally well for International Skeet, with a few additions:

- Practice, practice, practice shouldering. Have your shooters do it before and after practice using an empty gun — it must become second nature. Shoulder to straight-aways, then crossing shots — left-to-rights and right-to-lefts.

- If you don't have frequent access to an International field, crank up the American machines to the target's breaking limit and practice shooting from low-gun on International stations; the coach can release delayed targets. I caution against shooting American-speed targets International-style because it disrupts timing of both games.

- If the Station 8 target is too fast for your shooters, start them on Stations 1 low house (for low 8) and Station 7 high house (for high 8) and have them break targets until they hit them well — that shouldn't take long. Then they take a few steps toward Station 8, stop and shoot the incoming target until it is hit with ease, and so on. They progress as gradually as need be, sometimes expending a box or two of shells in the process, or quitting at a "sticking point" and resuming the exercise at the next practice. Once they

An incorrect low-gun hold position for International Skeet. The body is leaning too far forward (note the right foot coming off the station) and the gun barrel and stock are both too low, thereby putting the shooter at a considerable disadvantage.

have reached Station 8 and are comfortable with the shot, have them take a few steps off the station toward the house. If they can hit that, they'll be more confident next time on Station 8. This foundation training technique rarely fails.

- Begin your new International shooters on the simplest single shots, such as low 1, low 2, high 6, high 7 and low 7. Even though these shots are not included in a regulation round of International Skeet, they make excellent shouldering, sighting and timing shots. From there, of course, they can progress as their skill level develops.
- Start new shooters without the target delayed, but be sure they don't move the gun until the target emerges. Also, start newcomers with 1 1/8 oz. of shot instead of the regulation 1 oz. loads — the extra pellets will help success.

Trap

To become proficient in trapshooting in the same time that it takes to become proficient in skeet may require more drills. The reason is simple; skeet targets always fly along the same path — shooters practicing complete rounds know where to expect them and can adjust accordingly. Trap targets, on the other hand, are thrown at random angles. It may take many more trap rounds to learn the gun/target "sight picture" for each possible shot.

- The best practice for trapshooting is "machine setting." Machine setting or "locking" reduces trap to its component angles. Throwing targets that your shooters can anticipate helps them memorize or "imprint" the proper sight-picture for each category of targets, for example, hard rights, quartering lefts and so forth. To accomplish this, set the trap machine in the center hole, thereby throwing straight-away targets. Have your shooters take turns firing five-shot rotations from Station 3 (the center station). After they can disintegrate most of the straight-aways, move the squad over to Stations 2 and 4 for five shots on each, and then again to Stations 1 and 5. The shooters will gradually learn how to adjust from straight-aways to quartering right and left targets. Once they are hitting these targets, the next session can be coached similarly by setting the trap machine on angle shots. If the machine is set to throw hard lefts, for example, start your squad on Station 5, not the center station. The reason is fairly obvious — the hard left is a straight-away from Station 5. From there, you would move your shooters, one station at a time, to Station 1 where the angle is hardest. The opposite procedure would hold true for hard-right targets. In all likelihood, the only way to set the machine angle is to watch it oscillate (from a safe vantage point) and turn off the oscillating motor at the appropriate time.

- Shoot tougher targets — Set the machine on hole 3 or 4 (most ATA trap machines are set on hole 2). Being able to shoot hole-4 angles is a tremendous confidence booster for your students. When they return to ATA Trap, they will be amazed at how simple the game has become.
- Practice from handicap distances. Move your shooters back a few yards. The 16-yard shots will then become easier.

International And Wobble Trap

The principles of ATA trap machine setting can be applied equally well to International and Wobble Trap. However, the routine is modified for the varying target heights (International and Wobble Trap machines oscillate vertically as well as horizontally). In his book *Finding The Extra Target*, my former colleague, the nationally recognized collegiate trapshooting coach, the late John R. Linn, had this to say about International Trap drills:

> For the first series of shots, set a low hard left. Then readjust the trap machine and shoot a high hard left. For the third series of practice shots, set the trap to throw a low straightaway. Follow that drill with a high straightaway. The final two practice sets make use of a trap set to throw low hard rights then finally a series of high hard rights. Although International [and Wobble] Trap includes some targets that rise to the same height as American Trap, I do not find it necessary to set the trap [at ATA height] and practice them. Most shooters will hit ATA-height targets well by practicing for the low and high targets of the International game.

If no International or Wobble Trap fields are available, an American Trap machine can be adjusted to assist in practicing these events. Crank up the machine to the target breaking point, and then set it to oscillate on a wide angle. Adjust the height to practice the targets you wish.

Sporting Clays

Because of the variety of shots and courses, the best way to practice Sporting Clays or NSCA 5-Stand Sporting is to shoot different courses and repeat individual targets or stands. One problem facing many collegiate teams is that they have access to skeet and trap fields, but don't have the time, money or availability to practice NSCA 5-Stand or Sporting Clays. To practice for these events my Yale team shoots "Sporting" sessions after some of our regular skeet and trap practices. I create a variety of shots on standard skeet and trap fields to give my students some semblance of Sporting targets. We are fortunate to have our own fields and can shoot whatever we wish. Here are a few examples of what we have done, but remember, safety must be rigidly enforced. All shots are best performed with a skeet or Sporting Clays gun.

- Instead of simultaneous skeet doubles, release following pairs and report pairs.
- Shoot from various positions inside the skeet walkway, such as mid-point between Stations 3 and 8 or between 6 and 8.
- Back off the skeet stations to create longer shots requiring larger leads.
- On an exterior high house stairway, stand and shoot targets from the top step (ours is a platform).
- Raise or lower the skeet machines to change the target elevation (also see "Modern Skeet" and "Modern Trap" in Chapter 7 — Special Facility Games).
- Stand halfway between the trap house and the 16-yard stations after increasing the machine target angle from hole 2 to hole 4 or 5 and elevate the machine to throw targets as high as possible.
- Drop the trap machine elevation as low as possible to throw "rabbits" and stand on top of the trap house roof to shoot.
- Stand to the side of the trap house, parallel to the doorway, and shoot the hole-4 targets at various elevations. (Also see Chapter 3 — Novelty Games and Chapter 4 — Portable Hand Trap Games.)

ADVANCING INTERMEDIATE AND EXPERIENCED COMPETITORS

Coaching experienced gunners is often more difficult than working with beginners. First, the coach must be diplomatic because the person who has been shooting over a period of years is likely to be sensitive to criticism, even if he seeks help. Second, the coach must give a convincing reason why, for example, the shooter's stance can be improved even though he is "smoking" most of his targets. Some competitors' technique flaws developed because they were "hotdog" or show-off shooters. In other cases, the mistakes came from bad habits or lack of proper instruction. If it seems that such a participant might wish to join the team, it is worth the coach's effort to correct the shooter's defective style. He should approach the shooter

Before and after. The shooter hit this shot, but obviously his foot position and balance (note the heels lifting off the station) could be improved.

off the field and explain how these corrections will help his performance. The gunner should be assured that although his scores may dip until he acclimates to the change, they will ultimately be higher than they were originally. If his response to the coach's concern is lukewarm, or if he tries the suggested new system once to appease the coach, and then discards it, the coach may find his time better spent working with a more coachable shooter. As my father always preached to me: "The moment you think you know more than your teacher you are in trouble."

Missed targets have many causes. Yet, some of these causes occur more frequently than others. The following is a list of coaching techniques that may help your team perform better.

Practice Attitudes

Some shooters take practices too lightly. Their attitude is, "Well, the shots I missed were just practice — I'll just bear down more in competition." Practice must be shot like competition, your athletes should "compete as though practicing and practice as though competing." In other words, every target counts, whether it is in practice or not.

Self-talk

A positive outlook is important. Don't let your shooters get depressed after a bad day. Kicking themselves in the pants for the next week only brings stress and poorer results. Evaluating shooting performance with negative self-talk is programming the mind for failure. It downplays the good and accentuates the bad, instead of the other way around. The shooter should note his problems in a shooting diary, but only for corrective purposes, not to dwell on a poor performance. Then, he should focus on the things he did properly and resolve to improve the weaknesses. (See Chapter 8 — Sport Psychology, for more information on positive thinking.)

Despite having too deep a crouch (note the right heel coming off the station), this shooter had good scores. With a little help from a qualified coach, his performance would likely improve.

Observations

The day of the match, especially a big one, your team should arrive well ahead of time.

212

The shooters can then walk to their field(s) and watch targets. Sit on a nearby bench with the athletes while they acclimate to the background. Point out the wind's effect on the targets and the angle of the sun. Note the targets' flight and help your shooters make mental notes. Discuss appropriate eyewear tint for the conditions. Meanwhile, make sure your shooters disregard the other team's hits or misses — that is not the purpose of the visit. And, don't let them watch too many targets; eye fatigue can influence scores.

Key Thoughts

The "key thought" is used to unclutter the mind and permit the conditioned fundamentals of good technique to surface. More specifically, a key thought is selecting one thing to think about just prior to calling for the target. Concentrating on one thought and excluding all else from the mind is vital. For instance, if I had a high-strung, fast-paced shooter, I might have him use the key thought, "Stay relaxed." After he has positioned himself, loaded and mounted his gun he will say to himself, "Stay relaxed;" it is his only thought as the target emerges. This phrase helps prevent him from over anticipating the target, shooting too soon and having an abbreviated follow-through.

Another shooter's key thought might be "Watch the target." Again, this keeps the mind occupied and away from negative thoughts like "I hate this shot, I hope I don't miss it." Instead, the shooter is using visual concentration, forcing himself to look hard at the target and let the body do what he trained it to do. Because athletes differ in their needs, no two shooters on your team are likely to use the same key thought.

A Problem Target

First, identify the problem target(s). Do this by compiling practice and match score sheets and note where the misses occur. Next, on the field, have the athlete shoot a series of his best shots. The ease of the solid hits will build his confidence, reinforce proper sight pictures and put him in a positive mind set. The wrong way to coach is to just have your shooter step onto the field "cold" and start banging away at the trouble targets.

Don't rely on the old standby "You shot behind the target," or "You were over the target." Instead, watch the shooter. The coach should have a selection of probable causes that he considers in a given situation. A few problems to look for are head off the stock, not seeing the target properly, wrong hold position, improper foot position, excessive leaning, shifting body weight, moving too soon and flinching. Certain targets, of course, have more specific problems.

Coaching is sometimes a matter of trial and error; try a certain technique, and if it fails, try another one. Seek feedback from the shooter. Ask him what he thinks he saw and how the technique felt to him. Once the problem has been solved, have the shooter repeat several more shots to acquire the proper sight-picture, but don't tire him. Fatigue results in bad habits and mistakes. If you don't solve the problem completely, take a break; shoot some confident shots and return later.

Squad Rhythm

Squad rhythm usually refers to the "mount-pull-bang" cycle, especially in the trap games. Members of a smooth, consistent and well-timed trap squad will have improved scores. A problem occurs when one of your shooters draws a squad with a "lame duck" whose pace is off that of the rest of the squad. The only quick solution is to ignore it and concentrate harder on the pre-shot routine. A long-term solution is, of course, to practice and compete with a squad who your shooter is accustomed to.

Rhythm also applies to placement of shooters within a squad — skeet in particular. Determining inter-squad order is similar to selecting the runners' order in a relay team; you probably want your two best people first and last. The first shooter must be experienced and have enough confidence to lead off. His is the only position that will not see the targets beforehand. He should be a good shooter who sets an upbeat attitude for the station. The lead shooter is also the pacesetter who should step on and off each station smartly, and call for the target in a quick but unrushed fashion. The last shooter should also be an experienced shooter to "pick up the rear" and set the stage for the next station. Ideally, he would be a stalwartly individual because he must wait the longest to shoot. Your third strongest shooter could be put in position 3. The least experienced shooters can be sandwiched in positions 2 and 4 so that they have good examples preceding them and don't lead or follow the squad.

A shooter with a non-aggressive stance may also be the one whose rhythm is a bit slower than the rest of the squad. This shooter's feet are also turned too far left (note the foot positions of the shooters flanking him), causing difficulty with right-angle targets.

Flinching

Flinching has several causes. For the experienced shooter, flinching may result from hundreds of shots each week. Reducing the amount of shooting, of course, can alleviate this. But that is not always practical, especially if the shooter is training for national or world competition. Practicing with lighter loads and installing a custom recoil-absorbing device may help.

Flinching also occurs when a discrepancy exists between what the eyes see and what the mind believes is correct. For example, on skeet

Station 1 high house, suppose the target takes an unusual dive due to a stiff tail wind. Because of timing the mind subconsciously thinks, "Shoot now," however, the eyes see the gun/target relationship as incorrect and need more time to align the shot. The result is a jerked trigger pull or "flinch." The inexperienced competitor feels the flinch but doesn't know the cause. He blames the gun's trigger, a fast pull or other distractions. The solutions are to adjust hold positions to the conditions, be mentally prepared before saying "Pull" and to increase visual concentration.

For the less experienced shooter, check to see if he is closing his eyes in anticipation of the recoil. Or, perhaps ear protection is inadequate or fits poorly and the flinch is in response to the loud noise. For more information, see Chapter 13 — Flinching.

Competition Readiness

When constructive practices and well-planned physical and mental training are all said and done, a few things remain to be looked after on match day.

Equipment check. Be sure that the athletes have enough presence of mind to gather their gear: ear protection, vests or pouches, glasses, gloves, caps, ammo, guns, towels and so forth. Few things are as distracting as getting to the firing line ready to compete and discovering that ear plugs or ammo are back in the car. I have seen a shooter get halfway through a round before realizing that the gun he was using was a stranger's, which he had accidentally lifted off the rack. This discovery was soon followed by an embarrassing announcement over the P.A. system: "May I have your attention please! We are missing a gun...." Not a good way to start a competition.

Have the team be early, especially if dealing with students. When the squad is up, members of the team shouldn't be dashing around checking the cars and restrooms rooms to find "Joe," who has fallen asleep somewhere under a tree. Of course, having a shooter on "final call" break a sweat running to a distant field while bouncing shells out of his pockets is no way to start a match. Get them organized, and get them there early.

Give a short pre-contest pep talk. The best time to speak to your team is when they are together before walking onto the field. Keep it "short and sweet" and gear it to your athletes. Some shooters prefer to be alone with a headset listening to music; if that is what it takes, then let them be. But other personalities need a few positive, encouraging tips or remarks from the coach.

Practice Pressure

Athletes perform best under pressure. However, although a little pressure is good, too much pressure is detrimental. The proper amount of pressure might best be depicted as a bell-shaped curve.

One of the coach's jobs is to help the athlete control pressure. A

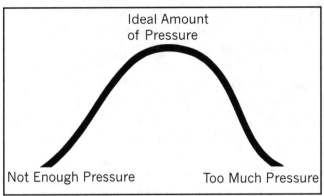

Ideal Amount of Pressure

Not Enough Pressure   Too Much Pressure

way to acclimate your shooters to moderate pressure is to create some during practices. Accomplish this by pitting half the team against the other, with the losers treating the winners to soda in the clubhouse after practice. Another way to create practice pressure is by buying three cases (30 boxes) of factory shells and offer one box of shells to the winner each week — it will be a worthwhile investment! If that is too costly, have the budget "absorb" a free round of targets for the winner. When a discrepancy in skill level exists between two shooters, simply spot one shooter enough targets to make the match a challenge to both. The practice match doesn't have to mean full rounds. Whichever drills you select for the team that week, count the last one as the match.

Practice pressure will occur automatically when six or more shooters of near equal ability are vying for only five positions. Select certain practices as "match days" and record each shooter's rounds. Set a number of qualifying rounds needed, and choose the team on a mathematical basis.

Shoot Offs

During a shoot off, don't let your shooters change or rush their pre-shot routines just to "get it over with." Hurrying to finish the match will only cause mistakes. Some shooters dread shoot offs. Have those shooters note that the more experienced shooters look forward to a one-on-one match-up. They go into the contest with a positive mental outlook, "Hey, I'm going to beat this guy, and I get to shoot for free while I'm doing it!" (Traditionally, the gun club pays for the targets and ammo for the shoot off.)

The nationally renowned shooting coach from George Mason University, the late John Linn, had this to say about shoot offs (you can explain it this way to your shooters):

Shoot offs are great because they get you used to shooting under pressure. They are certainly one of the more exciting parts of trap and skeet shooting and the most exciting for the spectator. Remember, a great many major and minor championships are won in shoot offs. I think it is a good idea to shoot every practice round just as though it was a shoot off for a major championship. How would you like to win that championship? If you win it outright, only people checking the scoreboard will know. If you win it head-to-head in a shoot off,

216

everyone knows. Enjoy that thrill; it is an important part of your motivation.

Basics That Experts Overlook

When expert shooters of equal ability meet in an important competition, the final standing invariably shows that only a missed target or two separate them on the scoreboard. After such a tournament, the best of shooters will ponder over particular targets missed: "Did I flinch on that station?" "Was I distracted?" "Was it a slow pull?" "Was my hold position too tight?" The few targets missed by the accomplished tournament competitor may not have been caused by one of the common faults discussed above. The difference between a shooter being in contention and falling out of the shoot-off may be the result of elements never considered by the gunners. The astute coach should review these factors when examining missed targets.

When was the last time your shooter had his eyes examined? As one grows older, eyes change and periodic exams are necessary. A slight change in eyesight, without a compensating change in lenses, will affect shooting. Also, as age advances, the eyes will not as quickly focus on moving objects. Have you considered fatigue? If arms, shoulders and legs have had no exercise to keep them in condition, shooting will suffer. Does he or she do any walking or running? Regardless of the type of job held, physical conditioning is important for clay target competition. If the shooter hasn't walked all week, walking and standing at the fields all day will increase fatigue.

Did your shooter drink too much coffee before a match? Coffee is a drug that stimulates the nervous system to the point where it may impact performance. What about alcohol? Did the shooter have "a few too many" at the pre-shoot social the night before?

Are you aware that breathing cigar or cigarette smoke raises blood pressure, whether or not your shooter is the one smoking? And that such a condition may subtly affect shooting accuracy? Secondhand-smoke inhalation is intensified during cold weather when small clubhouses are packed with shooters staying warm.

Did your shooter tire his eyes by watching someone else's targets from the sidelines for too long before shooting?

How is the shooter's personal life? Is work or school stressful? Did he or she have a big argument just before leaving home for the contest?

While on a station did the shooter drop a shell and pick it up, or did he or she bend over to tie a shoe? Bending over and quickly straightening to shoot may have affected equilibrium, causing a missed target.

The above factors may be subtle and appear to be insignificant to some coaches and many shooters. But they are valid and may make a crucial difference in performance. Further treatment of these and other variables can be found in Part II — Body and Mind.

NON-COACHABLES

In clay target shooting — as in other sports — "non-coachable" athletes are difficult to train. A non-coachable shooter may be a person who has tried to make a team but failed because he refused to take the coach's advice. Or, he may have made the team but remains a mediocre shooter because he thinks that he knows more than the coach does. Or, he may be the type of person who is unable to receive constructive suggestions from anyone on any subject. Such attitudes seldom change.

Shooters having the ability and experience to shoot in the area of 23 out of 25 targets need special handling because they are good, but may think that they are great. Those who will take coaching will be a blessing and will advance quickly to shooting straights. Those who openly resent constructive criticism should receive little further attention. The experienced coach will recognize such a situation as difficult and save himself much frustration.

COACH'S ATTITUDE

Don't overlook your own grumpy behavior — it will rub off on the team. If you've just had a quarrel with your spouse, you're hungry and you're standing in the rain watching your team perform poorly, don't let your attitude show. By intentionally or unintentionally communicating your depression or irritation, the squad may think that you've developed a non-caring attitude, and as a result, they may quit trying. Instead, remain professional and encourage your team at every opportunity; it will help their determination to shoot better. In other words, be a leader by example, it is hard for your shooters to listen to you preach the virtues of sportsmanship and positive thinking while you are walking around shaking your head, swearing and kicking hulls.

The author and coach of the Yale Shotgun Team is all business at the Intercollegiate Clay Target Championships. Being serious about the competition is one thing, but being overly emotional is unprofessional and it may impact your team's performance.

INCLEMENT WEATHER

Competitions are not cancelled due to wind, snow or rain. Your shooters must acclimate themselves to handling those competitive conditions by practicing in them. Some style adjustments may be needed; for example, a target with a headwind rises abnormally, and the shooters may need to raise their hold positions.

I do not coach "fair-weather shooters" who only shoot when the conditions are ideal. This holds true for every collegiate coach that I know. However, if the conditions are unsafe, such as a lightning storm or bitter wind-chills, I cancel the practice or postpone the match. Little is accomplished when the shooters are suffering in unsafe, cold conditions. And shooting in a thunder and lightning storm is just plain dumb.

I cancel shooting under less trying conditions if I have a group of beginners. Even when forewarned, novice shooters don't dress adequately for the conditions. Not only is little accomplished when the students are wet or cold, but if they have an unpleasant experience they may not return.

VIDEOTAPING

Modern technology has made at least one aspect of coaching more productive. Videotaping is a prime example of how technological visual aids can help the shooter. Two types of coaching videotapes

The 1977 Yale Trap and Skeet Team won the Intercollegiate Clay Target Championships. That victory probably wouldn't have occurred if the coach, Ed Migdalski (far right), had cancelled practice every time it was snowy or cold. Team captain, Brad Simmons (far left), was a member of the 1976 U.S. Olympic Skeet Team.

exist. The professionally, commercially manufactured "How-To" tape starring the "expert" shooter is useful for newer shooters. The tape provides an opportunity to "study" shooting at home and may furnish new ideas. The gun-mounted camera is particularly useful because it lets the viewer "see down the barrel" and watch the gun/target rela-

tionship in slow motion. A typical comment from one of my new shooters is "Wow! He put a big lead on that target." In other words, the shooter didn't realize how large a lead was really required.

The other type of video — the "homemade" video — is extremely useful to the intermediate and experienced competitors. Almost every coach has a video camera nowadays. If not, it is usually a simple matter to borrow a high-quality one from the school or club. The idea, of course, is to tape the shooters at practice and then replay the video in the clubhouse or in a classroom. It is a good idea to have another person scoring the round while the coach tapes. This way, when viewing the tape the shooter and coach will know if the target was hit or missed. For best results, the video camera should be mounted on a tripod and moved as needed. Also, if the team, school or club has the financial resources, a professional-grade VCR can be purchased that has a variable-speed slow motion and freeze-frame capacity. These features will greatly enhance the teaching and learning process.

If this trapshooter were videotaped by his coach, the gunner would see that his back foot is way out of position, causing difficulty making hard-left shots. The right foot should be parallel and in line with the left foot.

GOAL SETTING

The only person qualified to set personal goals is the shooter. The coach, however, can guide the shooter by helping him set challenging, yet attainable goals. How quickly the shooter wants to reach these goals is up to him; but the coach needs to know this to determine how rigorous to make the training. For example, the shooter who wishes to become his club's winter league champion will be trained much less strenuously than the shooter who strives to become a national champion or make the U.S. Olympic Team.

When coaching properly, the coach should move the shooter at the fastest sustainable pace while remaining consistent. To judge the rate of progress, it is necessary to establish goals as measuring devices.

Goals can be divided into three categories: short, intermediate and long term. The shooter and coach can plan a strategy for attaining the goals. The shooter can also set incentives for himself, if he wishes. These rewards should be determined in proportion to the degree of difficulty of the goals.

Let's use a first-year collegiate skeet shooter named "Joe" as an example. Having shot once a week for six months, Joe and his coach determined that it's time to set concrete goals. Joe's short-term goals are to shoot his first 25-straight and to hit six straight sets of Station 4 high and low house targets in drills within two months. To do this, he will need to increase his practice from two boxes of shells to three boxes per week. If he attains his goals he will treat himself and his girlfriend to a steak dinner.

Joe's intermediate-range goals are to make his team's top five shooters by the fall semester (in six months) by shooting a 23.5 average, and to place in the top 20 American Skeet shooters at the National Collegiate Clay Target Championships the following spring (in thirteen months). In order to attain the first goal, Joe will have to borrow his school gun, find a range near home and practice during the summer. If Joe makes the team, he will buy himself the new pair of shooting glasses he's wanted. To place in the top 20 at the Collegiate Championships (by shooting a 24 average) he will have to increase from three boxes of shells to four boxes shells per week and start keeping a shooting diary. If the goal is reached, his parents have promised him a better reloading machine.

Joe's long-range goal is to place in the top three American Skeet shooters at the Collegiate Championships in two and a half years; this will likely require a 24.75 average and maybe winning a shoot-off. To reach this goal, he and his coach have determined that he will need to start entering local registered shoots during his second season of shooting. His second long-term goal is to place in the top ten in International Skeet at the same Collegiate Championships, requiring a 21 average. To shoot a 21 average in International Skeet, Joe must learn International Skeet and add two rounds of International to his practice each week. If he attains both goals, his parents have offered to go 50-50 with him on his own gun.

Obviously, the goals can be much more or less lofty, depending on the individual, his determination and his monetary resources. One other tip about goal setting is that it must be flexible. If the shooter attains his goal(s) sooner than expected, he must set new ones. If the goal, for whatever reason becomes unobtainable, then the standards must be modified accordingly.

USING A SHOOTING DIARY

Shooting performance is closely linked to a series of variables that change periodically. By helping your shooters control these variables the less frustrated and the more consistent they will be. Such variables can be labeled as physical, mental and external. Physical conditions include energy, soreness, sighting, positioning, swing, practice, food and drink. Mental conditions encompass stress, imagery, negative and positive thinking, key thoughts, attitude and concentration. External variables are factors like guns and ammo, clothing, weather, lighting, distractions, location, referees, background and season.

The only way to have your shooter-athletes accurately remember these variables and use this information to their advantage is to record it. At least initially, it is probably best to review the entries with your shooters. After many written entries, or sometimes after only a few, you and the shooter(s) will see patterns develop that help or hinder scoring. You will discover what conditions influence each shooter and this, in turn, will help you coach them more effectively.

Diary entries read aloud, especially after a practice session with new shooters, is a good way to develop cohesiveness, encourage teamwork, reduce peer pressure and enhance learning. Have the shooters take a few minutes immediately after practice and record their thoughts and experiences. Then, while sitting in a circle, the individuals share their entries; those listening can then compare experiences and offer comments or suggestions

More detailed information and a sample a shooting diary format can be found in Chapter 17 — Keeping A Shooting Diary.

OFF-SEASON PRACTICE

Off-season "practice" should not be ignored. But I'm not just talking about some of your team members visiting the range for a few 50-target winter league shoots.

Many competitors put away their guns and don't do anything to enhance performance for the upcoming season. Or, perhaps they peek at their average card and resolve to hit more targets, or dream about moving up a class next year. But simply "resolving" to do something, like making a New Year's resolution, doesn't bring results without effort or change. Here are a few tips for your shooters to consider during the off-season, as well as a few reminders for the coach.

For The Shooters

- Work out. The off-season is a good time to start a strength and conditioning program. This improves shooting performance and reduces complaints about tired or sore muscles.
- Set goals. Review last year's goals, adjust current goals and set new ones. Write, in detail, the steps that must be taken to achieve these goals and list the rewards to be gained from attaining them.
- Examine shooting equipment carefully. Have personal guns inspected by a competent gunsmith. Check shooting glasses — are they bent? Are there any scratches on the lenses? Do ear protectors need replacing?
- Have your shooters start reloading shells to prevent last minute, late night rushes before shoots.
- Do your athletes need their vision checked? It's a good idea. Especially for those who wear prescription glasses.
- Reread shooting diaries from the previous year. Note any factors that may have been forgotten and incorporate them into the goals, if necessary.

For The Coach

- Examine shooting equipment carefully. Have school guns disassembled, cleaned and inspected by a competent gunsmith. Do the team vests need cleaning, repair or replacement? Should you order new team caps, shirts or jackets for nationals?
- Have you and the team planned fundraising events? Do T-shirts need to be ordered for contributors?
- Make some calls to get shoot schedules and line up competitions for the coming season. Is your team's expense budget ready? Have you ordered plane tickets for nationals? What about room reservations? Don't put it off until the last minute.
- Renew memberships for shooting organizations and monthly publications. Sit with a hi-liter, read and mark the latest articles on shotgunning techniques. Maybe you will find a few pointers to apply next season. If certain articles are especially good, copy and distribute them to your shooters as "required reading." Have you read Part II — Body and Mind in this book? The off-season might be a good time to study it.
- Inspect reloaders. Clean, oil it and replace any worn parts. Order new shotshell components.
- Take an inventory of team and school equipment. Check with your insurance company to make sure the program and guns are covered for the coming year.
- Is your recruiting done? Perhaps you need an organizational meeting, complete with refreshments and a short video, to recruit some new shooters.

- Have you taken a coach certification course? If not, isn't the off-season a good time to apply? If so, have you renewed your certification for the coming year?
- How is your first-aid and CPR certification? Is it about to expire? The off-season is a good time for a refresher course.
- And, how about *your* shooting? This is a great time to drive to the range and bust some targets without worrying about someone else's scores!

20.
Fundamentals of Skeet, Trap and Sporting Clays

Most of the important principles of the shotgunning games have been covered thus far: stance, shouldering, sighting, swing, follow-through and many others. What we have not discussed are the specifics of leads, hold positions and foot placement relative to the "Big Three" — American Skeet, American Trap and Sporting Clays

The treatment of these fundamentals will be comparatively brief because so many fine "How-To" books and videos already exist that explain the basics of placing feet on the stations, finding the proper sight-pictures and leading the targets. It is best, in my opinion, to present this material through photographs and diagrams because visual aids are effective teaching tools. This information is intended as a reference and starting point for the new clay target shooter. As the gunner reaches the intermediate and advanced stages of his skill, he will likely modify these fundamentals to suit his individual style and abilities. For example, the hold positions

Inside:

SKEET FOOT
PLACEMENTS

SKEET HOLD
POSTIONS

LEADING SKEET
TARGETS

TRAP FOOT
PLACEMENTS

TRAP HOLD
POSTIONS

SPORTING CLAYS

and sight-pictures that work superbly for one shooter may be almost useless for another.

One last clarification is in order. The following text, photographs and diagrams are, for the sake of presentation, geared toward the majority of shooters — right-handed gunners. It is quite simple, however, for the left-hander to do the opposite. If, for example, I indicate that in trap, the toes should be parallel to the right side of Station 5 — the last station, the lefty would put his toes parallel to the left side of Station 1 — the first (opposite) station, and so forth.

SKEET FOOT PLACEMENTS

As mentioned in previous chapters, the gunner's stance and "natural point-of-aim" should be oriented to where he expects to break the target, not to where the target is originating from. This way, the body is in its most comfortable attitude to the target breaking area. To find this position, stand on any station (Stations 1 through 4 work best). Place your feet so that the front right corner of the station splits your stance. In other words, if you took a piece of chalk and drew a diagonal line from the front right side of the station to the back left side of the station, your feet would evenly straddle that mark, with toes in line with each other.

This is a sound starting point for the first three or four stations in both skeet and trap; the remaining stations ideally require a stance farther to the right (a rule-of-thumb for skeet is that your belt buckle should always face the low house window). In other words, turn your feet slightly more to the right (relative to the station) as you progress around the field. We can now fine-tune your stance. But first, let me digress a moment.

A good starting position for the beginner is to face the forward, right corner of the station.

The reason that a right-handed shooter favors his right side is because he can turn much farther to the left than to the right (and vise versa for the lefty). To illustrate this, try the following demonstration. Using an unloaded gun when nobody is around you (a basement or garage works well for this), face a wall with your shoulders and toes parallel to it. Shoulder your gun and turn as far to your right as possible without moving your feet — you can probably turn about 90 degrees. Next, slowly swing as far as possible to your left — you can probably turn 180 degrees. Hence, to make this biomechanical idiosyncrasy work for you on the skeet and trap range, you must significantly favor your right side.

Now, back to fine-tuning your stance by incorporating your natural point-of-aim. Once your feet are on station as indicated earlier, close your eyes, shoulder your gun and, using your upper body, swing it back and forth in a pendulum fashion. Make each swing slower and shorter until you stop at your body's most comfortable pointing position. Now open your eyes and note exactly where your gun is pointing. Is this where you want to break the target? If not, slightly shift your feet toward the direction you want to be and repeat the procedure. Once the

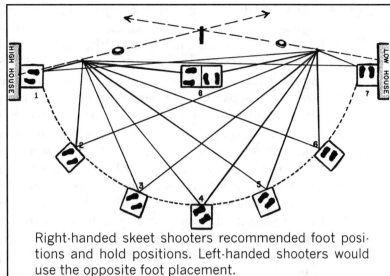

Right-handed skeet shooters recommended foot positions and hold positions. Left-handed shooters would use the opposite foot placement.

proper position is found, note your specific foot placement for future reference. You can take a few minutes and do the same on the other stations. Many experts take their natural point-of-aim one "tick" of the feet farther to enhance follow-through. Some skeet shooters use the same stance for high and low houses because they break both targets in the same area; others change their foot positions for the high and low houses. It is your preference. But, I urge you not to take foot placements casually. They make the difference between fair scores and great scores.

SKEET HOLD POSTIONS

Hold positions on the skeet field depend on the method used to achieve a lead on the targets. Two basic types of swings are commonly employed: the older "swing-through" or "come-from-behind" style and the newer "sustained lead."

Swing-through, as the name implies, entails holding the barrel near the target opening and letting the target emerge ahead of the gun (some shooters accomplish this by focusing out over the barrel, instead of back to the house). The gunner then swings faster than the target, thereby meeting and then passing it. The advantage of the swing-through method is that the target never gets an unintentional jump on the shooter. The swing-through method is popular with one-eye shooters who lack some peripheral vision (see Chapter 11 — Vision and Sighting) and must hold closer to the house. The drawback to swinging through is that shots are taken later than when using a sustained lead. The perceived leads are also smaller than those in sustained lead shooting because the muzzle is moving faster than the target; by the time the shooter sees the gun/target relationship, reacts to it and pulls the trigger, the barrel has already moved farther ahead of the target.

The intent in sustained lead shooting is to never permit the target to pass the gun barrel. To accomplish this, the shooter's hold position is farther out from the house, which compensates for the delay in reaction time (see "reaction time" in Chapter 11 — Vision and Sighting). The advantages of the sustained lead are that first, the target never gets in front of the barrel, and second, the target is hit sooner, which helps provide time for the second shot in doubles. Sustained lead is also the principle method used in International Skeet. The disadvantages of the sustained lead are that the shooter must be alert when he says, "Pull" and his hold position must be precise so that the target doesn't get ahead of his barrel. That would cause the shooter to suddenly revert to the swing-through method. The sustained lead hold positions should be such that the lead is correct when the gunner starts his swing. He then needs only to maintain that lead for a short while as he fine-tunes it and then slaps the trigger (a shotgun trigger should be quickly pulled or "slapped," as opposed to the slow, smooth "squeeze" used by rifle shooters). Doubles presents another quandary. The first target can always be taken as a sustained lead shot, but by the time new shooters have fired the first shell, the second target has already crossed their barrel from the opposite direction. This necessitates that the gunner "come from behind" and swing through the second shot. Experienced shooters can meet the second target quickly and maintain a sustained lead on it as it crosses the field. For example, if you were shooting Station 2 doubles and shot the high house target aggressively, say two-thirds of the way to the stake (target crossing point), you would have time to sustain lead on the second shot by about two feet. Yet, if you took the first (high house) shot late, perhaps hitting it past the stake, you must rapidly swing to come from behind for the second shot. Assuming that you then took the second shot as soon as possible, the apparent lead would be a foot or less (instead of two) because of the speed of your swing.

LEADING SKEET TARGETS

As mentioned in other chapters, skeet targets always travel along the same flight path. What varies is the shooter's position when moving from station to station. Because the stations are along an arc, the center stations are farther from the targets than the end stations, consequently, different leads must be used. I teach my first-time shooters an easy way to remember the leads: Station 1 needs a one-foot lead, and then add one more foot on each subsequent station as you progress to Station 4 (the farthest out). Hence, Station 4 requires a four-foot lead. Subtract a foot on each successive station as you travel toward the other end of the field (the low house), thereby ending with a one-foot lead on Station 7 and a zero-foot lead on Station 8. The leads for a sustained-lead shooter would look like this:

Station	Perceived Lead
1	one foot
2	two feet
3	three feet
4	four feet
5	three feet
6	two feet
7	one foot
8	zero feet

This system provides the beginner with many fine breaks (hit targets), however, it is not quite this simple. As your individual style and abilities develop, you will undoubtedly make subtle changes to these leads. For example, many shooters see no apparent lead on Stations 1 and 7; others see a foot. The reasons for this are swing speed and how individuals differ in perceiving distances.

The diagrams on the following pages show typical hold positions, leads and target breaking points.

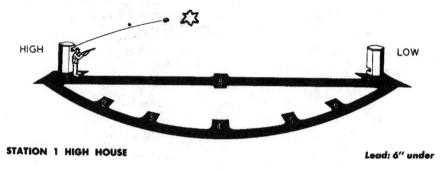

STATION 1 HIGH HOUSE

Lead: 6" under

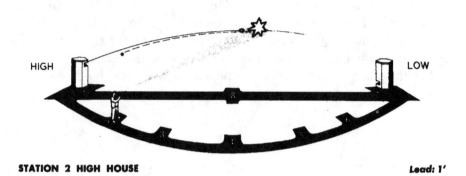

STATION 2 HIGH HOUSE

Lead: 1'

230

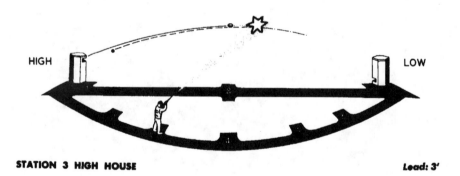

STATION 3 HIGH HOUSE

Lead: 3'

STATION 4 HIGH HOUSE

Lead: 4'

STATION 1 LOW HOUSE *Lead: 1'*

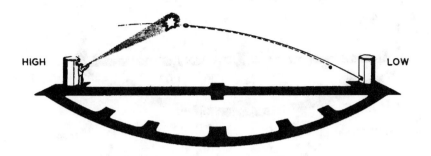

STATION 2 LOW HOUSE *Lead: 2'*

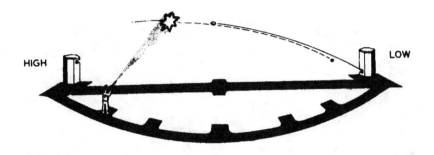

231

STATION 3 LOW HOUSE *Lead: 3½'*

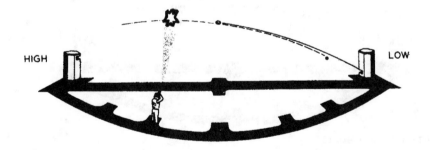

STATION 4 LOW HOUSE *Lead: 4'*

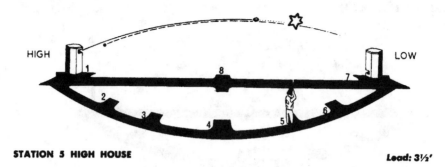

STATION 5 HIGH HOUSE

Lead: 3½'

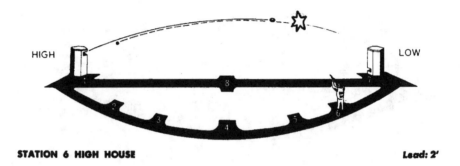

STATION 6 HIGH HOUSE

Lead: 2'

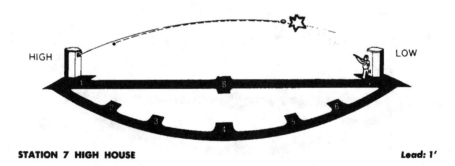

STATION 7 HIGH HOUSE

Lead: 1'

STATION 8 HIGH HOUSE

Lead: Blot out target with muzzle and slap trigger at same time

STATION 5 LOW HOUSE   *Lead: 3'*

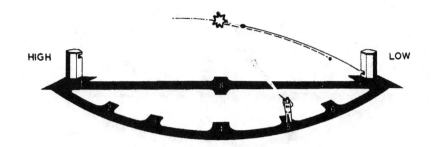

STATION 6 LOW HOUSE   *Lead: 1'*

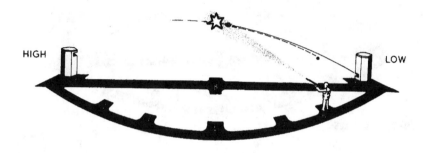

233

STATION 7 LOW HOUSE   *Lead: Point Blank*

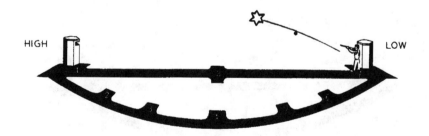

STATION 8 LOW HOUSE   *Lead: Blot out target with muzzle and slap trigger at same time*

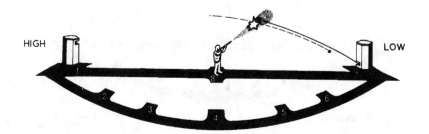

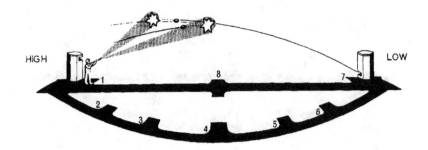

STATION 1 DOUBLES

Break High House Target First

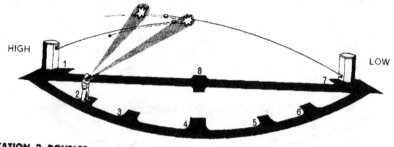

STATION 2 DOUBLES

Break High House Target First

STATION 6 DOUBLES

Break Low House Target First

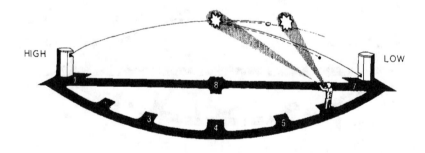

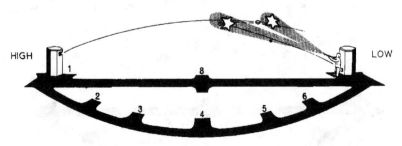

STATION 7 DOUBLES

Break Low House Target First

The following photographs are a sampling of proper stances and hold positions for selected shots in American Skeet. For International Skeet, the muzzle is held farther from the houses because of the faster target speed. Foot positions are also slightly farther over because the shots are taken later.

American Skeet — Station 1 high house stance and hold position

American Skeet — Station 2 high house stance and hold position

American Skeet — Station 3 high house stance and hold position

American Skeet — Station 4 low house stance and hold position

American Skeet — Station 5 low house stance and hold position

American Skeet — Station 6 low house stance and hold position

American Skeet — Station 6 high house hold position

American Skeet — Station 7 high and low house stance and hold position

American Skeet — Station 8 high house hold position

American Skeet — Station 8 low house stance and hold position

An Example

As an example of shooting a station in skeet, let's try one of the most difficult shots (because it requires the most lead) — Station 4 high house.

On Station 4 you will notice that you are standing midway between the high house on the left, and the low house on the right, in the middle of the semi-circle's perimeter. Your target will come from the high house, on your left. Now, ready yourself to break that target:

1. Assume the proper stance, which positions you to break the target at the crossing point, at centerfield. To do this, space your feet comfortably apart facing the forward right corner of the station and shift your body weight to the ball of the left foot. Crack the left knee and lean the shoulders and trunk of the body gently forward.
2. Mount your gun. Your left hand should be extended on the fore-end with the left index finger and thumb pointing along the left side of the fore-end in line with the barrel. Your right hand should be grasping the pistol grip with the thumb wrapped around it. Keeping your head erect, raise the gun toward eye level, so the front sight just floats on the top of the receiver. Raise and push

your right shoulder forward as you pull the gun butt firmly into the shoulder pocket. Lean your head forward and nudge that stock with your right cheek.

3. Now, without moving your feet, turn your body toward the high house. Point the gun at a spot about one-third of the distance out from the target opening to the target crossing point, in line with the bottom of the target opening (so that you don't lose sight of the target below the barrel). Look to the left of the barrel and focus in "dead space" a few feet in front of the target opening.

4. Get set. When you call "pull," the target will be released. The moment you see the target appear, focus on it and start your swing by pivoting at the waist and pushing with the left arm. Adjust your lead to about four feet (this will appear to be about four inches at the end your gun barrel). Maintain that lead, pull the trigger and follow-through by continuing to lead the broken pieces.

TRAP FOOT PLACEMENTS

The principles of foot placement in trap are simpler than in skeet for two reasons: First, there are only five stations instead of eight. And second, the body's range of motion is not as great in trap because the targets are traveling away from the shooter, not crossing as in skeet. Finding the natural point-of-aim, which we discussed earlier, does not apply as well in trap because the shooter does not know where he will break the target (remember, trap targets are thrown randomly from an oscillating machine). Feet are placed to

237

American Trap — Stations 1 & 2 stance

American Trap — Station 3 stance

American Trap — Station 4 stance

American Trap — Station 5 stance

give the shooter his widest range of motion while favoring the right-hand target. Similar to skeet, trap foot-placement is facing the forward, right corner of Stations 1, 2 and 3. Turn slightly more to the right on Station 4 and more so again on Station 5, where the toes should face the right side of the station. These more extreme foot placements on Stations 4 and 5 position the shooter to handle a hard-right angle target, if need be (a hard-left target from Station 5 is seen as a straight-away).

TRAP HOLD POSTIONS

Once again, I present a "rule-of-thumb" to help the beginner remember general hold positions. For Station 1, use the left, front corner of the house. Station 2 is halfway between the left corner and the center of the front edge of the trap house. Station 3 would be about over the center. Station 4 is halfway between the center and the right

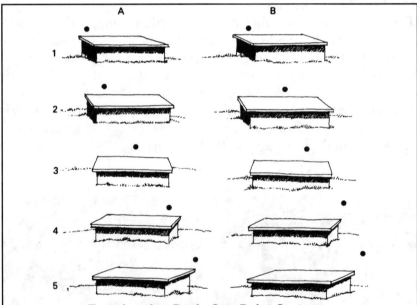

Trapshooting Basic Gun Point Systems

In 16-yard trapshooting the above diagrams indicate the two basic gunpoint systems most commonly used by experts. Veteran shooters do not agree on which method is superior. The new shooter should try both methods and find which one best suits his or her personal physical characteristics. Slight modifications in gun point and foot position may also help at "trouble stations." **A.** Take gunpoint about one foot above front edge at all stations. (1) One foot inward. (2) Quarter of the way in. (3) Above center. (4) Quarter of the way in from right. (5) Directly over right front corner. **B.** (1) About 1 1/2 feet high between middle and left front corner. (2) About 1 1/2 feet high over middle of house. (3) About 2 1/2 feet high, halfway between middle and right front corner. (4) About 2 1/2 feet high over right front corner. (5) About 2 1/2 feet high and 1 1/2 feet to right.

front corner of the house, and Station 5 would be over the right-hand corner of the house. Some shooters find that some of these positions do not favor the hard-right angle target enough, so they shift their hold point a bit farther to the right. For example, the hold position frequently used for Station 5 is one foot to the right of the front right corner of the house. For your reference, two different sets of commonly used hold positions are shown. As you develop into an experienced trapshooter, you may wish to vary these holds.

Thus far, we have only been concerned with horizontal hold positions, yet vertical holds must also be considered. Similar methods to the swing-through and sustained leads in skeet are used in trap. Some trapshooters hold their gun's front bead directly along the front edge of the trap house. One-eye shooters often prefer this style, otherwise the barrel initially obscures the target. Using this method, the shooter swings the gun from behind, catches up to and pulls the trigger as he "touches" the target. The speed of the swing compensates for horizontal lead, which is much less in trap than in most skeet shots. The majority of the trapshooters, however, hold their gun a foot or two above the front edge of the house to minimize gun swing. The higher hold is an advantage for the two-eye shooter because he can see below the barrel with his increased peripheral vision.

Most trap guns are designed to shoot high, which means that their point-of-impact is above where the gun points (this is the purpose of the elevated comb on a Monte Carlo stock). Trap guns shoot high to compensate for the vertical lead needed on fast-rising trap targets. Otherwise, the shooter would have to shoot above the target to account for vertical lead and the barrel would hide the target.

There is no practical rule of proper lead in trap without memorizing computed lead-tables, so the new shooter must rely on adapting the basic fundamentals he has learned about shooting moving targets. The principles of hold position, lead, swing and follow-through are applicable to all forms of shotgun shooting. In trap, just as in skeet, a stopped gun at the instant of firing is certain to cause a miss. Remember to continue your swing and follow-through as you fire. As the new shooter gains experience, he will acquire a memory image, or mental sight-picture of each lead. To speed the trapshooting learning process, refer to the drills recommended in Chapter 19 — How to Coach.

SPORTING CLAYS

Sporting Clays and NSCA 5-Stand Sporting require much more versatility than the skeet and trap games. Hence, "rules-of-thumb" are not easy to present to the beginner.

When assuming a stance, similar to skeet and most importantly, always place your feet in a comfortable position for the target breaking area and then turn at the waist to your hold position. When a squad arrives at a station or "stand" in Sporting Clays, competitors are permitted to preview a set of targets. Pay close attention to the

American Trap — Station 1 stance and hold position

American Trap — Station 2 stance and hold position

American Trap — Station 3 stance and hold position

American Trap — Station 4 stance and hold position

American Trap — Station 5 stance and hold position

targets' flight and locate the area that you would like to break the targets in. And, remember to favor your right side because, as we discovered earlier, a right-handed gunner can swing much farther left than right.

Experienced Sporting shooters can employ the sustained lead or swing-through methods in Sporting Clays, depending on the target that they expect. A third method of swing is also popular; it is called the "pull-away." The pull-away is a combination of the sustained lead

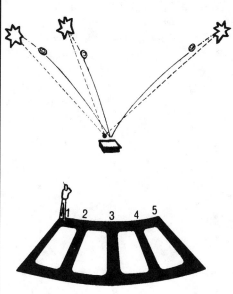

Station 1

At Station One, your feet should be placed with the left foot pointed toward the left corner of the trap house. Your gun should point about one foot above and one foot in from the left corner of the house. This point is shown here by a dot. Here, and in the next four diagrams, solid black lines indicate the flight angles of three typical targets you may encounter; dotted black lines indicate the swing and follow-through of your gun as well as the target breaking point.

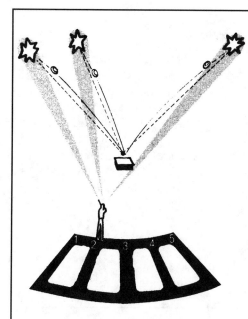

Station 2

At Station Two, your feet should be placed with the left foot pointed one quarter of the way in from left corner of the trap house. Your gun should point one foot above and about a quarter of the way in from the left front corner of the trap house, as shown by the black dot.

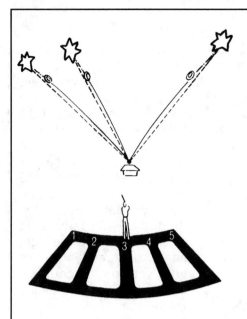

Station 3

At Station Three, your feet should be placed with the left foot pointed slightly to the left of the center of the trap house. Point your gun one foot above the center of the trap house as shown by the black dot.

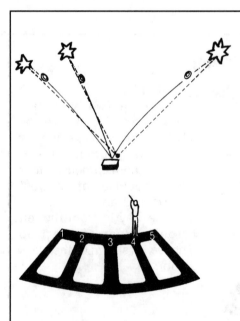

Station 4

At Station Four, your feet should be placed with left foot pointed one quarter of the way in from the right corner of the trap house. Point your gun one foot above and a quarter of the way in from the right front corner of the trap house as shown by the black dot.

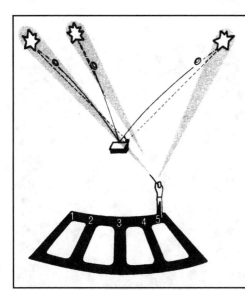

Station 5

At Station Five, your feet should be placed with the left foot pointed toward the right corner of the trap house. Point your gun one foot above and over the right front corner of the trap house, as shown by the black dot.

243

and the swing-through methods. The Sporting gunner comes from behind the target, similar to the swing-through, but instead of pulling the trigger as he passes the target, he pulls ahead of it to the proper lead, adjusts it momentarily and shoots. This method is used because few shooters swing fast enough to slap the trigger just as they are passing the target — the lead would be insufficient. Don't track your targets for too long; it is important to establish the lead quickly and shoot aggressively. As a beginner, you may feel rushed and be inclined to take snap or "poke" shots. Avoid doing this, as tempting as it may be. The poke shot simply means anticipating the target's flight, pushing the barrel straight-ahead to the spot you wish to hit the target, stopping the gun and pulling the trigger. You might hit a few targets this way, but you will never become a consistent or proficient Sporting shooter by just thrusting out and stopping your gun.

When establishing a hold position, you must give Sporting Clays targets a sufficient buffer. Your eyes will not be able to focus on the target as it leaves the trap, it is simply moving too fast and at too great an angle. Expect to focus on the target a short way into its flight, and adjust your hold position accordingly. You will have to acquire a knack for visualizing the proper hold points and leads as you arrive at each new Sporting stand, but that is part of the challenge and fun of this game.

The following diagrams and captions provide an idea of what to expect and how to shoot seven types of Sporting Clays targets.

NSCA 5-Stand Sporting — Stand 2. This shooter is preparting for a target originating from the right side of the field. He is aggressively favoring a right-side stance, indicating that he plans to break the target early in its flight.

The following diagrams were reprinted by permission, courtesy of Beretta U.S.A. Corp.

No. 1: The Crossing Shot

Targets may come from right or left, singly or in pairs...will usually be close and quick through trees and vegetation, simulating woodcock. Targets should be taken as quickly as possible.

Eye focal-point and gun hold-point should be close to the trap. Mounting the gun during tracking and swinging through target is imperative. Lead: minimal, due to closeness and rapid gunswing. Skeet shells and open chokes are best here.

For Report Pairs — Dismount and remount the gun for each shot. Simultaneous Pairs — Shoot rear target first and keep muzzle moving to swing through and break front target.

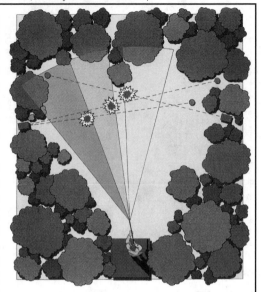

No. 2: The Driven Shot

Simulates driven grouse or similar birds, rapidly incoming toward shooter and rising. Eye focal point should be exactly where target is first visible, with gun hold-point below eye focal-point. When flying low, close and fast, cylinder chokes and number nine shot are recommended. Lead: no apparent lead needed; high-speed gun swing will provide sufficient allowance. Simultaneous Pairs — Must decide immediately which target in pair to shoot first. Any hesitation will likely result in second target being lost.

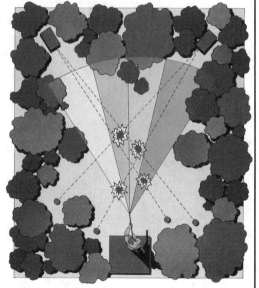

No. 3: The Going Away Shot

Targets may spring from behind as in Quail Walk, or from in front simulating a flushing pheasant. In either case, it is important to have weight on front foot and to pick up target as soon as possible. Number 7 1/2 or 8 shot and cylinder or improved cylinder chokes work best. Target will be most stable at peak of flight, before it begins to drop. If fired upon here, there will be little movement of the barrel between the focal-point and break-point. Lead: minimal, expecially if target angles away from you. Simultaneous Pair — Shoot target dropping fastest first, then point barrel at second target and dip barrel under it. You will not have time to dismount between. Shoot quickly and instinctively.

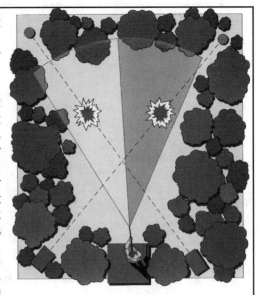

245

No. 4: Incoming Tower Shot

Simulates incoming waterfowl or pheasant, often from towers up to 100 feet high. You must be patient. With weight on front foot, eye focus-point is where target is first visible. Gun hold-point is just below. Give shot time to develop, swinging gun but not mounting till nearing break-point. Shoot targets as close-in and as nearly overhead as possible. Skeet loads and open choke give best results. Lead: minimal for close-in shots. Simultaneous Pair — Shoot first bird far enough out to allow time for tracking second. Report Pair — Dismount and remount to shoot second bird at about the same spot.

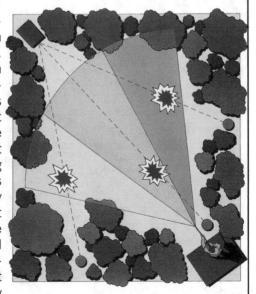

No. 5: Fur & Feather Shot

Simulates an erratic, bouncing rabbit and a crossing bird shot, usually as a report pair moving in same direction. Gun hold-point is toward rabbit break-point and just beneath it. This assures seeing the target whether it bounces or not. Pick up target at earliest point, but mount gun only when nearing break-point. Concentrate on breaking rabbit target, dismount gun to pick up flying bird target. Skeet load and open choke work best. Lead: up to a full gun length on fur; minimal on feather, as in crossing shot.

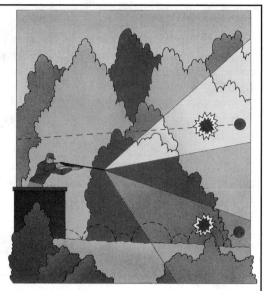

No. 6: The Springing Teal

Target is thrown rapidly up at about 70° and away from shooter, simulating a classic teal maneuver. Shooter's weight should be on front foot, and targets should be taken at or near their apex, where they have slowed to minimum speed. Gun hold-point should be high, so target is tracked at its slowest point. Fire just as you swing through target. Those that angle away near top will require more choke because clay will be edge-on as it travels away. These targets should be broken on way up when possible. Simultaneous Pair — Shoot clay with lowest apex first, then the higher one, thereby taking both as near apex as possible.

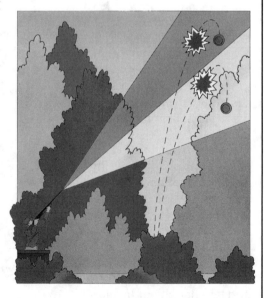

No. 7: Outgoing Overhead Dropping Shot

Simulates a darting dove coming from overhead. Weight on rear foot, lean back and tip bead backward to pick up target as early as possible. Muzzle straight up to point where target will pass overhead. Let target pass muzzle, mount gun, shift weight to front foot and track from behind. Keep muzzle moving and shoot just as you swing through target. Number 7 1/2 or 8 shot, and im-

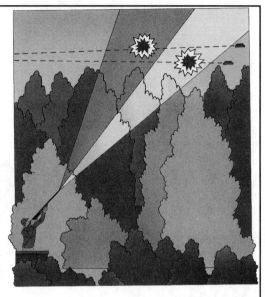

proved cylinder or modified choke. Lead: swing through should be enough. If falling very fast, open some daylight. Simultaneous Pair — Lean far back, take first target ASAP. This avoids a difficult edge shot at great distance on second bird.

247

PART IV:
The Equipment

21. Gunology

A tremendous amount of literature — books, pamphlets, brochures and magazine articles — specifically concerns guns, their history, development, use, performance and selection. This material is readily available to any shooter. The following review of basic gunology (the study of guns) is geared to serve as a guide for beginners as well as for instructors and coaches. Because this volume is concerned with the clay target games, the information mostly encompasses trap, skeet and Sporting Clays guns and associated items.

NOT A WEAPON

One of my particular peeves is to hear a person, especially an instructor or coach, refer to the clay target gun as "the weapon." Such terminology is a holdover from military rifle instruction, where such a reference was perfectly appropriate. Target shotguns are not weapons, but recreational or sporting firearms, and they should be referred to as such.

A BIT OF HISTORY

Today's shotguns are breech (the "action" where shells are inserted) loaders. But it was only a little more than a hundred years ago that all firearms were muzzle (the far end of the barrel) loaders. Various inventors tried to develop a breech-loading gun but all attempts were unsuccessful because such arms leaked powder at the breech, weakening the charge and, more often than not, burning the hand or face of the shooter. Breech-loading first became practical in about 1860 with the advent of fixed ammunition having metallic cartridge cases to act as gas seals.

In early firearms — arquebuses and blunderbusses, and later muskets and fowling pieces — the inside of the barrel was smooth. These "smooth bores" used lead balls, lead shot, or fragmented lead scraps, and were loaded through the muzzle.

The earliest muzzle-loaders were fired by a match put to a touchhole at the breech. The next development was the use of steel and flint to produce the sparks that ignited the charge. One of the models that employed the steel and flint arrangement was a "wheel-lock," which was wound with a key. Another, a more practical design, was called the "flint-lock." It was from these early guns that the term "lock, stock and barrel" originated as an expression of completeness. Flintlocks were "primed" by fine powder held in a "pan," into which were struck the sparks caused by the contact of flint and steel. When, at times, the priming powder jolted away from the "touchhole" and fired off with a flash that failed to set off the powder charge in the barrel, the result was called a "flash in the pan."

THE DIFFERENCE BETWEEN A RIFLE AND A SHOTGUN

Gun historians believe that a gunsmith in Germany discovered that grooves in a barrel afforded tighter fitting bullets to be rammed down the barrel more easily. And if the grooves were spiraled, causing the bullet to spin in flight, shooting accuracy was greatly improved. This process of grooving the barrels was called "rifling" — hence the name "rifle."

All rifles have spiraled grooves in the bore (lining of the barrel) and shoot bullets. Shotguns, on the other hand, are smooth bores and fire shotshells. The bullet is a single piece of lead that requires precision aiming at the target. The shotshell contains a number of small, round pellets or "shot," which spread over a certain area so that flying targets can be hit. And the gun is pointed, not aimed, at the moving target. Just as bullets come in a variety of types, so do shotshells vary in strength of powder and size of shot. The diameter of the shot pattern at an effective distance also varies. For example, a skeet shell was designed to perform best when approaching an approximate 30-inch circle from a distance of about 40 yards.

EVOLUTION OF THE SHOTGUN

The ancient bell-mouth blunderbuss was the forerunner of the modern shotgun. The fowling piece that followed it was a shorter, lighter version of the smooth-bore musket. The flintlock, on the other hand, which was slow to ignite, was used mostly for stationary birds. Gunners found that a smooth-bore musket loaded with a charge of shot pellets, produced favorable results when used on sitting ducks, but was almost totally useless against birds on the wing. Consequently, wing shooting did not become popular until the advent of the percussion cap, with its more rapid ignition.

As the rifled barrel replaced the smooth-bore, it became obvious that pellets used in bird shooting were unsuited for the rifled barrel. As a result, the shortened smooth-bore musket developed into a fowling piece or shotgun. Early shotguns were made with both single and double barrels and soon acquired the basic characteristics seen in today's shotgun. Although in use earlier, the breech-loading shotgun did not come into common use until about 1880, when the modern shotshell appeared.

CHOKE

Soon after the breech-loading shotgun appeared, choke boring was invented. It was discovered that by constricting or "choking" the bore at the muzzle, a narrower, denser pattern of shot was thrown, thereby extending the gun's effective range. The shotguns most commonly used in trapshooting today have a full choke. On the other hand, because skeet targets are at closer range and usually not going away as they are in trap, skeet guns have barrels that are minimally constricted at the muzzle. They are simply called "skeet choked." A "true cylinder" or "cylinder bore" has no constriction at all.

Several degrees of choke are available: full, improved modified, modified, improved cylinder and cylinder bore. Full choke barrels are designed for long range shooting; they make the shot-pattern denser at greater distances. Improved modified choke falls between full choke and modified choke; it is sometimes used in trapshooting. Modified choke is midway between full choke and improved cylinder. Some gunners, when shooting Doubles Trap or Wobble Trap, prefer to have one barrel with a modified or improved modified choke for the first shot and the other with full choke for the second, farther shot. Improved cylinder and cylinder bore barrels have little constriction and give maximum controlled spread of the shot charge for close shooting, as in skeet.

SHOT PATTERNS

Shot patterns are closely associated with choke. The amount of choke affects the spread or pattern of the shot. Patterns at 40 yards are used as a standard measure. Patterning a shotgun means shooting at a stationary target that will keep the marks of the shot hitting

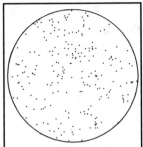

Shot Pattern, Skeet: 12 gauge — 3 drams — 1 1/8 ounces No. 9 shot; 30-inch circle. At 40 yards average pattern 35-40%.

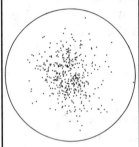

Shot Pattern, Trap: 12 gauge — 3 drams — 1 1/8 ounces No. 7 1/2 shot; 30-inch circle. Full choke at 25 yards average pattern 100%.

254

it. This can be done by shooting at a large paper target.

Each shotgun delivers a different pattern, and the pattern changes with each load. The pellet marks on the paper will denote whether the gun is shooting where the shooter is looking and whether the gun fits the shooter. A shotgun should be patterned before use, and certainly after any alterations have been made to it, to determine where it shoots.

HOW TO PATTERN A SHOTGUN

Set a large piece (perhaps 3' x 3') of cardboard or paper 40 yards from the shooting station. A bull's-eye on the paper is used as an aiming point. After firing, the target is inspected and a circle 30 inches in diameter is drawn to include the greatest number of pellet holes. Disregard the bull's eye; it may or may not be in the center of the drawn circle. After counting the holes in the circle the number is compared to the number of pellets known to be in shotshells having the same size and weight of shot. This will tell you the pattern density that your gun and ammo provide at 40 yards. Different size shot can be experimented with, which is especially important for hunting conditions where shot sizes vary widely. Chokes of particular constrictions will produce the following percentages of their total number of pellets in a 30-inch circle at 40 yards:

Full Choke: 65-75%
Improved Modified Choke: 55-65%

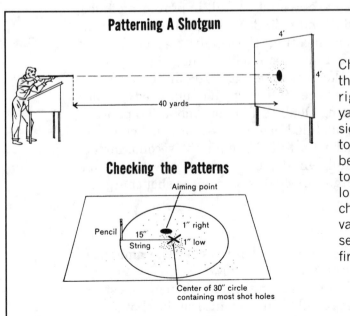

Patterning A Shotgun

Checking the Patterns

Checking the Pattern. In this case, gun shoots 1" to right and 1" low at 40 yards. If the shot holes inside the 30" circle — drawn to include maximum number of shot holes — add up to 70% of pellets in a full load, gun is shooting a full choke pattern. Patterns will vary from shot to shot — several patterns should be fired and an average taken.

Modified Choke:	45-55%
Improved Cylinder Choke:	35-45%
Cylinder Bore:	25-35%

Chokes that are an integral part of the gun are made either by cutting or by swaging. Cut chokes are formed by reaming the barrel, with the reaming tool carrying the shape, radius, and dimensions of the choke desired. Swaged chokes are first formed on the barrel's exterior with less metal ground from the muzzle end than from the rest of the barrel. When the muzzle is swaged in a heavy press the excess metal on the exterior of the muzzle is pressed inward, creating an interior constriction of the desired shape and dimension.

A tight choke may be removed or expanded by a competent gunsmith, but choke cannot be easily added. For instance, a full choke could be made into a modified choke, but not vise versa.

Several adjustable chokes are marketed, and interchangeable chokes that screw into a threaded muzzle are also available, which make the gun more versatile. These are not often seen at high level trap and skeet competitions where specialty guns are preferred. However, they have been well received in Sporting Clays, where a variety of target distances make screw-in chokes practical.

Dispersion

Imp. cylinder
Modified choke
Full choke

DISPERSION

No appreciable difference between 12-16-20 gauges — choke for choke

INTERCHANGEABLE CHOKES

A CUT CHOKE (Exaggerated)

Cylinder
Improved cylinder
Modified
Full

Outside

A SWAGED CHOKE (before Swaging)

Outside

A SWAGED CHOKE (after Swaging)

255

Porting

Porting is a professionally gunsmithed process that cuts grooves or drills holes, sometimes by way of laser (Light Amplification by Stimulated Emission of Radiation), near the end of the barrel. This technique allows expanding powder gases to escape sideways or upwards from the vents at the muzzle. Porting may help to lessen recoil, but its main function is to reduce muzzle lift or "jump," which is important to help the gun recover smoothly for the second shot in doubles. Besides the additional cost, the other drawback to porting is that the noise or "report" of the gun is magnified. This is not always well accepted on shooting ranges where other participants are standing close by. However, at least one laser-porting company (LAZER-PORTS, 1-800-833-2737) claims that their method does not produce louder guns.

GAUGE

The term "gauge," as it refers to guns and shells, is an archaic one. It is derived from the number of lead balls the diameter of the barrel needed to make a pound. For example, a 12-gauge gun had a bore that, if it had no choke, would accept one ball, 12 of which would weigh a pound. Although this outmoded means of measurement is no longer applied in marketing, the term has remained. Incidentally, most English gunners use the term "bore," which is synonymous with gauge.

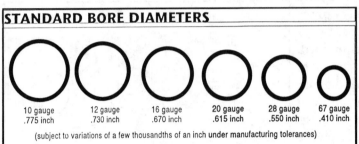

STANDARD BORE DIAMETERS

10 gauge	12 gauge	16 gauge	20 gauge	28 gauge	67 gauge
.775 inch	.730 inch	.670 inch	.615 inch	.550 inch	.410 inch

(subject to variations of a few thousandths of an inch under manufacturing tolerances)

Reprinted by permission. Copyright *1997 Black's Wing & Clay.*

In using gauge as an indication of measurement, the smaller the number, the bigger the gauge. In other words, 12-gauge guns have larger diameter barrels than 16-gauge guns, 16's are larger than 20's, etc. There is one exception: the .410-bore refers to the actual barrel diameter, .410 of an inch; being a relatively latecomer to the shotgun group, it got named using different nomenclature — it is actually a 67-gauge. Because the bore is larger, the 12-gauge can handle more shot than the 16, and so on. Hence, a larger gauge makes it easier to hit the flying target.

BARRELS

Modern shotguns are equipped with 26-, 28-, 30- or 32-inch barrels. A mistaken notion exists that the reason trap guns are longer than skeet guns is because they shoot harder, or they keep a denser pattern for a longer period of time, which is an advantage in trapshooting. This is not so. Let us backtrack a bit. A barrel has to be long enough to allow complete combustion of the powder. Generally, when the shot charge has moved about 20 inches from the breech, combustion has been completed; therefore, the trap gun's 30-inch barrel has no advantage over a skeet gun's 26-inch barrel in terms of combustion. Length of barrel has little effect on velocity. Skeet barrels are shorter because shorter barrels make for faster gun swinging at crossing skeet targets. On the other hand, the trap barrel's longer length, with more weight out front, steadies the swing and favors a more accurate point for the longer range, which is usually needed when firing at predominantly going-away targets. The current trend in skeet and Sporting Clays, however, is away from the shortest barrels because they don't swing as smoothly.

CHAMBER

The chamber, located at the breech end of all barrels, is larger in diameter than the remainder of the barrel. The chamber houses the live shell and is slightly longer than the shell so that the crimp (the closed, plastic end of the shotshell) can unfold when the shell is fired. Between the chamber and the barrel, the "cone," a funnel-like construction, narrows from the chamber to the barrel. The shell's rim (at the base of the brass) falls into a groove at the rear of the chamber. The chamber also has a cut large enough to allow the extractor or ejector to be held under the shell rim.

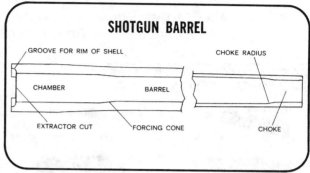

SHOTGUN BARREL

GROOVE FOR RIM OF SHELL CHOKE RADIUS
CHAMBER BARREL
EXTRACTOR CUT FORCING CONE CHOKE

In the United States, most shotguns are chambered for 2 3/4 -inch shells. Some guns used for hunting, especially for duck or goose hunting, have 3-inch chambers, which also accommodate 3-inch magnum loads for long-range pass shooting.

VENTILATED RIB

The barrels of many modern shotguns, including most clay target guns, are fitted with ventilated ribs. The rib, supported by stanchions leaving an open space between the rib and barrel, serves two purposes. First, it is a straight-edge, so to speak, to assist in gun pointing and sighting down the barrel. Second, it breaks up the heat mirage that shimmers up from a barrel hot from continuous firing, which otherwise may confuse the gunner's view of his target. Some more expensive over-and-unders also have venting between the barrels, which helps to lessen sideways wind force on blustery days, and also helps cool the barrels.

SIGHTS

Sights on a shotgun are not as important as those on a rifle because the shooter points the gun at the moving target. In rifle shooting, the sights are used for precise, usually slow, aiming. Shotgun sights are metal or plastic beads of various sizes and colors; one is just as good as another, so long as they are not distracting to the shooter. However, some shooters prefer smaller sights because, they claim, it makes the target appear larger. Sights help prevent canting the gun and also help in aligning the eye along the length of the barrel before the target is called for. In other words, if the gunner's eye is on the same level as the front bead but above the second or middle bead it will cause him to overshoot the target.

For consistent shooting, the eye should be in the same position for every shot, looking directly down the center line and slightly above

257

the receiver or rib, just high enough to see the target. Refer to Chapter 11 — Vision and Sighting for more information about how to look at targets.

STOCK

Manufacturers produce guns that have stocks suitable for people of average build. About 70 percent of shooters can adapt themselves to these "off the rack" guns. Shooters of average physique, who find that they are consistently placing their aiming eye improperly, need to have stocks adjusted to suit them. For example, a tall person with long arms may need a 1/2- or 3/4 inch spacer inserted between the butt of the gun and the recoil pad, thereby making the stock longer. In contrast, persons with arms shorter than average many need the stock shortened.

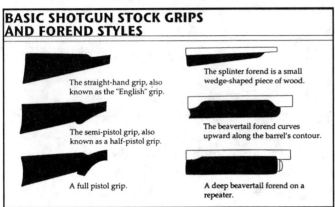

BASIC SHOTGUN STOCK GRIPS AND FOREND STYLES

The straight-hand grip, also known as the "English" grip.

The semi-pistol grip, also known as a half-pistol grip.

A full pistol grip.

The splinter forend is a small wedge-shaped piece of wood.

The beavertail forend curves upward along the barrel's contour.

A deep beavertail forend on a repeater.

Reprinted by permission. Copyright *1997 Black's Wing & Clay.*

Special Stocks

Stocks that are too short usually cause improper mounting of the gun, resulting in shoulder ache because of recoil. Or the point of the comb may dig the cheek. Or the thumb may bump the nose. Stocks that have too much drop at the heel hurt the face because they have a tendency to push upwards on recoil. Also, an excessive drop at the heel will not allow the entire butt to rest against the shoulder, and possibly cause bruising.

"Drops" are measured from a straight edge laid along the top of the muzzle and receiver, or along the rib if the gun has one. The comb is the top front of the stock; the heel is the top point of the butt. The distance from the straight edge to these points is the comb and heel drop. Stock length is measured from the front center of the trigger to the center end of the butt plate. Average shotgun stocks are provided with a 14-inch pull, that is, the distance from trigger to butt.

There is a major difference between the stock shapes of trap and skeet guns. Trap shots are fired at rising, going-away targets; therefore, trapshooters prefer stocks with a straighter or higher comb over those with more drop because it causes the gun to shoot slightly higher (thereby accounting for vertical lead). For clay target shooting, stocks should be equipped with a rubber recoil pad that eases recoil and helps prevent the gun butt from slipping from the shoulder pocket.

Shock absorbers or recoil reducers can also be inserted inside the length of the stock. Any good gunsmith is capable of adding the recoil pad, shortening or lengthening the stock or inserting an internal shock absorber.

TYPES OF GUNS

The two most popular types of clay target guns are the semi-automatic and the over-and-under. Also in use, but less popular, are the side-by-side and the slide-action or "pump" guns. The single-shot makes an excellent "youth gun" to use when teaching youngsters. All of these guns are manufactured in conventional gauges and chokes.

Semi-automatic

The semi-automatics are known as self-loaders, auto-loaders or automatics. However, they are not true automatics because, unlike a machine gun, the shooter's finger must be released from the trigger between shots. Semi-automatics are the most popular shotguns used in the clay target games for beginners because they are less expensive and the recoil is not felt as sharply as with the other styles of guns. This is because some of the recoil energy is used to eject the spent shotshell and re-set the firing mechanism. Although developed in America, they are now being produced in other countries and are imported in considerable numbers.

The semi-automatics are gas-operated shotguns, which are activated by gas pressure tapped from the fired shell in the barrel. They oper-

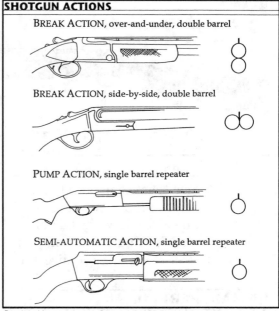

Butt Plate, Recoil Pad, Spacer Spacer and Recoil Pad. To change stock length attach a recoil pad. If more length is required a spacer is added.

The recoil pad is a rubber cushion that eases or softens the recoil against a shooter's shoulder.

SHOTGUN ACTIONS

BREAK ACTION, over-and-under, double barrel

BREAK ACTION, side-by-side, double barrel

PUMP ACTION, single barrel repeater

SEMI-AUTOMATIC ACTION, single barrel repeater

Reprinted by permission. Copyright *1997 Black's Wing & Clay.*

ate on a piston that is attached to the action. After causing the action to open, the spent gas escapes through a gas port as the piston returns under spring pressure. The takedown system is simple and barrels can be interchanged without factory fitting. Although the modern semi-automatic is very reliable and works well with reloaded ammunition, it must be kept clean and not over-oiled. Most of the semi-automatic "hang-ups" or malfunctions occur because the gun is not well cleaned. Some semi-automatics will not eject the hull (spent shotshell) with the new breed of "super-lite" ammo because the recoil is not sufficient to completely kick open the action.

OVER-AND-UNDER

The over-and-under is one of the most popular, reliable and safe of all shotguns. Over-and-unders are composed of two single barrels joined in the same frame, which prevents any chance of a third shell being accidently "hidden" in the gun (pumps and semi-autos can both hold three shells, although no more than two are ever needed in clay target sports). The double barrel also offers the advantage of different chokes: an open barrel for the first shot and a more tightly choked

Winchester Model 12 pump-action trap gun with regular stock

Winchester Model 101 over-and-under trap gun with Monte Carlo stock

Winchester SuperX Model 1 semi-automatic skeet gun

barrel for the second. Skeet guns, however, usually contain open or "skeet" chokes in both barrels.

Over-and-unders have a selector on the receiver, which lets the gunner decide what barrel to shoot first. The bottom barrel is preferred for single shots and for the first shot on doubles because the line of recoil is more direct, thereby reducing muzzle jump. This is especially important in preparation for a quick second shot.

One of the other advantages in the over-and-under is the single sighting plane that it provides along the top of the upper barrel. It can be aligned the same as a pump action or semi-automatic and gives

THE MAIN PARTS OF AN OVER-AND-UNDER SHOTGUN

CHAMBERS
EJECTORS
TOP LEVER
SAFETY CATCH & BARREL SELECTOR
RIB
ACTION
SINGLE TRIGGER
COMB
FOREND
PISTOL GRIP
HEEL
BEAD
STOCK
BUTT
TOE
CHOKED AREA OF BARRELS

the same "sight picture." Over-and-under malfunctions are substantially less than semi-autos because they have fewer moving parts.

SLIDE ACTION

The slide action, commonly called the "pump gun," is rarely seen on the skeet or Sporting Clays fields, where doubles are involved. Not many shooters can pump a slide-action gun as fast as they can get off two shots with a semi-automatic or an over-and-under. And, the pumping action creates excessive barrel movement.

The pump gun has a movable fore-end or forearm, usually made of wood, to work the action. After firing the shell the forearm is pulled back towards the shooter, thereby opening the action and ejecting the hull. When the forearm is shoved forward, a shell is loaded into the chamber and the action is closed. The gun is ready for firing. Pump guns can be single-loaded through the breech and into the chamber, or they can be loaded with one shell in the chamber and have a second shell slid into the "magazine." The magazine is a spring-loaded compartment that holds one or more shells beneath the breech. Both pump guns and semi-autos have magazines.

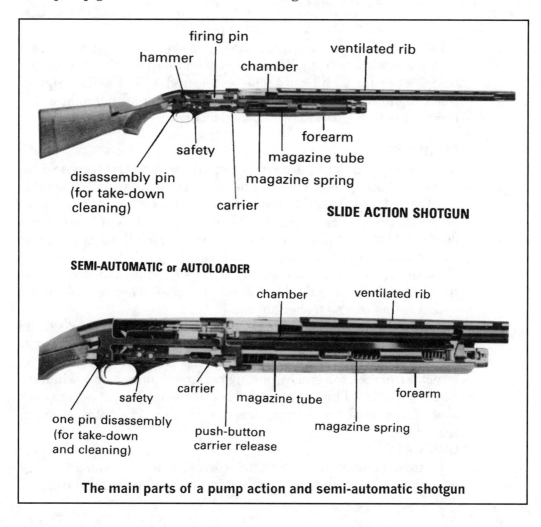

The main parts of a pump action and semi-automatic shotgun

In shooting 16-yard Trap Singles and Handicap Trap, the pump gun is not a liability. Only one shot has to be fired at a time and the speed of pumping the action and muzzle movement are not factors because they occur after the shot.

There are two general classes of shotguns:

1. SINGLE BARREL GUNS
- Single shot
- Slide action or pump
- Auto loading
- Bolt action repeater

2. DOUBLE BARREL GUNS
- Over-and-under
- Side-by-side
- A combination of one smooth bore and one rifle barrel

SIDE-BY-SIDE

The side-by-side has lost popularity as a clay target gun in America, but it is still regarded by many as the "classic" shotgun, not for clay target shooting but for upland game hunting. Most experts consider a well-balanced side-by-side to be the finest of all guns to handle. A good one is very expensive, which is one of the reasons why few appear on clay target fields. Some gunners claim that target sighting with a side-by-side is not as good as with an over-and-under because the width of two barrels tends to obscure the target.

Like the over-and-under, the side-by-side provides the advantage of two quick shots from differently choked barrels. Some have two triggers, one for each barrel. The better grades have single triggers that can be quickly set to fire either barrel first, plus automatic ejectors that pop one, or both, fired shells when the gun is opened.

SINGLE-SHOT

Single-shot shotguns are not commonly seen on the trap field because the good ones are very expensive. They are usually superbly constructed and choked to a degree of full choke sometimes known as "super pucker" or "extra full." These highly choked barrels produce a tight cluster of shot, which is perfect for Handicap trapshooters who often hit targets at distances of 50 to 60 yards.

On the other hand, some single barrel shotguns manufactured in the United States are the least expensive of all. They are all rugged and about as safe as a shotgun can be.

Because it is light, the single-shot 20-gauge, for example, is an excellent gun to use when teaching youngsters to shoot clay targets because it is light. But its best feature pertains to safety. The instructor can cock the gun by pulling back the hammer only when the gun is shouldered by the beginner and ready to shoot. And, only one shot can be loaded at a time, thus avoiding an accidental or errant second shot.

GUN CARE

Improved ammunition, with non-corrosive primers and all-plastic wads, has greatly changed gun care in the past 30 years. The plastic wad scrubs the barrel of much gunpowder residue each time the gun is fired. However, expert shooters often run a rag down the bar-

Breech of a single barrel shotgun. The breech is the rear end of a firearm where the shell is inserted into the chamber.

The breech of a double barrel shotgun.

rel between events and clean the entire gun after each day's shooting. The purpose is to remove plastic residue, which is built up from plastic wads being shot down the barrel. A lightly oiled rag or "mop" pushed through the barrel on a rod will remove dirt and moisture that forms in the hot barrel in the cooler air, but will do little to remove the plastic. Powder and moisture residues are held beneath the plastic and the chemicals mix to form acid that erodes the barrel's interior. This problem is the worst just in front of the chamber where the temperature gets the highest. If the initial residues are not removed, the problem gets worse more quickly — dirt collects on dirt more easily. This process causes pitting of the steel, and shot patterns can be effected due to barrel roughness. The solution, therefore, is simple: clean your gun after each day of shooting, being sure to run a wire brush down the barrel(s).

If the gun has been used in rainy or damp weather, an oily rag run through the barrel is required. Because wet shells will leave dampness in the chamber, light oil should be sprayed into the chamber and then wiped clean to prevent rusting. And, all the exterior metal parts of the gun should be wiped with a dry cloth as soon as possible. Always allow your shotgun to adjust to room temperature before wiping with an oiled rag so that any condensation is removed. Aerosol lubricants that contain a desiccant or moisture-replacing agent may also be used. The oil, of course, should be light gun oil. A light spray of WD-40 or similar product, with the excess wiped off, will do the job. Any excess oil should be wiped off the next time the gun is uncased for use. After oiling the outside of the gun, the metal should not be touched; hold it by the stock or forearm. If the metal is handled, fingerprints will be imprinted and the salt of the hand and fingers will cause rusting if left long enough. A good, basic shotgun cleaning kit, with instructions included, can be purchased at any gun shop or sporting goods store carrying hunting or target shooting supplies. Also, it is important to make sure that excess gun oil does not soak into the woodwork — it can cause swelling of the wood.

The double-barrel and single-shot guns require very little inside cleaning. A drop of oil on the extractors, on the area where the barrel hinges on the receiver, and on the action release on top of the receiver, is all the oiling required to keep the gun in good working order.

The slide action or pump gun must be given more care in oiling. The major flaw in oiling a pump gun is too much oil. A receiver full of oil will drastically retard the action and retain dirt and gunpowder residue. Occasionally remove the trigger guard and pop in a drop or two of thin oil on the trigger mechanism. If it is necessary to remove dirt, use a stiff paintbrush to wash the assembly in gasoline or gun cleaning solvent and allow to dry before applying the oil. Instant-drying "scrubbing" sprays are also available for this job. The semi-automatics require special attention if they are to perform well. The auto-loaders give the most trouble if not cleaned because they have the greatest number of moving parts. The gas system, within the fore-end, is the most important area requiring regular cleaning. Powder residue builds up gradually on the magazine tube along which the gas piston and action bar sleeve slide. If not cleaned for some time and over many rounds of shooting, this residue will build to hinder the movement of the auto-loading action and result in a mal-functioning gun. If a dirty gas system is the main reason for performance problems with the semi-automatics, the second reason is an over-lubricated gas system. Better to have no oil inside the gun than too much.

All auto-loaders should be cleaned completely after a day's shooting if 100 shots or more were fired. Cleaning the gas system will prevent residue build-up and assure a smooth functioning gun.

It is not a great chore to clean the piston rings, magazine tube and action bar assembly; the task requires but a few minutes. They should be wiped off with fine steel wool and a clean rag. No oil is necessary. Also, the gas parts in the barrel ring should be inspected to be sure they are not clogged with burned powder. Depending upon the amount of use the gun gets, it should be field-stripped occasionally. The trigger assembly and receiver should be cleaned with scrubbing spray. After allowing them time to dry, a little spray of fine oil should be applied to all moving parts and then wiped off. Some auto-loaders require extra cleaning of the gas cap. Before storing a gun for any length of time, a thorough cleaning and oiling are required. Again, be careful not to handle the metal portions of the gun once it has been oiled. Be sure to review your gun owner's manual or seek experienced help when taking apart and reassembling your gun for the first time.

Storage

The shotgun should not be stored for a long period in a leather, plastic or nylon gun case, especially the type that is lined with cloth, fleece or other material. The lining holds moisture and either rubs off or absorbs some of the oil, thereby exposing the metal to rust in spots. If a gun must be stored in such a manner, it should be inspected once a month to check for signs of rust. Store the gun in a locked wood or metal gun case. Some shooters have a special security rack situated in a "gun closet" behind a false wall that appears to be part of the room wall. An arrangement of this type hides the guns in case of burglary. The gun rack includes a metal bar that is locked into place to keep children from tampering with the guns.

Guns, of course, should never be stored loaded, and ammunition should never be stored in the same place as the guns. Steel gun safes with combination locks are a wise investment, and trigger locks can be attached to all firearms.

Storing shotshells safely.

Ammunition is easier to hide than shotguns, and that should be done if there is the slightest possibility of unauthorized hands getting at the ammo.

Transportation

When transporting a shotgun, not only should it be unloaded, it should be broken down (taken apart) and carried in a case. If you are traveling a short distance, such as to the gun club, leather or plastic cases are acceptable. However, the trunk-type case lined with foam cushions is by far superior. Such a case protects the gun from being damaged in the car. Also, the short gun case, where the gun must be broken down before recasing it, reminds the shooter that it should be cleaned. When using the standard, full-length, zippered case there is a tendency for the gunner to shove the gun into the case and forget it.

When travelling by train or by air, the shallow, hard, trunk-like case is a must. If the gun is carried in a full-length, form-fitting leather or nylon case, everyone knows it is a gun. But few people realize that the long, box-like case holds a firearm, and less eyebrows are raised. Be sure to check with local or state authorities if you are unfamiliar with area gun transportation laws.

The airlines require that the gunner advise the personnel at the check-in station that the case contains a gun. Arrive at the terminal early because air personnel will check photo I.D.'s and inspect your firearm in a back room. No ammunition is allowed to be placed in with the gun. Airlines allow a maximum poundage of ammo to be carried in a suitcase checked as baggage. Usually, one gun is allowed per person. Before even bringing the gun to the airport, however, the shooter should check with his airline for specific information about rules regarding guns and ammo as baggage.

Anyone who has traveled by air realizes that baggage takes a beating. Although the modern gun case is made of tough plastic or metal with reinforced corners, there is always a possibility that the locks may be tampered with or hit accidentally causing the case to open. After airline personnel inspect your gun, you should recase it and run strapping completely around the case in two areas, usually over the locks. The best strapping material is fiberglass packing tape, which is available in most hardware stores. It really sticks, and it is unusually strong.

When the Yale Trap and Skeet Team travels by vehicle I give them the following instructions:

1. The guns must be unloaded and open.
2. Record each gun's make, model and serial number and carry the information separately.
3. Place the guns in hard cases and lock them.
4. Set the cases in the trunk or the luggage compartment (someone should carry an extra set of keys). The cases should be on the bottom, covered by other luggage.
5. If it is an overnight trip, the guns must be taken into the motel rooms.
6. If, by chance, you have to prove to the motel management or anyone else that, in fact, the guns are for recreational shooting, someone in the group (usually I as coach) should have a copy of the shoot's program. You will find it best, however, to quietly put the cased guns in your room and slide them under the bed. If you are leaving the motel to go out to dinner, the guns are probably safer locked in your room than in the back of your car.
7. Never exceed the speed limit. If stopped for speeding, or any other traffic violation, the police officer may look through the car, and if he finds ammo or guns he may, at best, restrain the group for enough time to make the team late for the shoot. And worst of all, it is possible that the guns could be taken and held by the police, depending upon the area of travel. If police do stop you, it is advisable to tell the officer that you are transporting a firearm and the reason for it, before he or she discovers it accidentally.

FITTING THE SHOTGUN

A shotgun is correctly fitted when the gunner feels comfortable shooting it, and when no part of the gun interferes with the shooter's sight or swing. When a shotgun fits, the shooter's accuracy will be significantly better than with an ill-fitting gun.

In Europe, gun fitting is done with much more concern and fanfare than it is in the United States. There, generally only the more affluent participate in bird hunting and the clay target games. Some gun companies have talented gun fitters who tailor the guns exactly to the purchaser's physical build. American gunners who can afford it travel to England, for

GUNFITTING MEASUREMENTS

cast at heel
cast on   cast off
cast at toe

The gun fitter calculates the "cast" at heel and toe, as indicated

The vital statistics: **A** - drop at comb; **B** - drop at rear of comb; **C** - drop at heel; **D** - length.

Reprinted by permission. Copyright *1997 Black's Wing & Clay.*

example, to order shotguns that will be specifically designed to fit them. Such custom fitting is often done with a try-gun, first used by such fine English gunmakers as Purdey and Holland and Holland. The try-gun is a gun with an adjustable stock. The customer seats the gun to his shoulder and the expert then adjusts the length of the try-stock, extending the butt plate attached to bars that can slide in or out of the stock. Also, the mechanism that connects the stock to the gun can be raised or lowered. When both the expert and the purchaser are satisfied with the fit, an order is drawn up for a custom-built stock.

In America, where guns are produced in great volume, and sold at reasonable cost, manufacturers have arrived at a formula for making guns that will fit about 70 percent of the people buying them. Some of the remaining 30 percent will adapt themselves to a gun that doesn't fit very well, although they shoot under a handicap. This is like a hiker wearing a tight pair of boots; he will get to his destination, but his heels will be blistered. Shooters who use ill-fitting guns never shoot to their potential.

The stock is the major factor to consider in gun fit. If it is too short the gunner will lower his head to keep his cheek on the stock. This puts the eyes in the wrong relationship to the barrel. If the gunner sights too high along the barrel he will shoot over the target; if too low, he will shoot low. When the head is lowered to the stock it may also be tilted, placing the eye at an angle to the barrel, which causes the shot charge to fly either to the right or left of the target. If the stock is very short for him, the shooter may receive an unpleasant jolt from the thumb hitting the nose. If the stock is too long, the beginner invariably holds his head too high. And stretching the trigger hand forward may cause the shooter's face to leave the stock. A long stock also places the gun butt farther out on the shoulder or arm (instead of in the shoulder pocket) causing bruising.

Often, short and tall gunners shoot with these handicaps because they do not know the difference. Every gunner should take the time to analyze his particular gun-fit problems. One of the basic ways of discovering whether your gun has the proper length of pull (distance between center of trigger and center of butt plate) is to place the butt of the gun in the crook of the elbow. If the first joint of the trigger finger reaches the trigger comfortably, the stock is of reasonable, if not precise, length. If the first joint of the finger goes beyond the trigger, the gun may be a quarter to a half-inch too short. If the finger joint does not reach the trigger, the stock is too long. When a true gun fit is sought, however, the gunner must also take into account length of neck, length of arms, check bone structure and distance between the eyes.

Another test of gun fit can be tried. Hold the unloaded gun in the "off-shoulder" position. Then, with eyes closed, place the gun in shooting position with the butt cradled in your shoulder. Open your eyes. If the gun fits, your eye should be sighting down the top of the barrel in perfect shooting position with the nose about an inch from the thumb.

Of course, the most reliable procedure in checking for gun fit is to visit a competent gunsmith or qualified instructor, who will diagnose your fit. If the stock is short the gunsmith will add a recoil pad (or a spacer if your gun already has a pad). If the gun is too long he will cut the stock professionally. A stock that bruises the cheek may be too high at the comb or have too much drop at the heel. The stock can be made modified, if necessary. If that is insufficient, then the stock can be removed, the tang (rod that connects the gun to the stock) secured in a vise and bent.

The measurement of the comb in relation to the rest of the shotgun is extremely important, because it determines the position of the eye. For each shot, the eye must be positioned centrally over and only slightly above the rib or receiver groove. In other words, the gunner sees a flat, even surface as he sights down the barrel at the target.

It is easy to check your gun for correct drop at the comb. With the gun unloaded, open the breech, put the safety on, and mount the gun to your shoulder, being sure that the butt is secured in the hollow of the shoulder. Next, with your finger off the trigger, have a friend stand directly in front of you. With your cheek on the comb and your nose about an inch from the base of your thumb, point the gun barrel at his eye. If he sees the pupil of your eye just as if it were resting on the back of the rib or receiver, the comb of the gun is perfect. If there is considerable space between the rib and the pupil, more drop at the comb is needed to lower the eye to correct position. If the eye is partially or completely hidden, less drop is needed. This problem is easy to correct. Simply add a comb pad, available at any good gun shop, to the comb. Pads come in 1/8-inch, 1/4-inch, and 3/8-inch thicknesses. Another method is to add "moleskin" (a felt adhesive available in drug stores) to the comb until the necessary height is achieved.

Some gunners make these modifications themselves, cutting down the stock, adding a recoil pad, rasping the joint of the comb, and bending the tang. However, I advise any shooter who is not a skilled craftsman to let a good gunsmith do the job.

22. Shells

In England, shotgun shells are termed cartridges, but in the United States the term shotshells is so widely used it is now official. So shotgun shells are now referred to as "shotshells" or just "shells," and "cartridges" generally pertain to loaded rifle or pistol ammunition.

THE OLD SHELL

About 100 years ago the shotshell came into being in a form resembling today's shell. For most of those years the shotshell tube was made from tightly wound paper set in a brass head. The inside of the head was reinforced with a base wad of treated cardboard, and a centerfire primer was set in the rear or head of the brass exterior. Powder was poured over the base wad, and overpowder and filler wads of different sizes were set over the powder. The shot was poured into a tube and kept there by a cardboard top wad. The edges of the tube were then rolled down into a lip on the top wad.

Although the design of the modern shell remains basically the same as the shell of years past, it is far

Inside:

THE OLD SHELL

THE HULL

LEAD SHOT

THE WAD

POWDER

PRIMER

THE BASIC SHELL CATEGORIES

TRACER SHELLS

PROOF SHELLS

SHOTSHELL PARTS

HULL
The outer container of a shotgun shell, typically made of plastic or paper with a metal base

SHOT
Round projectiles, usually of lead or steel. Depending on shot size and load, a shell can contain from 45 to 1,170 shot.

WAD
Plastic or fiber separating powder and shot that forms a seal so that gasses eject shot uniformly down the barrel

POWDER
Gun powder situated above the primer where it will be ignited by flames caused by the detonation of the primer compound.

PRIMER
A compound contained in the middle of the base of a shotgun shell, where the firing pin strikes

Reprinted by permission. Copyright *1997 Black's Wing & Clay.*

superior to its predecessor, due to the great advancement of shotgun technology in recent years. The tube or hull is now made of plastic; the lead shot or pellets are enclosed in a plastic wad; the primer contains a non-corrosive priming mixture; and the brass head is tougher.

THE HULL

One of the greatest improvements in the construction of the shotgun shell occurred when the plastic hull or tube was invented. Because plastic is tough and will not swell under damp conditions, as paper shells did, plastic hulls became an immediate favorite with trap and skeet shooters who load their own shells. Plastic shells have other advantages. Their ballistic stability is superior to that of paper shells, because plastic helps eliminate the effects of changing temperature on powder. Plastic shells slide easier into the gun chambers, an important feature when used in autoloaders.

The advanced hull, and in the 1940's the plastic hull, was also responsible for an important improvement in the wad structure of the shell. The cardboard top wads, more often than not, mingled with the shot as it left the gun barrel, disrupting the shot pattern. Now, instead of a top wad and the rolled-down edge of the tube being used to secure the load, the new tube's edge was simply crimped or folded down. The new system eliminated the top wad. Now when the shell is fired the crimps open up and the charge goes flying out without interference.

A traditional method of making lead shot: the shot tower, nine floors high, with its associated facilities. After molten lead droplets fall into the pool of water that cushions their fall, the irregular pellets are culled, the shot is sorted for size, polished and stored in tanks.

273

LEAD SHOT

Shotgun shells are offered in a variety of shot sizes, the size depending upon the clay target activity or the type of game the hunter is pursuing. Here, however, we are concerned only with the ammunition used in the shotgunning games. Although steel shot has replaced lead shot in waterfowl hunting loads (because the birds may accidentally ingest the toxic lead pellets when feeding on the bottom), lead continues to be used in trap, skeet and Sporting Clays shells. Ballistically, lead is far superior to steel as a load in target shells, and it is much less expensive. One of the reasons why lead shot costs less than steel shot is because it is simpler to produce. Today, practically the same methods are employed in making lead pellets as were used when shotgun shells were first invented. Molten lead, when passed through a sieve-like device and dropped from a height, breaks into a spray of drops. Water, when dropped through a sieve from an equal height takes on a tear-shaped form. But lead emerges in near-perfect spheres.

The use of "shot towers" in the process of making lead pellets remains, in principle, the same as it was in colonial days. Metal pigs of alloys of lead, containing antimony and other hardening agents, are placed in elevators and transported to the top of the tower where they are melted. The lead is then poured into pan-shaped, sieve-like containers and strained, so to speak. The size of the holes on the bottom of the pan determines the size of the shot. The molten lead drops almost 200 feet from the pans into a tank of water. The lead becomes round almost immediately after leaving the pan. The water is not used to chill the shot, as is popularly thought, but simply cushions its fall. Next, the shot is dried and brought to the tower again, and polished in a tumbling process. Then the pellets go through a culling device, travelling down a series of inclined planes. The out-of-round pellets fall into a trough and are returned to be remelted and reprocessed.

Many attempts have been made to improve on this old fashioned way of making shot pellets, but as yet, no method has been found to be as efficient as the drop-tower operation.

The standard 12-gauge target loads contain 1 1/8 ounces of lead shot (and if it were size No. 9 shot, about 580 pellets, see chart below). The 20-gauge skeet shell holds 7/8-ounce; 28 gauge, 3/4-ounce; and the .410 has 1/2-ounce. Shells used for hunting upland and small game contain heavier loads of lead pellets, as do the steel (non-toxic) shot loads required for waterfowl hunting. For example 12-gauge magnum shells may have 1 1/4 ounces of shot.

STANDARD SHOT CHART — Diameter in inches

No.	12	11	10	9	8	7½	6	5	4	2
	.05	.06	.07	.08	.09	.095	.11	.12	.13	.15

APPROXIMATE NUMBER OF PELLETS TO THE OUNCE									
2385	1380	870	585	410	350	225	170	135	90

THE WAD

One major defect of shotgun shells, recognized by manufacturers for many years, was the abrasive action of the gun barrel upon the outer ring of pellets as they were pushed out. In exiting, they rubbed against the walls of the barrel and became flattened, consequently affecting the shot pattern and often causing it to fly wide of the mark. Technicians tried wrapping the pellets in various ways in order to protect the shot as it travelled down the bore, but none were satisfactory until manufacturers developed a method of using a thin strip of plastic in which to wrap the shot charge. The next improvement was a self-contained plastic wad and shot protector, with the rear end formed in an upside down, cup-like pattern that creates a gas-sealed chamber when the powder is ignited. The middle of the plastic wad progressively collapses at ignition, and absorbs shock that helps prevent pellet deformation.

POWDER

Contrary to common belief among non-shooters, gunpowder does not explode — it burns. The powder, when ignited by the primer, burns rapidly, forming gases which, in expanding, propel the shot out of the barrel. One of the great improvements in construction of the shotgun shells was the replacement of black powder with smokeless powder.

The shells used in 12-gauge clay target events contain either 2 3/4 or 3 "drams equivalent" of powder. The term "drams equiv." printed on boxes of shells refers to the unit of measurement used in the early days of shotgunning to designate the amount of black powder in the charge (the avoirdupois dram being equal to 1/16 of an ounce). When the first smokeless powders came into use they were made to load in a volume equal to that of black powder. For example, three drams of smokeless powder had about the same ballistic capabilities as three drams of black powder. As smokeless powder continued to be improved, however, the volume-for-volume concept ceased to be valid. Nevertheless, the original terminology was retained, since gunners were familiar with it. Consequently, manufacturers still designate the smokeless powder loads as equivalent to black-powder drams, even though the smokeless powders now represent only a part of that weight. Most shooters prefer the 3 drams equiv. when participating in Handicap Trap and International Skeet and Trap because of the added distance and degree of difficulty in those sports. Shells used for hunting hold larger amounts of powder; for example 12-gauge magnums may contain 3 3/4 drams equiv. or more.

PRIMER

The primer is a small metal cap that fits into the center of the brass head. It contains a sensitive explosive compound which, when struck by the firing pin, ignites the powder. It was in the 1920's that a non-corrosive priming mixture was introduced, which made gun care significantly easier.

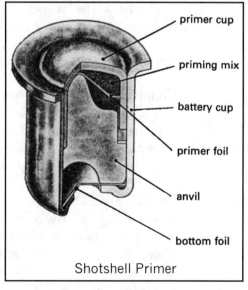

primer cup

priming mix

battery cup

primer foil

anvil

bottom foil

Shotshell Primer

THE BASIC SHELL CATEGORIES

There are two basic categories of shotgun shells: those used in the clay target games, and those used in the field for hunting, including long range and magnum shells. A variety of powder and shot-size combinations, as well as gauges, is available in each category. The brass bases of 12- and 20-gauge clay target shells are low in comparison to the bases of long-range and magnum shells. The shells used in clay target shooting create lower internal pressures on ignition than do long-range loads; therefore, they do not require as much metal as the high-base hunting shells to contain these pressures. Low base shells in 12-, 16-, and 20-gauge are generally used in hunting small upland game and birds. The 28-gauge and .410-bore target shells are high base. The standard length of both high and low base shells in 12, 16, 20 and 28 gauges is 2 3/4 inches. In 10-gauge, standard shells are available in 2 3/4 and 2 7/8 inches. The .410-bore guns are nearly all chambered to accommodate the 3-inch shells, but they will take the 2 1/2-inch shells as well.

Magnum shells are available in both 2 3/4- and 3-inch lengths. These shells are never used in clay target shooting; they provide extra power for hitting game at long ranges.

Rifled slugs and buckshot shells are not used in flying-target shooting. The rifled slug used in deer hunting is a solid cylindrical lead projectile with rifling grooves cut into its outside face. The grooves cause the slug to spin when fired from the smooth bore of a shotgun. A buckshot load, also used for hunting, contains a group of large lead pellets, many fewer but much bigger than those found in standard shot sizes.

TRACER SHELLS

Another type of shotshell, used mostly to correct clay target shooting faults, is the "tracer shell." These tracer loads vividly show, under all light conditions, the actual path of the shot column, and they eliminate any doubts as to how a target was missed. But it's not that easy. Determining where the shot went is one thing, but determining why it went there usually requires a qualified coach or instructor (see Chapter 19 — How To Coach).

A word of caution: the tracer shells contain an ignited substance and are for use only in areas where there is no possibility of the tracer igniting ground material. A distance of at least 100 yards should be allowed for the tracer to burn out.

PROOF SHELLS

"Proof shells" are especially produced for use by firearms manufacturers to test the strength of a gun's chamber, barrel, and action. These shells are loaded with much heavier charges of powder than any clay target or hunting ammunition. Manufacturers use proof shells to check the quality and safety of a gun by firing one or more of these potent shells. All proof firing is done under rigidly controlled and supervised conditions. Such testing proves that the gun is safe for use with commercial ammunition. In the United States, the manufacturer proofs the guns and affixes a "proof mark" (a symbol or letter) to the gun. In some countries, the proofing is supervised by government inspectors and the gun is stamped accordingly. Proof shells are conspicuously marked and loaded into hulls of atypical coloration. However, the danger lies in the fact that some shotgunners, who make a hobby of collecting shotgun shells, include live proof shells in their collection. A proof shell, fired by mistake in a trap or skeet gun, could be dangerous.

The term "proof shells" also refers to the one or two spare shells that a competitor may shoot just prior to the start of competition. These shots are safely fired down range, but not as a practice at targets. Proof shells in this situation are the same as those the competitor uses in the match. The purpose of firing proofs is to insure that the gun's safety is off and that the gun is functioning properly. Some shooters who have the utmost confidence in their guns still fire proof shells; the reason is simple: to help reduce pre-match nervousness.

Manufacturers continue to develop "specialty" shells for different types of shooting, not only for various kinds of game in hunting, but also for the clay target games. One of the latest breakthroughs is the "super-lite" shell, which has reduced kick and less noise. These lighter shells are helpful for women, small-framed men, beginners and those who shoot many boxes of ammo during frequent practice sessions and are concerned with recoil.

The shells used in skeet must comply with the standards of shot and powder set by the NSSA. Those used in trap are guided by the rules of the ATA. Sporting Clays ammunition is governed by the NSCA and USA Shooting monitors the International events (see Appendix B).

23. Reloading

WHAT IS RELOADING?

Reloading is a "do-it-yourself" process by which an empty shotgun shell or "hull" is refilled to form a new shell that is as useable and as potent as the original. Rifle and pistol cartridges can also be reloaded.

When a shotgun shell is fired, its components — pellets, wad and powder — are discharged. The plastic hull or shell, including brass head and detonated primer, remains in the gun until popped out of the chamber by the ejector. It is this empty hull that is retrieved before or after it hits the ground and saved for reloading. The value of the hull is between two and six cents apiece, depending on who is selling it.

WHY RELOAD?

The primary reason for reloading is economy. Generally speaking, a box of shells can be reloaded for about half the cost of new factory-loaded shells. *Black's 1997 Wing & Clay — Shotgunner's Handbook* cites this average cost breakdown for a box (25 shells) of 12-gauge, 1 1/8-ounce target loads: store price —

An over-and-under ejecting two hulls (spent shotshells). Usual gun club policy states that any hulls hitting the ground become club property. If this skeet shooter wants to re-load his empties, he should catch them by placing his hand over the ejectors as the gun is opened.

280

$5.75; reloaded price of components — $2.27; savings per box — $3.48. As you can see, avid clay target shooters can realize a substantial financial saving over a year by reloading their own shells.

The advent of the plastic hull, and the development and availability of a wide selection of manual reloading machines, is at least partly responsible for the ever increasing number of participants in the clay target games, as well as for the upsurge of collegiate shotgunning. Without the financial advantages of reloading trap and skeet shells, the collegiate world of recreational and competitive shooting would soon fold.

Reloading is also an enjoyable hobby, either alone or with a shooting companion. And, you get the satisfaction of breaking targets with shells you reloaded, which is like catching a trout on a fly that you tied or growing you own vegetables.

GETTING STARTED

Getting started is easy. If the beginner does not have a friend to instruct him or her, easy-to-follow instructions can be found in the free pamphlets and brochures made available by various ammunition manufacturers. Also, very precise step-by-step directions are presented in booklets that come with every new reloading machine. The National Reloading Manufacturers Association (NRMA) offers a booklet, *Set Yourself Up to Reload!*, which details the basics of reloading, a source guide for catalogs, literature and videos, as well as plans for a reloading bench. Send $5.00 to NRMA, One Centerpointe Drive, Suite 300, Lake Oswego, Oregon 97035.

Many companies produce reloading machines, which vary in price and capability. For a complete listing of ammunition, component and reloading machine manufacturers, see *Black's Wing & Clay — Shotgunner's Handbook* in Appendix C.

RELOADING MACHINES

The type of reloader a gunner uses depends upon how often he shoots. A single gunner who shoots two to four boxes a week can get by with an inexpensive type of reloader, one that is capable of reloading perhaps a couple of boxes of 25 shells in an hour. At the other extreme are the large reloading machines installed at some clubs for use by members. These can produce many hundreds of shells per hour. The most popular reloaders lie in between these extremes. They produce between 100 and 250 rounds per hour. Any well-supplied gun store carries reloading machines or can supply price information and the addresses of the manufacturers.

COMPONENTS

The components — shot, wads, powder and primers — all come neatly packaged. The shot usually comes in 25-pound canvas or cloth bags; the wads are carried in plastic bags, usually in lots of 250; powder is available in metal cans of various sizes; and the primers are housed in shallow trays, usually 100 to the tray. Fish and game clubs usually purchase components in large quantities for resale to members; their prices will be lower than those of gun shops.

A typical, at-home reloading station includes a reloader, bench, chair and storage containers, as well as the shotshell components: hulls, wads, primers, powder and shot

281

THE OPERATION

Operating a reloader is so simple and the results are so gratifying that the beginner will be amazed. As a lever is pulled down, a circular disc moves about 1/2 dozen hulls around in assembly-line fashion. The primers, shot and powder are fed automatically. The operator's main task, besides pulling down the lever, is placing hulls onto the first reloading station. The sequence of steps is as follows: punching out the old primer; seating the new primer; dropping a measured powder charge; seating the wad; dropping a measured shot charge; partial crimping and last, the final crimping.

SAFETY

Two principal safety concerns must be exercised. The powder and primer must be properly stored, and the operator must be alert while reloading. Although care should be taken in all reloading activity, the hobby itself is not unusually hazardous. Every year the number of reloads almost equal the number of new shells manufactured!

Skeet shooter and grounds manager of the Yale University Trap and Skeet Club, Richard Wick, claims that he can produce up to 12 boxes (300 shells) in an hour with this reloader.

The great majority of these are loads for trap, skeet and Sporting Clays shooting. Misinformation about safety factors therefore should not deter the beginner from doing his own reloading.

The following paragraphs were taken from a booklet published by the National Shooting Sports Foundation:

STORING RELOADING COMPONENTS

Contrary to popular belief, modern smokeless powders do not create an explosion hazard. They don't even create a fire hazard if properly stored. In fact, smokeless powder is less flammable than many liquids commonly kept in the home, such as solvents, cleaning fluids, and polishes. Powders can be safely kept in the home by taking these steps:

Keep propellant powder in the container in which it was originally shipped or stored. These containers are specially designed to prevent explosion and spontaneous combustion. Never store powder in a severely confining container.

Powder containers should be kept under lock and key in a wooden cabinet. The heat-conducting properties of metal cabinets make them hazardous in the event of fire.

Propellant powders should be stored away from fire hazard areas. However, they should not be kept in either damp cellars or unventilated — and possible very hot — attics since they will deteriorate under such conditions.

Similar rules are applicable in storing primers. They should be kept in the original package until used and stored in a locked wooden box. In addition, the National Fire Prevention Association suggests limits on the number of primers that should be kept in the home or transported by vehicle: 10,000 in the home and 25,000 in any vehicle.

If reloading components are kept in the home in large quantity, it is a good idea to check fire insurance policies to make certain that coverage is not affected by the presence of primers and powders. Also look into state and local fire regulations to ensure that storage and quantity limits are met.

The next two treatments are quoted from a booklet issued by Winchester-Western, titled *Ball Powder Loading Data for Shot Shells, Center Fire Rifle and Pistol Cartridges*.

RELOADING PRECAUTIONS

Follow these precautions to help assure maximum enjoyment and safety in reloading and to assure uniform performance of your reloads. Remember that you can be badly injured or suffer severe burns if the strictest safety precautions and housekeeping rules are not enforced.

1. Exercise care at all time and wear safety glasses while reloading.
2. Never load in haste.
3. Never smoke while handling powder or primers or during the reloading operation.
4. Handle primers carefully; they are the most hazardous of all components used for smokeless powder loads.
5. Keep powder and primers away from heat, sparks and open flames.
6. Store powder in a cool, dry place at all times.
7. Never use a powder unless you are certain of its identity.
8. Do not mix powders.
9. Devote full attention to reloading operations; avoid distractions.
10. Keep powder and primers out of reach of children.
11. Use components as recommended; don't take shortcuts.
12. Never exceed maximum recommended loads.
13. Develop a loading routine to guard against mistakes.
14. Examine every hull before loading to insure good condition.
15. Double-check every operation for safety and uniformity.
16. Check powder charge level in hulls to avoid double charges.
17. Do not decap live primers; it is safer to destroy them by firing the empty shell in a firearm.
18. Do not substitute components; it will result in a significant change in ballistics, and could result in an unsatisfactory or even dangerous load.
19. Do not allow children to play in the vicinity of handloading operations.
20. Observe all local fire regulations and codes with respect to quantities of powders and primers stored and conditions of storage.
21. Store powder only in its original container. Never transfer it from one storage container to another since this increases the possibility that it may become mislabeled.
22. Keep these "Reloading Precautions" posted where you do your reloading. Reread these precautions periodically.

RECOMMENDATIONS FOR POWDER STORAGE

- STORE IN A COOL, DRY PLACE. Be sure the storage area selected is free from any possible sources of excess heat and is isolated from open flame, furnaces, hot water heaters, etc. Do not store smokeless powder where it will be exposed to the sun's rays. Avoid storage in areas where mechanical or electrical equipment is in operation. Restrict from the storage areas heat or sparks which may result from improper, defective, or overloaded electrical circuits.
- DO NOT STORE SMOKELESS POWDER IN THE SAME AREA WITH SOLVENTS, FLAMMABLE GASES OR HIGHLY COMBUSTIBLE MATERIALS.
- STORE ONLY IN DEPARTMENT OF TRANSPORTATION APPROVED CONTAINERS.

283

- DO NOT TRANSFER THE POWDER FROM AN APPROVED CONTAINER INTO ONE THAT IS NOT APPROVED.
- DO NOT SMOKE IN AREAS WHERE POWDER IS STORED OR USED.
- PLACE APPROPRIATE "NO SMOKING" SIGNS IN THESE AREAS.
- DO NOT SUBJECT THE STORAGE CABINETS TO CLOSE CONFINEMENT.
- STORAGE CABINETS SOULD BE CONSTRUCTED OF INSULATING MATERIALS AND WITH A WEAK WALL, SEAMS, OR JOINTS TO PROVIDE AN EASY MEANS OF SELF-VENTING.
- DO NOT KEEP OLD OR SALVAGED POWDERS.
- OBEY ALL REGULATIONS REGARDING QUANTITY AND METHODS OF STORING. Do not store all your powders in one place. If you can, maintain separate storage locations. Many small containers are safer than one or more large containers.
- KEEP YOUR STORAGE AND USE AREA CLEAN. Clean up spilled powder promptly. Make sure the surrounding area is free of trash or other readily combustible materials.

24. Targets

SIZE AND COMPOSITION

Today's standard target has a diameter of 4 1/4 inches; its total height is 1 1/16 inches; and its weight is 3 1/2 ounces. Composed basically of asphalt pitch and ground lime, it has to be strong enough to withstand the shock of being launched at high speed by the arm of the target-throwing machine, yet fragile enough to break when

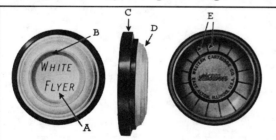

The Standard Target has a diameter of 4 1/2 inches; total height is 1 1/16 inches; weight is 3 1/2 ounces. It is basically composed of asphalt pitch and ground lime. Targets are available with domes of different colors. A — poker chip; B — Ledge; C — Flange; D — Dome; E — Scorings.

hit by a few No. 9 pellets at 30 or 40 yards.

COST

Clay targets are not expensive. They are packaged 135 to a standard case. A squad of five shooters needs a minimum of 125 targets for a round of skeet or trap. The extra ten birds are usually consumed in the same round; some are thrown for the initial viewing by the squad, others serve as replacements for any targets that are broken by the machine or for repeating early or late pulls.

COLOR

The color of the target's dome varies, depending upon the surrounding environment and the preference of management and shooters. Originally, white dome (the rim or "flange" remained black) targets were mostly used, then yellow became popular; then orange domes came into vogue. The latest rage is for complete (rim and dome) fluorescent orange; they seem to flash on dark or overcast days, in early morning and at dusk. Many shooters claim that these targets are the easiest to see. Some Sporting Clays targets are signigicantly smaller than skeet and trap targets, and they are all black, making them more difficult to see.

CLAY TARGETS

STANDARD
4 ¼ inches in diameter, 1 ⅛ inches thick; dome shaped; standard in trap and skeet.

ROCKET
4 ¼ inches in diameter; ⅝ inch thick; deceptive in flight; appears to float, but retains more velocity than the standard.

RABBIT
4 ¼ inches in diameter; ½ inch thick; rolls and bounces on the ground; thick rim, density prevent shattering on impact with ground.

BATTUE
4 ¼ inches in diameter; ⅜ inch thick; "flying razor blade," difficult to pick up edge-on; does rolls and wingovers.

MIDI
3 ½ inches in diameter, ⅞ inch thick; smaller size make it appear farther away than it actually is; retains initial velocity longer than other targets.

MINI
2 ⅜ inches in diameter, ⅝ inch thick; deceptive because small size makes it appear to be moving faster than it actually is; slows quickly because it's light.

WHERE AND HOW TO BUY

Clay targets can be bought by the case, and sometimes in a half-case, in most stores that sell guns and ammunition, but they are also available in cases by the truckload. Many clubs buy them this way because money can be saved and the fees per round to club members can be lowered. However, it requires a group of volunteers to unload the huge trailer-truck. Also, a large weatherproof storage area must be available, though not necessarily at the shooting grounds. An occasional trip to the storehouse with a pickup truck is all that is necessary to transport 50 or 60 cases and maintain a field's supply of targets.

A standard case holds 135 clay targets, enough for a five-person squad to shoot one round of 25 shots each, plus ten extras used for checking target flight and accidental breakage. These White Flyer targets (see Appendix C) have an all-orange top (flange and dome), which is probably the most popular and easily seen target color.

STORING

The lower section of the high house on a single skeet field can be used for storing cases of targets so that they are easily accessible if needed. About 25 or 30 extra cases can also be stored in the high house and low house without interfering with the loading or function of the throwing machines. The trap field house also has plenty of room to store targets.

Cases of targets should be kept dry. Rain, roof leakage or excessive moisture will weaken the clay targets, not to mention the cardboard boxes they are packed in, and the result will be broken targets thrown from the machine. In all houses with concrete or earth floors, the bottom row of target cases should be stacked on wooden planking to prevent moisture damage. This is especially important in trap houses because they are below ground level and are prone to dampness and flooding. A handy, inexpensive shelf can be made by placing a few concrete blocks on the floor along the back wall of the house and bridging them with a couple of 2" x 8" planks. The other advantage of a shelf is that the person loading targets will not have to bend down to the floor to stack or access the bottom row.

Targets should not be stacked more than about six cases high. Any more than that may cause the targets in the bottom boxes to be crushed from the excessive weight.

THE TARGET-SETTING HOOP IN SKEET

The target-throwing machines are usually set before the day's shooting takes place, preferably under a "no wind" condition. Once set, it should not be necessary to change the spring tension or machine elevation during the shoot, unless the trap becomes defective. In skeet, the machine's

Clay targets can be quickly and gently loaded into a skeet machine by holding two fingers beneath the stack.

spring is adjusted to a tension that will just reach the 60-yard stake, passing near dead center in the target-setting hoop. The hoop, a three-foot circle of steel rod, narrow copper tubing or plastic pipe (the latter two are lighter and will not rust) is held in position alongside the center stake or target-crossing point, 13 1/2 feet above the ground. The post to which the hoop is attached may be of wood or, better yet, of a straight length of copper tubing (to which a copper hoop can be soldered). The ideal arrangement is to have a two-inch pipe set in the ground, as the target crossing point stake, and filled with sand or other material up to ground level. Then the post can be set into the pipe when the hoop is being used.

Not every gun club has a perfect "hoop" to check target flight. This club makes do with a square, which was probably easier to construct and support on a pole.

With the hoop having a three-foot diameter and the post being 13 1/2 feet high, the center of the hoop will be located at 15 feet, establishing the official target-height. If both high house and low house targets whiz through any part of the hoop and land in the vicinity of 60 yards from the house then the field is considered to be legal. The target-setting hoop is a piece of permanent equipment at all skeet fields.

Three people are ideally needed to quickly check the target flight on skeet fields. One person standing on Station 1 to ensure that the targets are not to either side of the circle, one on Station 4 to check that doubles cross through the hoop at the same time and height, and one person to hold the pole and hoop vertical.

THE TARGET-MEASUREMENT ROD IN TRAP

The official ATA rules for target flight in American trap specify that "targets, whether single or doubles, shall be thrown between eight and 12 feet high, ten yards from the trap. The recommended height is nine feet. The height at a point ten yards from the trap is to be understood to mean height above an imaginary horizontal straight line drawn through the firing point and the trap."

Generally, if trap targets fall between 48 and 52 yards in a straight line from the trap house (50 yards is the recommended distance) they are legal targets and the height is usually considered acceptable. To meet the requirements, an appropriate measuring rod should be devised, one that will take into account the drop in terrain below that of the shooting stations.

A length of any type of pipe, about an inch in diameter, will do as a measuring rod. While being held vertically ten yards straight ahead of the trap in a line with Station 3, the pipe should be wrapped with a piece of tape at a point level with the grade of the station. Then the targets should fly between eight and 12 feet above the tape marker. The eight and 12 foot points on the pipe should also be marked with tape.

If the grounds have more than one trapshooting facility and the terrain in front of the houses is not at the same level, each trap field must have its own target-measuring rod, if the field is to meet official ATA rules concerning target flights.

25. Facilities

Shotgun shooting facilities vary greatly from a single trap field and no clubhouse to 40 or 50 fields or more with numerous structures and buildings. However, they all have some features in common. At this point, we are more concerned with addressing the questions and needs of the new or aspiring gun club owner or field manager rather than trying to critique existing fields and their layouts.

TEN MAJOR PARTS OF A SHOOTING FACILITY

A shooting facility generally consists of ten major areas:

1. The 300-yard shotfall zone may seem excessively large for a safety dropzone for trap and skeet pellets. Actually, at that distance, the shot comes down like light rain. However, even at that distance, there is still a possibility of a pellet hitting someone's eye and causing serious injury, so we stick to the 300 yards. Of course, that prescribed distance is needed only in the direction of the shooting, and for the area in which the shot actually drops. *Black's Wing &*

Inside:

TEN MAJOR PARTS OF A SHOOTING FACILITY

REFEREES

291

Clay — Shotgunner's Handbook recommends that 52 acres be allowed for shot fallout for the trap games, 58 acres be allowed for the skeet games and 100-200 acres be reserved for a Sporting Clays course.

2. The walks are constructed of concrete or asphalt. Obviously, such factors as costs and climatic conditions are to be considered when the material is chosen. Professional advice should be sought. Rod and gun clubs, schools and other organizations with limited budgets can build an attractive trap or skeet field without specially built walks. The stations can be outlined by sunken, pressure-treated 4' x 4's cut and nailed together to form a three-foot-square frame; the wooden frame is imbedded in the ground and the exposed upper edges painted white or yellow. Another option is to make the stations out of three-foot-square slabs of concrete, about two inches thick and imbedded in the dirt to ground level.

The trap and skeet field layouts must be built to meet exact specifications. The most easily accessible and complete skeet and trap field layout diagrams are found in the centerfold pages of the "Rules and Regulations" booklets sent to all members of the ATA and NSSA.

3. The structures that house the machines (houses) can be constructed

Skeet houses are usually constructed from concrete blocks or wood. This wooden house was stained brown to enhance its rustic appearance. Note the gun rack against the protective fence.

of various materials, depending upon the finances of the organization building them. They can be made of wood, of cinder or concrete blocks with wooden stairs, or they can be built with a combination of wood and blocks. International Skeet uses the same houses as American skeet.

Also, the Wobble Trap can be accommodated by the same house as that used in American Trap. International or Olympic Trap requires a highly technical and very expensive construction involving a pit housing a 15-target throwing machine. USA Shooting is the organization to query for detailed construction plans (see Appendix B).

4. Each of the electrically controlled skeet machines, one in each house, throw targets in one set direction. The body of the machine does not move. The target drops into position when the throwing arm is automatically cocked. The puller activates the mechanism by pressing the appropriate button at the end of the portable cord.

The machines used for American Skeet can be, and usually are, used also for International Skeet. But special springs are wound tighter in order to throw farther (faster) targets. International Skeet also requires a special electrical device that is attached to the cord and releases the target at an undetermined time — from instantaneous to three seconds later — as prescribed by International Skeet rules.

The trap machine, on the other hand, oscillates back and forth. The gunner does not know in which direction the target is going to fly, because the machine's throwing arm is released in whatever direction it happens to be pointing when the release button is pushed.

An interior view of a standard trap house, at least half of the structure is below ground level. The walls, floor and roof are made from poured concrete, but the door was constructed from 3/4' plywood.

The Wobble Trap machine is different from the American Trap mechanism in that it moves up and down, as well as oscillating back and forth, so that the height of the flying target is also unknown to the shooter. Manual traps, which are far less expensive than automatic loading machines, require a person to stay in the house and hand-load each target released. Portable traps, the type that are used in informal shooting, such as in the novelty clay target games (See Chapter 3), are also part of the regular equipment at many trap and skeet fields. They are surprisingly rugged and light in weight. Some of them weigh no more than 11 pounds. They come complete and ready to use, and are excellent for use in a "do-it-yourself" Sporting Clays course. The portable trap, such as "Trius Trap" (produced by Trius Products, Inc., Box 25, Cleves, Ohio 45002, phone 513-941-5682), throws regulation targets, and does not require much effort to cock. The trap is loaded by simply laying the target on the arm, and the direction of target flight is ascertained by the position of the target on the arm. Also the height of the target flight is determined by adjusting the trap vertically. By placing clay targets side-by-side on the arm, the trap will throw horizontal doubles. And when placing one target on top of the other the trap will throw vertically spaced doubles. Sporting goods stores that sell guns can help with information concerning portable traps. Or, you can reference *Black's Wing & Clay — Shotgunners Handbook* (see Appendix C).

5. Licensed electricians, of course, should install electrical systems in the skeet and trap fields and houses. The specific plans and diagrams involved with electrical supply to target throwing machines, and the machines themselves, are available from the companies that produce the traps, see *Black's Wing & Clay — Shotgunners Handbook*.

The gun rack is a critical piece of equipment at all shooting ranges.

294

6. Gun racks are necessary at the shooting field, in shelters by the fields where gunners wait their turn to shoot, and also in the clubhouse. At the field, the gun rack may be one of many designs, although they all basically serve the same purpose. The triangular type is the most popular. The racks found in shelters are usually built-in over one of the railings. And in the clubhouse the racks are best recessed into a wall, so that people will not trip over a rack that has an extended base.

7. Fences are necessary to prevent spectators, as well as gunners who are waiting their turn to shoot, from encroaching too closely on the shooters. It is unsafe, and extremely disconcerting to the squad, if people are talking and moving about close to the shooting field. The fences can be constructed of attractive split rail or cedar, or they may have wooden posts supporting cattle fencing, or the fence may simply be composed of the least expensive posts available, erected eight or ten feet apart and connected by sections of rope. In other words, some sort of barrier should be erected, or a walkway established, as an indication that only shooters in action are permitted beyond it. There is a great laxity in many fields around the country, including some of the best, where persons not shooting jaywalk around the field because no visible restrictions exist.

8. At some fields, shelters may seem to be a luxury. But where no clubhouse exists, or the clubhouse is some distance away from the fields, a protective roof should be provided for shooters or spectators who might otherwise have to wait in the rain or under the blazing sun. Shelters may be built in attractive and yet practical designs. A prospective designer might wish to travel to other clubs to observe shelter designs.

The B. Robert Wood Shelter, located at Yale's trap field, is a fine example of a large, rustic structure to protect spectators and gunners from the weather and provide comfortable seating. Mr. Wood is an avid Sporting Clays competitor and friend of the Yale Shotgun Team.

9. Shooting fields that are without clubhouse facilities must provide (by law in most states) comfort stations — either outhouses or chemical toilets. The old time outhouse is not as unattractive as non-outdoorsmen may think. They require a minimum of maintenance. A five-gallon can of powdered lime, with a scoop, should be provided. After each use, the pit should be lightly dusted with the lime, thereby keeping everything "sweet." Inexpensive lime available in

hardware or garden stores should be used.

Portable chemical johns can be rented for the season or for a tournament. The company that rents the port-o-

The Clubhouse

johns also services them. On a year-round basis, the portables, usually constructed from durable but light plastic, should be purchased outright, and only the services contracted for. Eventually, a sizeable amount of money can be saved.

10. The parking area should be placed as far as conveniently possible from the shooting fields. True, many people like to have their vehicle close by, but car parking should not be allowed up against the fence of the shooting field (except for physically-challenged access). There is always noisy activity around cars, and that is a disadvantage to shooters.

Any person interested in more information on construction or layout of a shotgunning games facility may obtain it from the NSSF's 24-page manual *How to Develop New Places to Shoot*, item #008, for only $1.00. And, for those wishing to evaluate other shooting facilities, you can purchase the 36-page, state-by-state *NSSF's Directory of Public Shooting Ranges*, item #099, for only $2.00, (plus .75 shipping for up to $5.00 worth of materials). Write to: Promotional Materials Department, National Shooting Sports Foundation, 11 Mile Hill Road, Newtown, Connecticut, 06470, phone 203-426-1320.

REFEREES

Along with any shooting facility must come referees or "pullers." Three general types of referees officiate clay target competitions. First, and by far the most numerous, are the volunteer referees, who may or may not be completely familiar with all the technicalities. Generally, however, an experienced squad of shooters will police each other and will advise the referee, who may simply be doing the squad a favor by pulling (releasing targets) and scoring. Obviously, the advantage of a volunteer referee is that he doesn't have to be paid, although he should certainly be thanked for his help. Such a referee serves adequately for weekend recreational shooting at the local club. But where serious competition takes place the referee, if he is a volunteer, must have had experience in competitive gunning. If an organization must rely on volunteer referees for its more serious intra-club tournaments, the volunteer should be from another club.

The primary reason why experienced volunteer referees are difficult to secure is because the job is a thankless one. Few clubs show any real appreciation for this type of service. Refereeing in a competition requires standing or sitting for hours and being extremely alert;

COST & ACREAGE REQUIREMENTS OF SHOTGUN SHOOTING DISCIPLINES & GAMES

DISCIPLINE/ GAME	ACREAGE & COST ESTIMATES				THROUGHPUT OF SHOOTERS		
	ACRES		COST (in thousands of dollars)		CONSTRUCTION COMMENTS	SHOOTERS PER HOUR	TIME PER SHOOTER/ SQUAD	NO. OF TARGETS
	Construction	Fallout *	Machine	Construction				
TRAP ** (ATA, ABT, DT)	.25	52	7-9	2.5-8	Layout, trap pit, walkways, electr.,floodlights	18-25	13-16 min./ 5 shooters	
OLYMPIC TRAP	.38	52	42-65	12-28	Large pit for traps, walkways,electr., floodlights	18-24	15-18 min./ 6 man squad	
UNIVERSAL TRENCH	.32	52	14-22	8-16	5 trap pit, walkways, electr., floodlights	18-24	15-18 min./ 6 man squad	
ZZ BIRD	.38	52	.5-9	.2-1	Layout & small fence	6-12	6-8 min./ shooter	
SKEET (NSSA/UIT)	.34	58	8-9	8-12	Layout, buildings, walkways, elect., floodlights	10-12	25 min./ 5 shooters	
SPORTING ***	20-30	100/ 200	M: 12-16	4-23	Stands, trap mounts, gun racks, shelters, walkways	50	1 hr./5 man squad	50
			A: 73-92	12-45	As above + trap houses & electr.			
FITASC	15-30	100/ 200	M: 18-32	8-30	Stands, trap mounts,racks, shelters, walkways	20	2 hrs./5 man squad	200
			A: 90-150	18-68	As above + trap houses & electr.			
CRAZY QUAIL	1	58	M: 1 / A: 5-9	1	Trap pit	12-15	5 min./ shooter	25
TWO-MAN FLUSH	.20	48	A: 5-9	1-1.8	Trap house/ shooting platform	60-80	34 sec./ 2 shooters	24
TRAP HOUSE	6	100	7	0	Trailer with 10-20 M traps	10-40	25-35 min./ 5 man squad	50
5-STAND SPORTING®	.80	58	A: 18-30	0	Skeet or empty field	10-15	20-25 min./ 5 man squad	25
QUAIL WALK	0.5-2	50-60	M: 3-9	1-4		4-10	15 min./ shooter	25
			A:18-40	3-15	Including electr.			
SUPERSPORT	10-30	150/ 200	A: 80-140	15-25	12-25 traps & electrics	4-10	15-25 min./ shooter	50
TOWER SHOOTING	.2	160	A: 7-10	2.5-15	Tower	10-20	6-10 min.	25
PRO-SPORTING	1	58	A: 15-18	1.5-5	5 traps	360	36-50 sec./ 6 man squad	25/ squad
SUB-TRAP	1	58	.6 - .8	.1-1.5		18-25	10-25 min./ 5 man squad	25
FLUSH AND FLURRIES	0.5-2	50/ 110	M: 1.2-2 A: 4.8-6.6	.1-1.5 .6-2		100-300	36 sec./ 4,5 or 6 man squad	25/ squad
STARSHOT	.34	58	48	3-25		15-30	3 min./shooter	25
DOUBLE RISE	.25	52	7.6-9.2	2.5-8		18-25	16-22 min./ 6 man squad	25

* No shot larger than 7 1/2.   ** For a Skeet/Trap overlay field, the combined construction costs would be $10,000-$17,000.

*** Quality of landscaping varies price.   M = Manual   A = Automatic   Source: The Shooting Academy it is a long, tiring job. Most of the time the shoot management forgets about the volunteers. A show of appreciation, such as bringing him a drink and a doughnut or a sandwich, will go a long way toward persuading him to volunteer again. A gift box or two of shells with a "thank you" note attached will help immeasurably. Perhaps a cap or T-shirt with "REFEREE" printed on it may appeal to the volunteer; it will give him some recognition and it will only cost a few dollars. Shoot managers should not take the volunteer referee for granted.

The referee at work. During long shoots, this custom-built chair provides comfort for the referee while elevating him for better vision and adding professionalism to the job.

The second type of referee is the experienced shooter who is paid for his services by being allowed to shoot for free. This type of refereeing has severe drawbacks, for both the referee, who is to participate in the shoot, as well as for the other shooters in the competition.

Hiring a certified chief referee is, of course, the best arrangement. Such an official may be expected to help set the machines for target flight, distribute squad sheets, call the squads, and in general run the fields and supervise the other referees. Such an arrangement takes the load off the shoulders of the shoot management in controlling the fields. In large tournaments, management is stressed trying to satisfy everyone; a paid, certified referee, in most cases, is a Godsend.

With some study and much practice, any experienced shooter can become an NSSA, ATA or NSCA licensed referee. If you are interested, the procedure is simple. First, join the organization. You will receive a copy of the Association's most recent "Official Rules and Regulations." Study that manual from cover to cover. To be a licensed referee, you must pass a written, "open rulebook" examination, given by the state association or affiliated club. True, it is easier to to take an open notebook exam, but every answer must be correct. Eye examinations are also required. Official NSSA referee cards and emblems are given to candidates who successfully meet the requirements.

The referee is responsible for the conduct of the shooting on the field to which he has been assigned. He has jurisdiction on the field used by other shooters and spectators. He must be completely familiar with the shoot program and with the rules of the event(s). He must stay constantly alert, impartial, and courteous though firm in the handling of shooters. A referee is the sole judge of the decision of whether a target was hit or missed, regardless of the opinion of the spectators or other members of the squad. And, the referee has the responsibility to record the correct scores and to ensure that the shooters verify them before they leave the field.

Appendix A — Classification Systems and Tables

Governing bodies of the different shotgun sports disciplines administer shooter classification systems to permit shooters to compete for awards against others of similar ability.

American Trap (ATA)

Class	Average (16-yard)
AA	97 and above
A	94 to 96.99
B	91 to 93.99
C	88 to 90.99
D	87.99 and below

International Trap (USA)

Class	Average
AA	94 and above
A	88 to 93.99
B	82 to 87.99
C	76 to 81.99
D	70 to 75.99
E	69.99 and below

Doubles Trap (ATA)

Class	Average
AA	93 and above
A	89 to 92.99
B	85 to 88.99
C	78 to 84.99
D	77.99 and below

Double Trap (Olympic)

Class	Average
AA	91 and above
A	85 to 90.99
B	79 to 84.99
C	73 to 78.99
D	67 to 72.99
E	66.99 and below

Handicap Trap (ATA)

The ATA Handicap system is a method where shooters whose ability to win has been demonstrated and shooters whose ability is unknown are handicapped by shooting a greater distance from the trap house. The minimum handicap is 19.0 yards and the maximum is 27.0 yards. A shooter's yardage is determined by yardage earned by high scores placed in registered events or by known ability and 1000 target reviews.

Number of Shooters	High Scores and All Ties			
	1st	2nd	3rd	4th
15-24	1/2 yd			
25-124	1 yd	1/2 yd		
125-249	1 yd	1 yd	1/2 yd	
250-499	1 1/2 yd	1 yd	1/2 yd	
500-1499	2 yd	1 1/2 yd	1 yd	1/2 yd
1500 and above	2 1/2 yd	2 yd	1 1/2 yd	1 yd

Automatic Trap (USA Shooting)
Identical to International Trap

American Skeet (NSSA)

Class	Average (12 Gauge)
AAA	98.50 and over
AA	97.50 to 98.49
A	96.00 to 97.49
B	93.50 to 95.99
C	90.00 to 93.49
D	85.50 to 89.99
E	Under 85.50

International Skeet (USA)

Class	Average
AA	95 and above
A	87 to 94.99
B	81 to 86.99
C	75 to 80.99
D	69 to 74.99
E	68.99 and below

Sporting Clays (NSCA)

There are six classes in Sporting Clays: AA, A, B, C, D, E. In addition, a Masters Class exists for AA shooters who are consistent winners in the Open category. Because Sporting Clays courses vary so widely, a specific percentage of hits is not used for classification. Instead, shooters earn their way up in class by shooting the high score(s) or tying for the high score(s) in their class based on the number of participants in an event. For example, in a large tournament with 200-299 entries the top two scores and all ties in each class will move up one class.

For further information regarding classification systems, rules and regulations, contact the appropriate sport's governing body. Brief descriptions, addresses and phone numbers for these organizations may be found in Appendix B.

Appendix B —
Organizations

The six largest and most important organizations in the United States dealing with shotgunners and the clay target games are the Amateur Trapshooting Association (ATA), the National Rifle Association (NRA), the National Shooting Sports Foundation (NSSF), the National Skeet Shooting Association (NSSA), the National Sporting Clays Association (NSCA) and USA Shooting. They have all been referred to frequently in this book. Any shooter interested in a particular segment of the shotgunning games should contact and join the associated governing body. Several other organizations are also listed below.

ASSOCIATION OF COLLEGE UNIONS INTERNATIONAL (ACUI)

The Association of College Unions International is a non-profit, higher education organization whose individual members are union directors, student personnel administrators, student activities directors, recreation managers, food service administrators, program coordinators, fiscal officers and deans. ACUI is a professional association that is dedicated to enhancing campus life through programs, services and facilitates. The Association has existed since 1914 and has nearly 1,000 member institutions.

The ACUI sponsors the Annual (1998 will be the 30th Annual) Intercollegiate Clay Target Championships, which is held on about the third week of April each year. Most recently, these Collegiate Championships have been hosted by the National Gun Club, home of the NSSA and NSCA, in San Antonio, Texas. For more information on the Collegiate Championships, see Chapter 2 — The Competitions. ACUI's central office is in Bloomington, Indiana, adjacent to the Indiana University Campus. You may contact ACUI at 812-332-8017, or fax 812-333-8050.

AMATEUR TRAPSHOOTING ASSOCIATION (ATA)

A regulatory body for competitive trapshooting, the Interstate Trapshooting Association, was formed in 1892. Eight or ten years later this organization began promoting National Championship shoots. It was from these beginnings that the Amateur Trapshooting Association was founded in 1923 in Vandalia, Ohio. A year later the permanent home grounds were built there.

The Association is the focal point of all registered trapshooting in the United States and Canada, and it computes and records the results of all registered trapshoots in the two countries.

Annually, each member of the Association receives a card on which are recorded his averages and handicap for every registered match shot in the preceding year. Also recorded are the member's scores and percentage average of hits on his handicap and doubles events. The gunner's handicap yardage is punched along the edge of the card at the time of mailing. These cards must be presented to the management of any registered shoot in which the member wishes to participate. By using the data on the card, the shoot supervisor assigns the proper yardage and classification to each gunner.

Every registered trapshooter in the United States, Canada, and several foreign countries is listed by state, and in alphabetical order, in the Association's "average book," which is available from the ATA office for a nominal fee. The known shooting ability, that is, handicap yardage, etc., of over 50,000 shooters can be easily ascertained. The official publication of the ATA is the monthly magazine *TRAP & FIELD*; a one-year subscription is $25.00 (see Appendix C).

The ATA sponsors the Grand American, the largest of all participating sport tournaments (see Chapter 2). This spectacular ten-day shoot has been conducted on the Association's home grounds in Vandalia, Ohio, since the field's completion in 1924, previous tournaments having been held in different parts of the country).

Every gunner in the United States and Canada interested in trapshooting should join the ATA. One-year membership dues are $15.00. Application blanks are available from the ATA office, 601 W. National Road, Vandalia, Ohio, 45377. Phone 937-898-4638. Fax 937-898-5472.

NATIONAL RIFLE ASSOCIATION (NRA)

Strange as it may seem to the uninformed, the National Rifle Association is an important organization for the promotion of shotgun shooting and the clay target games.

The NRA has excellent basic firearms education and training programs, instructor and coach certification programs and collegiate shooting support. Annual membership dues are $35.00 For more information, contact the NRA at 11250 Waples Mill Road, Fairfax, Virginia 22030. Phone numbers: General and Membership — 800-NRA-3888; Education and Training — ext. 1500; Youth Programs —

ext. 1591; Training Department — ext. 1430; Collegiate Shooting Promotion — 703-267-1473.

NATIONAL SHOOTING SPORTS FOUNDATION (NSSF)

The National Shooting Sports Foundation was chartered in 1961 to promote shooting sports in America and to give the public a better understanding of recreational shooting. It continues to play an active role in educating the public in the safe use of sporting firearms and in furthering the conservation of our natural resources.

The Foundation's center of operations supplies informative brochures and pamphlets dealing with shotgun sports, firearms ownership, gun safety, shooting sports promotions and the shooting industry. The NSSF's programs and activities include The SHOT Show, Sportsman's Team Challenge, *Shot Business Magazine*, *Shooting Sports America* TV Show, School Programs, Video News Releases, *Boy's Life* magazine Insert, a 25-title Literature Program, *Gun Club* newsletter, National Hunting & Fishing Day, Women's Shooting Sports Foundation, Dealer Commercials, Cooperative Efforts and Grants, United States Shooting Team Support, Summer Biathlon, General Norman Schwarzkoph Video and Strategic Planning Marketing Surveys.

To Join the National Shooting Sports Foundation, contact the NSSF at Flintlock Ridge Office Center, 11 Mile Hill Road, Newton CT 06470-2359. Phone 203-426-1320. Fax 203-426-1087; dues are $50.00 per year. To Join the Women's Shooting Sports Foundation, write WSSF 1505 Highway South, Suite 101, Houston, Texas 77077. Phone 281-584-9907; membership dues are $25.00 per year.

NATIONAL SKEET SHOOTING ASSOCIATION (NSSA)

In a manner similar to the Amateur Trap Association, the National Skeet Shooting Association is the governing body for all official American Skeet shooting activities in the United States. In the NSSA book of "Rules and Regulations" the Association is described as a nonprofit organization owned and operated by and for its members: sportsmen who are dedicated to the development of those qualities of patriotism and good sportsmanship which are the basic ingredients of good citizenship, and in general to the promotion of the interests, welfare, and development of skeet shooting and related sports (a brief history of the NSSA can be found in Chapter 1).

In addition to governing American Skeet, the NSSA has an International Skeet division for gunners who wish to shoot under the rules used in International-style competition.

As the controlling center for all registered American Skeet shooting in the United States, the Association computes and records the results of all registered shooting. All members of the Association receive the monthly *Skeet Shooting Review*. In the "Records Annual" of the *Review* the yearly national averages of all NSSA members are published. Like ATA members, NSSA members annually receive an averages card, on which is recorded every registered match shot during the previous year. The card is shown to the manager of any registered shoot in which the member wishes to participate during the current year. The shoot manager, by using the information on the card, assigns the participant to the proper classification.

The Association hosts the prestigious NSSA Annual World Championships at the National Gun Club (now also called the National Shooting Complex) in San Antonio, Texas. This week-long event is described in Chapter 2. In 1970, the NSSA inaugurated a Hall of Fame to honor its people who had contributed greatly to the development of the game or who had been outstanding competitors over a lengthy period. Six famous gunners were elected the first year, and five more have been added each year since. The names of the distinguished members of this famous institution are usually listed in the "Records Annual," which can be purchased from the NSSA. The home grounds and headquarters of the NSSA are located at the beautiful grounds of the National Gun Club in San Antonio, Texas. Annual dues are $30.00. Membership applications may be obtained from most gun clubs or by writing to NSSA Headquarters, 5931 Roft Road, San Antonio, Texas 78253. Phone 210-688-3371.

NATIONAL SPORTING CLAYS ASSOCIATION (NSCA)

The National Sporting Clays Association is the largest governing body for Sporting Clays in the United States, with approximately 12,000 members who own and operate this non-profit organization. About 600 NSCA clubs exist nationwide with representation in all 50 states. Membership benefits include *Sporting Clays* magazine, rental car discounts, gun insurance discounts, instructor certification courses and tournament, state, zone and national shoots. Rates are $40 for a regular one-year membership and $500 for a lifetime membership. Call or write NSCA Headquarters, 5931 Roft Road, San Antonio, Texas, 78253; 210-688-3371

SPORTING CLAYS OF AMERICA (SCA)

This organization governs the new sport of International Sporting Clays in the United States. Call or write SCA, 9257 Buckeye Road, Sugar Grove, Ohio 43155-9632; 614-746-8334.

USA SHOOTING

USA Shooting is the governing body for all International-style shooting sports. As a member of USA Shooting, you will receive *Quickshots*, a publication that lists upcoming competitions throughout the country. The Competitions Division of USA Shooting is the main force behind all National Teams, National Development Teams and Olympic Shooting Teams; they are headquartered at the U.S. Olympic Training Center, One Olympic Plaza, Colorado Springs, CO

80909-5762. Phone 719-578-4883. Fax 719-578-4884.

305

APPENDIX C — Shotgun Sports Equipment and Publications

Bob Allen Sportswear
214 SW Jackson
Des Moines, IA 50315
800-685-7020

AmericanZZ
(ZZ Bird targets & launchers)
171 Spring Hill Rd
Trumbull, CT 06611
203-261-1058
Fax 203-452-9359

Beretta U.S.A. Corp.
(shotgun manufacturers)
17601 Beretta Drive
Accokeek, MD 20607
301-283-2191

Black's Wing & Clay
(Shotgunner's Handbook)
Box 2029
43 W. Front St.
Red Bank, NJ 07701
908-224-8700

Cabela's
(shooting equipment and apparel)
812 — 13th Ave.

Sidney, NB 69160
800-237-4444

Decot Hy-Wyd
(shooting glasses)
Box 15830
Phoenix, AZ 85060
800-528-1901

The Hunters Pointe
(PDQ Twister)
Larry Cero
14264 SW 50th St.
Benton, KS 67017
316-778-1122

L.L. Bean
(shooting equipment and apparel)
3 Campus Drive
Freeport, ME 04034
800-221-4221

NRA Shooting Education Update
(publication)
National Rifle Association
11250 Waples Mill Rd.
Fairfax, VA 22030
800-672-3888

Quack Sporting Clays, Inc.
(Modern Skeet and Trap oscilla-
tors)
Box 98
Cumberland, RI 02864
401-723-8202

Quickshots
(publication)
USA Shooting
One Olympic Plaza
Colorado Springs, CO 80909
719-578-4670

Shooting Sports USA
(publication)
National Rifle Association
Box 708
Herndon, VA 22070
703-267-1583

Shotgun Sports Magazine
Box 6810
Auburn, CA 95604
800-676-8920

Shotgun Sports Magazine
Shootin' Accessories, Ltd.
(shotgun shooting books, videos
and products)
Box 6810 Auburn, CA 95604
800-676-8920

Skeet Shooting Review
NSSA
5931 Roft Rd.
San Antonio, TX 78253
800-877-5338

Slapshot
Simulated Live Pigeon (SLP)
Jim Lee at Blakewood Sporting
Estate,
England, 011-44-179-887-5605

Sporting Clays magazine
5211 S. Washington Ave.
Titusville, FL 32780
407-268-5010

Sporting Planes
"The Red Baron Game"
Sporting Planes, LTD.,
Saratoga, CA
408-395-0049

Trap & Field magazine
1000 Waterway Blvd.
Indianapolis, IN 46202
317-633-8804

Trius Traps
Box 25
Cleves, OH 45002
513-941-5682

White Flyer Targets
East 800-423-6077
Central 800-647-2898
West 800-872-7888

Appendix D — Shotgunning in Education

An important place exists for the shotgunning games in both the high school and the collegiate world. That fact is emphatically substantiated by the interest in intercollegiate shotgun shooting throughout the nation. Many of the faculty and administrators at our universities now understand the benefits of the lifetime sports as opposed to the highly competitive, team-oriented varsity sports. Consequently, trap and skeet activities find a special niche in the ever-increasing physical education, recreation and club sports programs.

Club sports programs provide an activity of some type for every individual, regardless of height, weight, and physical prowess (for instance, we carry as many as 35 club sports at Yale University). And the activity of clay target shooting is a perfect example of a sport in which persons of small size and with an average degree of physical dexterity can excel. On the skeet field nobody raises an eyebrow when a five-foot-four, 120-pound female is outshooting a six-foot-three, 230-pound male.

What is so special about the collegiate shotgun shooting activities? And what does it have that most of the other sports do not have? They are especially valuable because they offer both recreation and competition, a competition that is friendly even if it is serious and tough. And, both men and women can compete together and against each other. Also, graduate students can compete with undergraduates, which is normally not permitted in varsity sports programs. These factors are apparent at the Intercollegiate Clay Target Championships, held annually since 1969, where thousands of students, male and female, representing over 50 colleges and universities from throughout the United States have met over the years for several days of shooting. When in action, the teams work as intently and with as much dedication as any other athletic team. But when each squad finishes its course of shooting there is no animosity; instead, there are congratulations — or condolences — and always camaraderie and sociability.

What benefits does the individual accrue? Few people can deny that competitive sports have a positive value in the development of person and personality. I have seen remarkable changes of personality in some students once they have learned to shoot and compete; confidence has replaced shyness. All students want to excel, although the desire may be hidden at times. Trap, skeet and Sporting Clays offer them an opportunity to be good at something "athletic." Shotgunning, by its very nature, demands self control, concentration and, most importantly, discipline. It also has value as a way of releasing tension. It can be immensely satisfying and healthy for a student to purge pent-up classroom frustrations by getting outdoors in the fresh air and banging away at fast flying targets.

The shotgunning games are now accepted as unique educational tools and valuable recreational and competitive activities for students in high schools and colleges. They will continue to be accepted as such, unless undue importance begins to be placed on winning, rather than on the recreational aspects of the sport.

College students interested in forming a shotgun club should seek a faculty advisor or "coach" and contact their school's Student Union or Club Sports Department (those club advisors new to clay target shooting can gain a wealth of information by referring to Chapter 18 — Methods of Instruction and Chapter 19 — How to Coach). Full-time students are eligible to participate for five years in the Intercollegiate Championships.

Other information on collegiate shooting can be found in Chapter 12 — Starting a Scholastic Shooting Program, in the book *Finding the Extra Target* by John Linn and Stephen Blumenthal, which is available through *Shotgun Sports Magazine* (see Appendix C). You can also contact the department of Collegiate Shooting Promotion at the National Rifle Association (see Appendix B).